AMONG THE BROS

AMONG THE BROS

A Fraternity Crime Story

MAX MARSHALL

HARPER

An Imprint of HarperCollinsPublishers

HarperCollins books may be purchased for educational, business, or sales promotional use. For information, please email the Special Markets Department at SPsales@harpercollins.com.

FIRST EDITION

Designed by Michele Cameron

Library of Congress Cataloging-in-Publication Data has been applied for.

ISBN 978-0-06-309953-1

23 24 25 26 27 LBC 5 4 3 2 1

To Rachael and Charlie

They made it back up front to their seats just in time to sing with all their friends: "The road goes on forever and the party never ends."

—*Todd Snider, "Beer Run"*

The joy of feeling at home everywhere belongs only to kings, wolves, and robbers.

—*Honoré de Balzac*

CONTENTS

CONTENTS

AMONG THE BROS

CHAPTER 1

WOLVES OF KING STREET

When Mikey Schmidt entered the College of Charleston as a freshman in the class of 2017, he'd just finished a seven-inch growth spurt. For the first three years of high school he'd remained five feet zero, and some boys called him "Little Mikey." During JV basketball games, opposing coaches thought he was a twelve-year-old trash-talker playing above his level, not a seventeen-year-old whose voice hadn't changed yet. Classmates told him he was going to be a legal midget forever, and his mom took him to a specialist for a bone age scan. The doctor told them a spurt was coming, and senior year Mikey began to grow. Every morning for three months he woke up with leg pain, and his jeans started to look like capris. By August he left for college with a deeper voice and a new wardrobe courtesy of his mother. Still, Mikey had topped out at five feet seven, just small enough to stay "Little Mikey" for the rest of his life.

Mikey had picked the College of Charleston for the same reasons a lot of boys do. He'd enjoyed visiting Charleston on vacation, and he'd read that the college had a nearly seven-to-two girl-to-guy ratio. At C of C, he'd choose between swimming off Folly Beach and golfing at Wild Dunes. He could sell his mom on the small class sizes and eighty-minute flight home to Atlanta, and he could also go out four or five nights a week.

Even before his growth spurt, Mikey had been a rowdy kid. He hadn't been afraid to drink before class or leave campus in his 1990s Mercedes to smoke outside Chick-fil-A. After driving through his Saint Francis High School classmate's front yard, he'd dated the cutest girl at the Mount Vernon School, even though his voice was almost as high as hers. He knew the lyrics to most Gucci Mane and Future songs, and one time he showed a younger kid on the JV basketball team $10,000 in cash that he'd made from selling weed. Still, Mikey wanted a different social life at C of C. In college, his stepfather couldn't ground him for downloading Ludacris's "Move Bitch" on iTunes, and his friends wouldn't need to know that his voice had only just changed. When he got on campus, he'd be a prep school kid with good hair and a drop-top SL500. After he woke up and smoked a blunt without a towel under his door, he could put on an Augusta National shirt or a Southern Tide visor and try to join a good fraternity.

✦ ✦ ✦

I learned about Mikey Schmidt thanks to a press conference held during the 2016 College of Charleston summer break. Standing under a photo of $100 bills, Charleston's police chief, Greg Mullen, announced one of the largest busts in the city's history, a six-month collaboration between local police, state law enforcement, the DEA, the FBI, and the US Postal Service. Chief Mullen pointed to a row of tables to show what they'd seized: five pounds of marijuana, a pound and a half of cocaine, seven firearms, a Tac-D grenade launcher, $214,000 in cash, and forty-three thousand pills worth $150,000. During his speech, he also said that the case was related to the murder of Patrick Moffly on the first Friday of that year's C of C spring break. Detectives had found Moffly, the son of a luxury real estate developer and a Charleston school board member, lying on the floor of his house a block from campus. He'd been holding a Chipotle napkin to a wound in his chest, and his body had been surrounded by a few hundred loose pills marked GG249. When a reporter asked about the link between the killing and the drug arrests, Mullen refused to discuss it more. Instead, he added that the college ring had sold everything from MDMA to LSD to Xanax, which "seems to be a drug of choice right now." He gripped the podium and said that the suspects operated in a network and knew one another, but "they were not thought to be part of a gang."

Chief Mullen then switched the TV display from piles of money to rows of mug shots. Up on the screen, the suspects' frowns hid their dimples. They looked like guys who put in time at the gym, and maybe at the beach, and definitely at the putting green. Next to the pictures, the Charleston PD listed their names and ages:

Michael Schmidt, 21
Robert Liljeberg, 22
Zackery Kligman, 24
Benjamin Nauss, 23
Jonathan Reams, 19
Daniel Katko, 25
Russell Sliker, 22
Jake Poeschek, 21*

The first thing I noticed looking at the photos was the haircuts. Most had feathery bangs, which they either pushed to the side or parted in the center. They looked like kids who'd played lacrosse at my prep school in Dallas. The lacrosse group was known at my school as "the bros," and they drove bigger SUVs and seemed a little older than the rest of our class. Most weekends they threw wild parties at nice houses with girls from the Episcopal School of Dallas, and I think I unconsciously copied their hair. When I joined a fraternity my freshman year of college I swept my bangs to the right, and I kept a

---

* Poeschek's girlfriend, Samantha Hincks, was also listed in the original press release, but her charges were dropped a year later.

flowy haircut until I stopped paying dues my senior year. After that I grew out a semimullet and moved to Northern Vietnam to work as a journalist, but the Charleston mug shots took me back to that place again.

The photos also got my attention because of what the suspects had been arrested with. I didn't know whether the drug network should've been considered a gang or not, but I agreed with Chief Mullen that Xanax was a "drug of choice right now." I'd seen benzodiazepines flying around college fraternity life, and I'd watched my friends get addicted while other friends dealt to them. After college I learned that a few of the Dallas "bros" had joined fraternities and then dropped out of school to deal with benzodiazepine dependencies, and a few of our mutual friends had died. When I started working as an investigative reporter, I wondered if this problem extended beyond my surroundings, and I'd Googled something like "Xanax arrest fraternity." Soon I was reading Chief Mullen's press release, looking at forty-three thousand Xanax pills and two rows of the "frat swoop" haircut.

Mikey Schmidt was the lead name on the press release, so when I flew to Charleston for what I thought might be a good story about Xanax and fraternities, I started asking people about him. I arrived a few months after he'd been sentenced to the Wateree River Correctional Institution for ten years without parole, though, so I couldn't reach him myself. My investigation had to begin as a "write around," where I talked to sources who knew him and the other boys in the mug shots. One friend said that Mikey had a wealthy grandfather and good taste in rap music. Another tried to explain why he did well with women: "He just had mad game. He had this little swag to him, and the hottest girls always wanted guys that don't give a fuck." (His high school girlfriend wasn't available to confirm this.) No one mentioned his growth spurt.

The first time I visited the College of Charleston, I tried to imagine what Mikey saw when he got there. While sunlight ran through cypress leaves, I walked toward a gate with a Latin motto above my head. C of C has the oldest campus south of Virginia, and students were walking to antebellum mansions in heirloom Rolexes or Tory Burch sandals. Sitting under a palmetto tree, I looked up the Latin quote from the gate. It comes from the *Aeneid*, and it means "Someday, it will please you to remember even these present troubles." On the university's website, a C of C professor calls it a reminder for those who read it "to set aside their current misery in favor of feasting, heavy drinking, and some sleep."

After that, I started interviewing kids about the Xanax ring. The Charleston police didn't answer my first emails, so I asked C of C alumni linked to the 2016 bust to tell me about their school.

Kappa Sigma from South Carolina: The school has some nicknames, like Camp Charleston. It's more like a country club for rich New Englanders. Which feeds directly into the drug ring. I don't know where to start.

Delta Delta Delta from Connecticut: You walk around, and everything is bright and sunshiney, and you walk into happiness. You get up on a Saturday morning, and instead of sitting hungover in some shitbox house, you, like, drive to the beach.

Kappa Alpha from Georgia: You see the divide at the College of Charleston immediately. The really rich kids just live differently, from the places they eat, to their circle of friends, to what road they live on. Everything.

Sigma Alpha Epsilon from Maryland: I remember my off-campus house one year was on the market for like $900,000. It was a brand-new house, and we were the first people to live in it. Everyone's riding golf carts around from house to house.

Sigma Nu from South Carolina: It just builds up from day one. Not only is this place so gorgeous, it's got nightlife, it attracts money, it attracts women. And then you throw some eighteen-year-old boy in there.

Kappa Sig from South Carolina: I think an issue at the College of Charleston is the ratio of men to women. It's like 25:75. That means easy picking for guys. It's like, "If I go out every night, I can fuck a different girl every night." For really rich frat guys, it pays to be a shithead, which also ties back to the drug ring.

Lacrosse Player from Virginia: It was not one ring, it was several spread out among all these different connections. You could throw a rock a few feet and hit somebody who sold Xanax. And the same goes for cocaine, and for everything.

Kappa Sig from South Carolina: The police basically didn't catch one-fourth of what was actually going on.

Kappa Alpha from Georgia: There were a lot of drug dealers within my frat.

Kappa Sig from South Carolina: There's real money driving serious crime. There are assault rifles and millions of dollars in cash and people dying, all under the guise of fraternity.

GDI* from South Carolina: The fact is, I'm one of the very few people who's willing to talk about it openly, because it still subliminally affects me. It definitely has affected my anxiety, it's affected how I can trust people, what I think about corruption.

High-Dollar Local Defense Lawyer: Have you read *Motherless Brooklyn*? There's a phrase in there [about the secret forces that control things]: "wheels within wheels." And it's kind of a joke. It's like, "Yeah, man, I get it, wheels within wheels." But it's real. There are wheels within wheels, and there are conspiracies within conspiracies.

GDI from South Carolina: There's a larger beast in Charleston that's out there. To understand it, we'd need a corkboard, man. If we took a string and connected all the dots, we'd need a corkboard the size of a warehouse.

I wasn't sure how seriously to take this chatter. A $400,000 drug network organized by five fraternity kids and three friends was wild enough, but the conversation about deaths and millions of dollars felt like subreddit talk. For that reason, I started interviewing the boys' criminal defense lawyers. The suspects had hired some of the best orators and backroom dealers in South Carolina, and

---

* Fraternity members often refer to non–fraternity members as "GDIs," which is short for "goddamn independents."

Mikey Schmidt alone had hired four attorneys. His first lead attorney, Tim Kulp, had been an FBI special agent in Miami during the late 1970s, and his four-decade career in criminal defense led to appearances on *Dateline* and in the *New York Times*. The first time we talked, he was eating a sandwich when our conversation got interrupted by a whooshing sound over the ceiling. "Oh shit! Hold on." He put his hand to his ear while jets flew overhead from Joint Base Charleston. "F-16 afterburners. The sound of freedom!"

Kulp sat on the third floor of his wood-shuttered building in the French Quarter, his food spread on his desk. Above him were photos of his sons, one of whom serves as a first lieutenant in the air force and another of whom stars in a *Southern Charm* spin-off on Bravo. I asked Tim how far the College of Charleston drug conspiracy ran, and he stopped chewing. "These guys, the fraternity guys, were overlooked by the police and the school. I tried to write a screenplay about it, didn't get very far, called the *Wolves of King Street*, because the KAs [Kappa Alphas] actually had T-shirts printed up that said that. . . . It was not just KA but it was Sigma Nu and SAE [Sigma Alpha Epsilon], and the notion is that they traveled all over the southeast serving UNC Chapel Hill, Duke, the University of Georgia, and beyond. We're talking about a huge fucking operation." *

When I asked for proof, Kulp emailed me a police affidavit that hadn't been released to the public. The document stated that on April 1, 2016, Charleston detectives had raided a

---

* No members of Sigma Nu were arrested or charged in connection with the 2016 bust.

storage locker belonging to one of the boys in the mug shots. In the locker, they'd confiscated an ounce of cocaine and two firearms, but they'd also found 6,947.62 grams of counterfeit Xanax. During the summer 2016 press conference, the Charleston Police Department had announced the seizure of forty-three thousand alprazolam pills worth $150,000, but according to this document, they'd discovered more tablets and never disclosed it. Because each Xanax bar contains 2 milligrams of alprazolam, the nearly 7,000-gram seizure yielded somewhere in the ballpark of 3.5 million pills. By Chief Mullen's own math of $3.50 a pill, his team had uncovered $12,250,000 of black market Xanax. By Tim Kulp's $6 estimate, the boys had been caught with $21,000,000 worth. Whatever the pricing model, the Charleston police had underreported the amount of Xanax they'd seized by more than 8,000 percent, and they hadn't charged anyone for the pills.

CHAPTER 2

MOUNTAIN WEEKEND

After his mom dropped him off in Charleston, Mikey left his dorm room in McAlister Hall to tour the school's annual Student Activities Information Fair. Hundreds of kids gathered in the Cistern Yard, with ivy growing on the walls and moss hanging from the trees. Walking near a buried Civil War cannonball, Mikey approached rows of picnic tables belonging to student clubs and organizations. Older kids with sign-up sheets tried to make eye contact with him, but he kept walking. Mikey wasn't going to play Quidditch. He wasn't going to join the Chucktown Trippintones a cappella singers either, but he knew which tables he wanted to find. He wasn't sure what he wanted to major in, but before he'd even left high school, he'd planned on joining one of the best fraternities at C of C.

The college's Greek organizations set up booths outside the Stern Student Center, next to the other clubs. Mikey first ran into two upper-middle-tier fraternity options, Kappa Sigma and Sigma Nu. Kappa Sig was known for its big pledge classes and rowdy compound on Spring Street, and Sig Nu thrived with its Phish vibe. Mikey put his phone number on the Kappa Sig spreadsheet, but he didn't like Widespread Panic, so he passed Sigma Nu. After that he looked for the tables belonging to the top-tier chapters.

By consensus, the two best frats at C of C were Pi Kappa Alpha (Pike) and Sigma Alpha Epsilon (SAE). Mikey heard that Pike recruited northerners from towns like Greenwich, Connecticut, and felt like a New England boarding school without the nerds. These boys seemed older than Mikey, in part because the boarding school kids had lived away from home before, and in part because some of them had already tried cocaine. Entire tristate-area friend groups came to Charleston for the southern coastal lifestyle and the two-hour flight home to LaGuardia, and Pi Kappa Alpha had a pipeline of Connecticut recruits to choose from.

Mikey was proud to come from Georgia, and he didn't want to join a clique of boys from Fairfield County. Instead, he wanted to rush Sigma Alpha Epsilon. He'd heard about C of C SAE before he'd left Atlanta. The chapter recruited boys from old southeastern families, but it also attracted tristate kids who liked a mix of northern and southern rhythms. A Charleston SAE might drive a F250, but he'd prefer EDM to country and salmon-colored pants to Wranglers. Some other C of C fraternity members disliked the SAEs. A member of the midtier Kappa Alpha Order called them "fuck boys with less morality." Still, one Tri Delt sister from Connecticut summed up the elite sororities' view: "SAEs are good-looking douchebags. Honestly, I think of taller guys." Even the haters talked about their lake house parties, bar tabs, day parties, bottle-service nights, house parties, and boat charters. Other fraternities could only try to compete with their photos from the Carolina Cup and Pat O's, and many sorority members wanted an invite to SAE Mountain Weekend. For these reasons and others, Sigma Alpha Epsilon had a claim at being the best fraternity at the College of Charleston.

From the outside looking in, many people find it hard to understand what makes a fraternity the "best." If the best baseball team is the one that wins the most games and the best hospital is the one that has the highest likelihood of saving your life, it's difficult to tell what makes one group of fraternity kids better than any other. One key trait, though, is that elite fraternities like to recruit members from elite backgrounds, which usually means they come from money. Accepting boys from "good" families and rejecting ones from "random" suburbs means higher budgets for parties and better connections in the job market, and these benefits accrue over time. When Mikey and I showed up to college at the start of the 2010s, for instance, many Greek websites had a quote like one found on a Cornell University Greek life site: "While only 2 percent of America's population is involved in fraternities, 80 percent of Fortune

500 executives, 76 percent of U.S. senators and congressmen, 85 percent of Supreme Court justices, and all but two presidents since 1825 have been fraternity men." Less publicized but just as wild is this fact: Greek alumni give approximately 75 percent of all money donated to universities.

In terms of this gilded recruitment pool, the best fraternity chapters never change too much. If you compare an Alabama SAE membership photo from 1882 and a chapter Instagram from 2022, you'll see a similar concentration of swoopy haircuts and powerful last names. In terms of their public-facing behavior, though, the best fraternities have really morphed over the last fifty years. For a long stretch of the twentieth century, the top chapters branded themselves as stereotypical Richie Rich kids, with chapter sweaters and official songbooks for crooning. As Nicholas L. Syrett writes in *The Company He Keeps: A History of White College Fraternities*, houses often competed for top status by recruiting as many campus leaders as possible. Among other things, wealthy chapters wanted men of public virtue who'd run the student government or cheer with the pep squad. By 1970, though, fraternity membership hit an all-time low, and in 1978 rich fraternities were stereotyped as the boring snoots of *Animal House*'s Omega Theta Pi. At parties, the Omegas pinned flowers or name tags to their blazers and entertained with piano and cookies.

No audience member left *Animal House* wanting to be an Omega Theta Pi, but everyone wanted to party with Tim Matheson and John Belushi. While the Omegas built parade floats and called the dean "sir," the brothers of Delta Tau Chi destroyed parades and seduced the dean's wife. Belushi and his crew were lovable jesters, and they'd found a way to mix countercultural freedom and old-timey male order. On the one hand, the Deltas fought the power. They smoked pot back when that was a radical thing to do and hit golf balls into ROTC drills. On the other hand, they were the kind of guys who liked to golf. They slept with every woman and girl they desired, and they hired Otis Day and the Knights to make them dance. In the grand scheme of things, they had all the power in the world. The movie ends when Belushi dresses like a pirate and kidnaps the prettiest sorority girl at Faber College. The credits predict their future: "Senator & Mrs. John Blutarsky, Washington, D.C."

By the 1962 logic of fictional Faber College, the Omegas were the best fraternity on campus, and Belushi and his friends were the worst. But by the 1978 logic of the movie itself, their status flipped. The campus leaders were the uptight losers, and the wild boys had all the fun. *Animal House* laid the groundwork for *Old School* and other man-child films of the next century, but it also opened a new path for America's real-life snooty fraternity chapters. The best fraternities were still made up of rich kids from elite families, but as one fraternity lobbyist told me, "No wealthy fraternity wants to be known as the cardigan guys anymore. They want to be the crazy ones." The new fraternity king asserted his rule by breaking the rules, and he became the man by acting like a bro. During the 1980s, fraternity membership boomed again. In 1988, four Alabama SAEs were arrested for selling cocaine. By 2013, the fraternity lifestyle website *Total Frat Move* wrote, "Greek life today makes *Animal House* look like a Pixar movie."

During my early reporting, I tried to get a sense of why Sigma Alpha Epsilon was one of the best fraternities at the College of Charleston. Two of the boys in Chief Mullen's mug shots had been SAEs, and their chapter house sits across the street from campus. Gold lions guard the entrance, and an engraved list of donors looms above the porch. When Mikey was a freshman, Sigma Alpha Epsilon operated on 230 college campuses, and it had initiated over 300,000 brothers since 1856. The national organization was founded by a ministerial student in Tuscaloosa, and an 1899 Bridgewater College grad wrote its creed, which begins, "The True Gentleman is the man whose conduct proceeds from goodwill and an acute sense of propriety, and whose self-control is equal to all emergencies; who does not make the poor man conscious of his poverty . . . who appears well in any company, a man with whom honor is sacred and virtue safe." The College of Charleston chapter was founded in 1881, and its members still memorize the creed. But for a sense of why Mikey and so many other kids wanted to join C of C SAE in 2013, people told me I needed to learn about Mountain Weekend 2012.

Tri Delt from the Midwest: This was fall 2012, three weeks into my freshman year. All the older girls in my sorority were like, "There's Mountain Weekend coming up. You should definitely go."

MOUNTAIN WEEKEND

Christina Arnold:[*] Girls would skip class so they could paint a frickin' cooler. They'd say, "I should study for this test, but I have to paint my cooler instead."

Tri Delt from the Midwest: I got invited and so did my best friend Christina [Arnold]. On Friday these two SAEs pick us up.

Christina Arnold: It was the four of us.

Tri Delt from the Midwest: We get in, and [the guys] tell us, "We're in the drug car." They had giant suitcases full of drugs. Weed and coke but also acid, probably Xanax too. I was like, "I guess this is what happens in college."

Christina Arnold: We all drank the whole drive down there. Flavored Burnett's, you know, shitty vodka.

Tri Delt from the Midwest: Night comes and our car breaks down on the side of the highway. The two guys freak out. "We have all these drugs—we need to be with Mountain Weekend!" One of them runs to find a mile marker for Triple A, and as he's running down the side of the highway, he trips and falls on a dead deer.

Christina Arnold: Literally fell on a deer carcass.

Tri Delt from the Midwest: He comes back covered in blood. Horrifying. Finally one of the SAE pledges comes to pick us up.

Christina Arnold: When we got to the campsite people were raving. They were so excited. But it turns out Mountain Weekend wasn't in the mountains. We were in the woods.

---

[*] Another C of C Tri Delt, Christina was the only person from Mountain Weekend 2012 who let me print her name.

Tri Delt from the Midwest: It was probably, I would say, ten cabins owned by the state of Georgia, spread out around this lake. The first thing that happens when I walk in is I slip and fall in somebody's vomit. My back is covered in throw up, and my date says, "Well, there's no showering here."

Christina Arnold: My date brought a blow-up mattress that had a hole in it.

Tri Delt from the Midwest: We hadn't slept, so Christina and I decide to take a nap before everyone starts partying. When we wake up there are hunting knives stuck above our headboard.

Christina Arnold: They were throwing knives at the walls, having challenges where they tried to hit different spots. After that, they pulled all the mirrors and photos off of the walls and just started doing lines and lines of cocaine.

SAE from the Southeast: On our way there I'd gone into this bait and tackle shop and bought every single cricket they had. It was like three hundred dollars' worth of crickets. Then I broke into my friend's car and released all the crickets. No one knows that I did this.

Tri Delt from the Midwest: Christina and I are like "It's so pretty here! We should go for a hike!" We go, and when we get back people are wearing Viking hats, smearing paint on their faces, playing in the leaves. They're covered in mud. And we're like, "What is going on here? Like, we haven't been gone that long." One of the older girls in our sorority is like, "Oh, half of the Mountain Weekend, they took acid, so they're tripping right now."

SAE from the Southeast: One of my pledge brothers on shrooms emerged from the woods covered in mud. No shirt, no shoes, nothing.

Tri Delt from the Midwest: Like obviously, this is a frat party, so people are hooking up everywhere. Literally having sex in plain daylight.

Christina Arnold: Stripped in the sand by the lake.

Tri Delt from the Midwest: I didn't want anything to do with my date, so they started a rumor that Christina and I were lesbians who wanted a free trip to Mountain Weekend.

Christina Arnold: People were dancing on all the coolers, so of course they got destroyed.

Tri Delt from the Midwest: Then we walk down to the water. Someone had driven their Hummer into the lake.

SAE from the Northeast: There was some off-roading going on, and a brother drove his truck into the pluff mud.

Tri Delt from the Midwest: The wheels were in the water. They considered using a barge to tow it out, but they ended up needing a truck.

SAE from the Southeast: This guy goes to his car to see if he can tow the Hummer out. He opens his door, and the crickets come out like the plagues of Egypt! He was like, "What the fuck is going on?!"

Tri Delt from the Midwest: A bunch of people decide to go swimming in the lake, and they come out covered in red clay. But they're all tripping, so they're like, "Oh my God, we're covered in blood."

SAE from the Southeast: One guy's on top of the Hummer, humping it, trying to get it out of the mud. The tow rope breaks, and it misses his head by half a foot. It would have squished him like a watermelon.

Tri Delt from the Midwest: At this point it's noon. They kept going at it.

SAE from the Southeast: We're all fucked up, drunk, breaking shit, throwing shit, burning shit.

Christina Arnold: It's nighttime now, and a girl tells me, "If you don't want your stuff thrown in the fire, frickin' pack it and put it in the car real quick."

Tri Delt from the Midwest: They started burning so many things.

Christina Arnold: Pillows, sleeping bags, cleaning chemicals.

Tri Delt from the Midwest: It was a full-on bonfire. My date was like, "Rip anything off the wall and just throw it into the fire," and I was like, "I don't want to." But I ended up burning a shower curtain.

SAE from the Southeast: Every single thing that was burnable was burned.

Tri Delt from the Midwest: They're taking all the couches from the inside and throwing them into the firepit.

SAE from the Southeast: One guy lit a broom and used it like a torch. People doused a football in hair spray and started playing fire football. And then a forest ranger shows up.

Tri Delt from the Midwest: A park ranger comes, and there's no furniture left inside the cabin.

SAE from the Southeast: He comes up to the flames, and he's like, "What in the *hell* are y'all *doing*?" And my friend takes the fire football and hikes it between his legs. "Hike!"

Christina Arnold: I thought we were gonna get arrested.

SAE from the Southeast: I think he tried to stop us, but he was so beyond the pale of his authority. I don't think he wanted to deal with the paperwork. It was two in the morning, so he told us all to go to bed. We just kept going.

In the weeks after Mountain Weekend, the managers at Tugaloo State Park tried to find the boys who'd rented the cabins. The rooms had been stripped to nothing, and the walls had been punctured by hunting knives. Everything flammable had been burned. According to a source at Tugaloo, the SAEs had made the reservations pretending to be students at Charleston Southern University. After the park rangers called Charleston Southern and read out names from the rental agreement, the dean of students said, "That ain't us. Try the College of Charleston." A month later, one Tri Delt's date told her that if C of C investigators reached out, she should claim that she never went on Mountain Weekend. When I asked an SAE what happened in the end, he said, "There wasn't really any fallout with the school, I don't think? I don't really remember. Back in Georgia, I think I got some kind of minor charge, like destruction of state property."

At the C of C activity fair one year later, Mikey Schmidt walked past the irrelevant Sigma Chis, who were playing with their dog. Then he made his way to meet the SAEs. Listing it before the religious organizations and after the geology club, the College of Charleston website described Sigma Alpha Epsilon as promoting "the highest standards of friendship, scholarship, and service for our members based upon the ideals set forth by our Founders and as specifically enunciated in our creed." For certain kids on campus, the SAEs were elite in part because stories like Mountain Weekend showed what they could get away with.

Before he reached their table, Mikey saw a booth for another fraternity he recognized. He'd heard about the C of C Kappa Alpha Order from older kids in the Atlanta suburbs, and his new roommate had talked about Kappa Alpha too. Sitting behind the KA table was a boy in khaki shorts and a fire-engine red T-shirt. He wore a backpack on his shoulders, and he was eating a foot-long Subway sandwich. He reached out his hand and introduced himself as Rob. His blond hair curled above his ears, and he had gold Kappa Alpha lettering on his chest. From the way Rob's eyes looked at the foot-long sub, Mikey could tell Rob was very high. Rob was sitting with a friend who was making fun of him for eating Subway. Mikey asked them if they smoked, and Rob said, "Yeah, we burn." They talked for a minute, and then Rob looked up and said, "I live across the street. Wanna hit my bong?"

Even though his memory might be colored by everything that would happen over the next four years, Mikey later said he could tell that Rob was smooth. Forgetting the SAE booth, Mikey responded: "Word."

CHAPTER 3

RECRUITMENT

Robert Liljeberg III lived only a block and a half from the Stern Center, but he belonged to a separate campus, away from kids who played Quidditch in cargo shorts. His block on Montagu Street was lined with $2 million or $3 million homes with white facades and blackened fireplaces. Magnolias bloomed over courtyards, and Tri Delts and Chi Os [Chi Omegas] parked their Cayennes at the end of the street. Looking at the house at 7 Montagu, Mikey saw three stories of wood shutters and a Preservation Society of Charleston medallion. He wasn't focused on whether the architecture was Federal or Colonial, or if the paint was charcoal or taupe, but he knew he'd entered the bubble.

Walking in, Mikey looked into the dining room, where he

saw a beer pong table under a chandelier. He followed Rob into his room, a converted wood-paneled study with a mattress and a box spring on the floor. Sitting down, Rob opened a big red tomato can and pulled out a vacuum-sealed bag of weed. He loaded his HiSi glass bong and passed it to Mikey, who lit the bowl and watched the hexagonal chamber fill with smoke. Mikey later described Rob's marijuana as "shitty-ass fucking outdoor dark-green bullshit weed," but in the moment he felt giddy. He handed the bong back to Rob, and they giggled under the exposed beams. Looking around, Mikey saw more red tomato cans, which by his mental math came out to several pounds of weed. They passed the hexagon back and forth. To Mikey's joy, Rob had no problem keeping up with him.

Robert Liljeberg III wouldn't speak to me for this book, but it seems like he behaved better as a child than Mikey did. He grew up the son of an orthopedic surgeon and a registered nurse in Hickory, North Carolina, a forty-thousand-person town known for its lake culture and handmade furniture. A photo from middle school shows him next to the local priest at Saint Aloysius Catholic Church, with his ears flopping out from his curls. He's wearing an Ad Altare Dei pin on his Boy Scout shirt, proof that he studied the seven sacraments. The photo ran in the *Catholic News Herald* under the headline "Devout Scouts."

As far as I could tell, Rob was not a bro in high school. He was not only a devout Catholic but also a soccer team leader and an Eagle Scout. His varsity soccer coach told me he was "good natured . . . hardworking . . . passionate and dedicated . . . a tireless attacker at the flank who did well in school." He also called Rob "quiet," and, really, so did almost everyone else I asked. Before he rebranded himself in college, he seemed to have devoted much of his social energy to his girlfriend. Rob wrote her public Twitter devotionals, posting things like, "Got the best girlfriend ever @Jenniep773" and "Gotta love someone as perfect as @Jenniep773." When he accepted an offer to play soccer at Elmhurst College outside Chicago, he promised to try a long-distance relationship.

Rob and Jennie stayed together, but his freshman year didn't go well. Chicago's suburbs were a long way from the Blue Ridge Mountains, and after hearing Rob's North Carolina accent, one Elmhurst student thought he was from Australia. During the soccer season Rob took one shot and scored zero goals, and he looked for a school closer to home. He got into the College of Charleston, but when he came back southeast, his parents left North Carolina. His father was in trouble for an episode outside Hickory's Viewmont Surgery Center, where, according to a North Carolina Medical Board consent order, security cameras recorded him placing a nail under a coworker's car tire. He lost the right to work at Viewmont, and he met with a Board-certified coach about "deal[ing] more effectively with any frustrations or pressures in the workplace." Soon after, the Liljebergs left Hickory for a small town in central Alabama.

While Rob settled into Charleston in 2012, he didn't have an easy answer if people asked his hometown. He was fit but skinny from soccer, and his hair was an unshaved bush of curls. He tried his usual way of making a life for himself, volunteering with the student government association and joining the Catholic Student Association as a Eucharist minister. He stayed devoted to his high school sweetheart, ignoring the boys who'd look down on monogamous "girlfriend guys" and their earlier bedtimes. But the College of Charleston isn't the kind of place where Eagle Scouts have social pull, and his classmates from Connecticut hadn't heard of Hickory, North Carolina, let alone Troy, Alabama. After a semester of marine biology and volunteer work, Rob took a step toward becoming someone that more kids wanted to be friends with by exploring the Greek system, and he found a spot in the Kappa Alpha Order.

No one I met in Charleston ever accused Kappa Alpha of being the best fraternity at C of C. Whereas the SAEs had a historical marker next to their house, the KAs didn't have a house. The same Tri Delt sister who called the SAEs tall and handsome described the KAs as "random." "Where the obnoxiously good-looking frats would be like, 'Oh, we're hot shit, we're gonna have all these hot girls at our parties,'" she told me, "the KAs would just be like, 'Oh, we have a keg.'" A Kappa Sig called Kappa Alpha "steady middle tier," and an SAE told me that "they weren't on my radar." When Rob arrived, their chapter GPA hovered around the national 2.7 minimum, and their community service hours were near zero. Their budget allowed only a simple social calendar. One older KA said, "We just got fucking hammered off bourbon and Natty Lights all the time."

If the Kappa Alphas were known for anything, it was being southern. They recruited boys from Atlanta, Memphis, Fort

Worth, and around South Carolina. Many of them liked to hunt and ride ATVs. For a good KA, there was no shame in wearing whitewashed Wranglers and throwing in a cheek of Red Man, and, unlike the SAEs, they weren't afraid to like country music. Since its founding at what became Washington and Lee University in 1865, the Kappa Alpha Order national organization has seen itself as "southern in its loves." Before the end of the century, Kappa Alpha voted to ban expansion north of the Mason-Dixon Line, and although the policy has been reversed, all but a dozen or so of its 130 or so chapters remain in the South. This concentration gives the fraternity a rare level of cohesion. Where a Delta Sigma Phi at Penn State and Georgia Tech might not have much in common, almost every Kappa Alpha I've met has something to say about chewing tobacco.

Rob fit in with this southern crew. His dad and uncle had been KAs at Tulane, and he drew on their roots. Talking to the C of C Kappa Alphas, Rob didn't share much about Hickory or Troy, but he talked a lot about New Orleans, where the Liljeberg name meant something. Rob's grandfather once imported a fifteen-foot statue of Saint Jude from Italy to stand in front of a major Louisiana hospital complex he partially owned, and Rob's uncle was a parish judge with eyes on the Louisiana Supreme Court. Rob liked to tell people that he'd missed only two Mardi Gras in his life, and he knew a lot about LSU Tigers football. In fact, several KAs I interviewed thought Rob had grown up in New Orleans instead of North Carolina and transferred from Louisiana State instead of a Church of Christ–affiliated college in suburban Illinois.

After a semester of recruitment and pledgeship, Rob joined the Kappa Alpha Order. He also started going to the gym and bulking up. After tweeting things like "Great weekend lsu won and I got to see my baby. Can't wait for thanksgiving!! Love you @Jenniep773," he retweeted things like "The derivation of the word 'bride' is from an old English word that means 'cook,' whereas the word 'groom' came from 'male child.' Hahaha." On a road trip to a Clemson–Auburn game with other KAs, Rob made a good water bottle bong with some tape and a lug nut. His new brothers thought of him as a chill, southern kid who drank Coronas and still got his work done, and they started to know him as a guy who could sell them weed too. He didn't stand out among C of C fraternity kids—he was still a long-distance-girlfriend guy, and one roommate described his family wealth as "somewhere between well off and okay"—but now he had friends outside the Catholic Student Association. Before the 2013–2014 school year, Rob got invited to move into the off-campus house on Montagu Street with three other KAs. Two of the roommates were from Greenwich, and the third's father was the CEO of a for-profit college based in Virginia. The college CEO purchased the house as a gift to his boy for $885,000.

Mikey arrived in Charleston only a few weeks after Rob moved into 7 Montagu. When Rob invited him to smoke in his room, he introduced Mikey to the unofficial side of fraternity recruitment, also known as rush. Officially, recruitment was a sober and regulated process. Mikey and other underclassmen would meet chapter leaders at the activity fair, pay thirty-five dollars to enter the applicant pool, and take a few house tours. After that, the candidates might sit through career-fair-style interviews, and active members would select boys who fit their organization's written values.

Unofficially—at least for the good fraternities that Mikey wanted to join—rush was actually a big competitive party. He'd go to SAE's and KA's pregames, darties, booze cruises, boozy golf trips, beach kickbacks, postgames, and late nights, and he'd get tested on how good he was at going out. To start, he had to know how not to dress. This meant no V-necks, ankle socks, male jewelry, hair gel, Abercrombie/Old Navy/American Eagle, or cargo shorts. Then he had to answer questions about his hometown and high school sports without making things awkward. After that, he couldn't embarrass himself at beer pong, and he'd need to shotgun without asking for help making a hole in the can. As he got drunk, maybe drunker than he'd ever been in his life, he'd need to hit on a few girls and make new friends without saying things that kids would hold against him later. He'd also have to do these things without looking like a "try-hard." Older fraternity guys can smell a try-hard's desperation from across the lawn, because he takes their social cues and turns them to eleven. Not only will he wear a Vineyard Vines button-down, but he'll have whales on his belt and socks too. In general, he'll pour an obvious amount of energy into fitting in, which is an easy recipe for social death.

One of Mikey's first tests during rush was KA's Catalina Wine Mixer. Like "Boats N' Hoes," the theme was inspired by a scene in the movie *Step Brothers*, and the idea was to wear pastel and drink boxed wine. Before Mikey arrived, he chose between his Augusta National merch and shirts by Southern Marsh and Southern Tide. Walking on Vanderhorst Street, he approached a skinny wood house that a few KAs rented and had nicknamed "Vandyland." From the sidewalk Mikey could see inflatable pools in the driveway. Above him, boys and girls jumped off the porch into the water. After they dried off, they took the plastic pouches out of wine boxes and "slapped the bag." Joining in, Mikey and the other rushees held the plastic above their faces, slapping the pouch while they chugged from the spigot. After Mikey wiped his mouth, he made his way up to the top balcony, where he remembered why he liked the KAs. Unlike the SAEs, whose rush parties involved EDM on weeknights, the KAs were happy to smoke on the porch all afternoon.

Mikey didn't know it, but some KAs didn't like him. In their eyes, he told stories designed to make him seem cooler than he probably was. One brother told me, "I was a little skeptical. He'd be like, 'Aah, towards the end of summer, like, we were soooo drunk at this kid's house,' and we were like, 'Sick, dude.'" Another KA said that "he definitely had a bit of an insecurity—small guy, hanging out with older guys, wanting to prove himself, wanting approval." A third said that "he was a little full of it," and the first added, "He's a nice kid, but he was almost trying a little bit too hard."

Lucky for Mikey, he had Rob. Besides the fact that they both dealt some weed, they connected over other things. They drove the same car, a Mercedes SL coupe from the 1990s. They riffed with each other's dick and fart jokes, and they both loved to sit back and people-watch. Even for eighteen-to-twenty-year-old boys, they were also both exceptionally good at video games, with Mikey specializing in *FIFA* and Rob winning at *Super Smash Bros.* In *Smash*, Mikey liked to play as Samus, and Rob picked blue Donkey Kong. While Mikey levitated around in a flashy suit, launching missiles and shooting electric charges, Rob sat back and let the other players fight. Once they'd injured each other, he'd wind up Donkey Kong's Giant Punch and grin while other characters flew off the screen. After that, they'd bring out the HiSi bong or roll another joint, and Mikey got to connect with guys who'd be making his rush decision. These KAs liked that Mikey was down to smoke, and that he sold weed and other things too.

Since 1984, when the minimum legal drinking age rose from eighteen to twenty-one, US law has baked criminality into the lives of fraternity kids. Even though they're committing a range of misdemeanors when they purchase and consume alcohol, most eighteen-to-twenty-year-olds who join fraternities drink. To access the promised fun of college, underclassmen usually need a fake ID. A decent fake will pass UV light and hologram tests, but the holy grail is one that gets past barcode readers and box scanners. When I was eighteen, the most common source for those fakes was IDChief.com, a website that took in a kid's address and passport photo and mailed back scannable cards wrapped in Chinese newspapers. But after a bipartisan team of US senators raised the alarm that America's teens were sending their personal information to Guangzhou, the site shut down. After that, good IDs were harder to find. Some kids bought easier-to-fake cards from harder-to-believe states like Idaho or Hawaii, and others sent their money to websites that turned out to be scams.

Mikey found his opportunity to sell fake IDs through one of his best friends in Atlanta. His friend, a rave lover we'll call Flip, was a year younger than Mikey and better with computers. They liked to break stuff together, and in high school they robbed a smoke shop and buried the stolen bongs in Flip's mom's backyard. Around the time Mikey graduated, Flip bought an Epson R280 and a laminate attachment to make ID cards. Using something he called the dark web that Mikey didn't understand, Flip found software to program scanner strips. The results felt flimsier than top-tier fakes, but they worked at most King Street bars. As a freshman, Mikey started bringing dozens of ID orders back from Atlanta. He paid Flip $20 per card, and after he hid them inside his blue dorm mattress, he sold them for $200 each.

In comparison with some college rackets, Mikey's ID operation was relatively small time. I got one of my fake IDs from a UT Sig Ep whose process involved an HD scanner, several operating systems, and five printers. On the floor of his freshman dorm in West Campus, he rigged a top-level Epson, a black light printer, a rare 1980s hologram printer remade by a dark web mechanic in rural China, and a hole punch printer programmed to punch 238 dots in the shape of Texas. He bought a burner phone and answered texts as "the Owl," and I once ran into him on 6th Street in Austin lifting a magnum of Dom

Perignon with both hands. Later that night I saw him with his arm around a former Longhorns starting quarterback. "I could walk up to almost any fraternity and get into their parties," he told me later. "[I'd think], 'Well, I made your ID, I made your ID, I made your ID.'"

The Owl in Austin and Mikey in Charleston found that demand for their product was almost limitless. Also, unlike with drugs, there was nothing taboo about it. A few of the Owl's customers' parents showed up to pay for their kids' fakes themselves, and my friend's dad framed his ID from the early 1980s next to his son's from 2012. For a certain type of college boy, fake IDs carried little to no risk. On my twentieth birthday, for instance, my friend and I were arrested with fakes that the Owl had made for us. The policeman who booked us threatened to charge us with identity theft, but we walked away with "misrepresentation of age by a minor," a class C misdemeanor little worse than a speeding ticket. It actually turned out better than a speeding ticket, thanks to a mutual acquaintance named John Gioffredi. Mr. Gioffredi is a defense lawyer who, if I remember right, used to make beer cozies that said, "*Don't Drink and Drive, But if You Do, Call John Gioffredi.*" I called John Gioffredi, and he got the "misrepresentation of age" charge erased from my record for something like $120. Many kids in Greek life know a Mr. Gioffredi, a family friend who can make a minor in possession arrest or a public intoxication charge disappear.

Of course, Mikey and the Owl risked far more than their customers did. Because fake IDs are tools for fugitives and terrorists, the federal government takes them seriously. Still, neither Mikey nor my UT friend were ever arrested for their operations. The Owl sold over one thousand IDs at a price of $200 a card, and he now works for a Big Tech company.

Mikey later said that at one KA rush party, Rob called him over and asked, "What the fuck you got going on in that dorm now? Are you gonna show me how to do it?" Mikey responded, "Naw, I'm not your pledge yet."

After rush week at the College of Charleston, the local chapters gathered their brotherhoods to vote on slideshows. Recruitment chairs showed Instagram pictures with boys' names and hometowns below them, and members commented on each slide. If the candidate was popular, the commentary might sound something like "Solid kid, played golf at Jesuit," or "Chill, pulls." If the boy was unpopular, the actives might call him a cheesedick or describe his high school girlfriend as beat. If an active member had a vendetta against a particular kid, he might try to blackball him. (The term comes from an old process in which fraternities voted on members with black and white marbles, and a single "black ball" could knock a boy out of contention.) Some slides flashed up on the projector for a forty-five-second yes vote or rejection, and some led to twenty-minute arguments.

After interviewing 124 sources for this book, I still don't know if Mikey got a bid to join Sigma Alpha Epsilon. He told people that he got one, but the SAEs I talked to said they didn't remember meeting Mikey as a freshman. Rush voting is a semisecret process without much paperwork, and the truth might be lost to local history. Regardless, despite a few protests that he was a try-hard, Mikey got a bid to join the Kappa Alpha Order. After voting, Mikey went over to Rob's house, and he, Rob, and the for-profit college CEO's son all sat on the red couch in one of Montagu's two living rooms. Rob kept things casual. "Yo, you got a bid, if you want it."

Mikey didn't tell the KAs if he'd accept Rob's offer until Bid Day in the Cistern. At the end of rush, every interfraternity council organization met next to the seafoam green shutters of Randolph Hall. It was the only time all year the fraternity bubble stood in one place, with the Pikes swaggering next to the sweet, irrelevant Sigma Chis. When it got to his turn, Mikey went up on stage and faced a few other hundred kids. He stood on the platform and listened to the IFC president announce "Michael Schmidt: Kappa Alpha Order," and he watched the KAs blow up in celebration. Then he walked into the crowd to get embraced by Rob and his new group of boys.

"Right after that, the whole weekend is a party," one Kappa Alpha from his year told me. He said that the KAs threw a combined mixer with the Kappa Delta, Alpha Delta Pi, and Tri Delt sororities, and the ratio was eight girls for every guy. "You gotta seem legit for one week, and KA did it. They really put on a great face," he said. "But then Sunday comes, and you're a pledge now, and you're getting the shit beaten out of you, and you're like, 'Yo, what the fuck did I just get myself into?'"

CHAPTER 4

PLEDGESHIP

After Mikey accepted his bid from the Kappa Alpha Order, he received a book called *The Varlet*. It looks like a skinnier bible, with a hard case surrounding a gold cross on the cover. The cross sits inside a shield that rests between two lions, which paw at what the book calls "an arm wielding a battle-ax in the act of striking." Under this coat of arms is the French motto "*Dieu et les Dames*," which means "God and the Ladies." The first 150 pages are illustrated with smiling photos and original art, and the last fifty contain the KA Order bylaws. On one of the non-bylaw pages, the book compares new Kappa Alpha members to medieval varlets, European page boys who trained in noblemen's castles to become knights. During this training, "a candidate was prepared in the arts and techniques of war and was familiarized with the code of chivalry. . . . The title of this book, Kappa Alpha Order's membership education manual, is taken from this initial stage of learning on the path to knighthood."

The Kappa Alpha Order national organization, headquartered in an eighteenth-century Virginia plantation manor called Mulberry Hill near Lexington, takes a strong official stance against hazing. *The Talisman*, KA's guide for recruits and parents, calls it "the fratricide of brotherhood," and *The Varlet* says, "Hazing, like some forms of assault, is about power." KA nationals officially banned the practice in 1903, and the *Talisman* concludes, "If you care about brotherhood, modern day chivalry, integrity, being a leader and having a KA undergraduate experience, be the better man and REFUSE TO ACCEPT IT, REPORT IT, and STOP IT." Instead, Mulberry Hill's new-member education curriculum teaches boys how to be modern gentleman knights. The program includes weekly coat-and-tie meetings with quizzes and guest lectures, plus a book called *To Manner Born, To Manners Bred: A Hip-Pocket Guide to Etiquette for the Kappa Alpha Gentleman.*

Near the front of the book, *The Varlet* has a chapter titled "Chivalry and Gentility." It begins with an illustration of a Kappa Alpha knight riding his KA horse away from a KA castle. After that comes readings on Charlemagne and the decline of feudalism, but the goal is less of a history lesson than a rulebook for life. "A man is chosen for membership in our Order because his conduct reflects the true chivalric code, a code modified only slightly to suit contemporary society." According to *The Varlet*, Kappa Alpha initiates are taught to behave like gentlemen and revere God. They are "brought privileges of class," which also bring the responsibility to protect the poor and defend women's purity. Their Order is "military in organization and religious in feeling," which means its national executive, the knight commander, has the "ruling authority of a top military officer" over every brother. KA calls itself an order, and not a fraternity, because its "members are bound by the same ideal and philosophy of life—the epitome of the chivalric knight of the Middle Ages, especially the Knight Templar. Kappa Alpha Order then, is a contemporary order of knights."

KA isn't the only fraternity to treat its boys like young Lancelots. The Sigma Nu preamble talks about the Knighthoods of Love, Honor, and Truth, and SAE built a neo-Gothic headquarters with stained-glass knights in the chapel and a mural of gnomes in the basement. Medieval heroes are part of the classic fraternity man blend, a mix of Greek philosopher, feudal knight, Victorian gentleman, and American world leader. Unlike other fraternities, though, KA views one historical man as the embodiment of all those traits. After its section on the decline of feudalism, *The Varlet* begins a chapter titled "A True Gentleman, the Last Gentle Knight" dedicated to Robert E. Lee. General Lee was president of Washington College (now Washington and Lee) when Kappa Alpha was founded there in 1865, but the order sees him as more than an administrator. "Kappa Alphas have never claimed that Lee was an initiated member of the Order, but they do rejoice that KA was born under the white light of his noble life. Members are immensely proud and honored that his ideals were woven into KA's soul, and that he is, in a profoundly real sense, our spiritual founder." According to *The Varlet*, KAs placed a wreath under his Richmond statue in 1915 and designated him the organization's spiritual founder in 1923. Near the end of the chapter, the book defines a gentleman as "the chivalrous warrior of Christ, the knight who loves God and country, honors and protects pure womanhood, practices self-respect to ill-gotten wealth," and adds, "Lee in his daily walk, was this perfect gentleman."

Once a pledge reads *The Varlet*, including the fifty pages of rules in the back, Mulberry Hill considers him ready for his initiation ceremony. *The Varlet* doesn't describe the official KA ritual, but it promises that it will be a life-changing event. It assures the reader that it will distill wisdom of ages past while penetrating his mind and heart. It quotes one of Kappa Alpha's founding fathers, saying, "I once heard a distinguished Kappa Alpha say that but three books are needed for the formation of the perfect man—Shakespeare, the Bible, and the Kappa Alpha Ritual." Beyond that, it doesn't give anything away. Nervous initiates have tried to find copies of the nineteenth-century text in stores or even in the Library of Congress, but it's never been made available to the public. Online, the only information I could find was Kappa Alpha's "ritual supplies" list. It includes tunics, capes, crowns, jewels, spurs, blindfolds, an urn, a fireproof lockbox, and something called the Excalibur Sword.

At the College of Charleston, parts of Kappa Alpha new-member education varied year to year. A fall 2015 pledge told me that his term began when the actives made the new members arrive at an off-campus apartment in a white T-shirt and disposable sneakers. After the brothers walked in and gave a welcome speech that no one really remembers, they locked the pledges in a bathroom with a handle of Fireball whisky. Once the boys drank the 1.75 liters, they were led upstairs to the living room, where they saw a tarp covering the floor. The older brothers pulled out a trash can and told the pledges to form a circle around it. They gave them a handle of Evan Williams and said it was time for a bourbon circle. It's a simple game: a pledge holds the handle of Kentucky whiskey to his lips, chugs as much as he can, and passes it to the next pledge, who does the same, sending the bourbon around until it's empty. (In my fraternity, we called it "Don't Fuck Your Brother," because the less hard alcohol you chug, the more your pledge brothers have to chug for you.) The KA pledges had to finish seven or eight handles of Evan Williams, a little under twenty shots a person, and they vomited a good chunk of it into the trash can. "That was the first day," the KA told me. "It was definitely hazing, but it was, you know, more celebratory than violent."

Regardless of the year,* the real work of pledgeship started when the boys met to learn the rules for the semester. Every morning, the new members reported to active members' apartments to cook and clean. Most days, they delivered the brothers'

---

* For recollections of the C of C KA new-member education, I spoke to one boy who pledged in the spring of 2012, one who pledged in the fall of 2013, another who pledged in the fall of 2015, and one who pledged in the spring of 2016.

lunch and ran things around town as couriers. They also had to wear a uniform at all times; one semester the boys alternated between formal suits and white T-shirts with dirty New Balances, and during Mikey's term they wore neckties and Velcro shoes from Walmart. One boy had to wear a Disney Princess backpack all day, and another had to store his backpack in the freezer each night. The 2015 pledge with the longest hair had to shave his head, and every boy had to keep Marlboro Reds or Lights and a red or gold lighter in his pocket. They submitted their schedules to the pledge master, and they were on call for errands if they weren't in class. Thursday, Friday, and Saturday nights they'd be "pledge drivers," chauffeuring brothers to and from house parties and King Street from nine p.m. to two a.m. Other nights they'd have lineups, and at the end of the semester they'd have Hell Week, but in the meantime they had the daily routine of being a pledge.

Forced drinking in secret rooms gets more news coverage, probably because it kills an average of one college student every year, but it's the daily hazing errands that fraternity kids often hate most. Chugging bourbon over a tarp at least means drinking with your friends, but there's nothing fun about working as older boys' menservants. When Mikey and I were in college, these servile tasks were coordinated on GroupMe, a messaging app that can handle bigger groups than iMessage. The pledge class would join the group chat, which they'd title something like "Shotcallerz OG" or "Eatin' Pussy Kickin' Ass," and fill it with memes, nudes, college football talk, and pledge requests. The boys would elect a pledge class president (PCP), a prestigious-sounding title that's mostly a phone operator job, who listened to members' needs and found pledges to fill them. The PCP would text the GroupMe things like, "Clint needs three pledges to hand wash his Tahoe," or "Lonnie wants a McRib and a pic of 1 pledge kissing 2 girls on the street." In some bigger fraternities, pledges were also expected to do "builds," hauling lumber and hammering nails to construct bars and stages for theme parties. By themselves, none of the tasks felt that bad, but combined they became a full-time job. In certain parts of the South, prospective employers understood that fraternity boys' GPAs would dip during their pledge term, because most guys had little time for homework and others didn't make it to class.

Mikey had no problem missing school. One of his first college lectures was an introductory government class, and on the first day he watched the professor wheel in a bike from the Cistern Yard. The man wore purple socks with Godzillas on them, and when he took the podium he started complaining about Charleston's lack of protected bike lanes. When Mikey looked down and saw his "GOATS" pledge class GroupMe light up, he left the lecture and never came back. He later told an older guy, "The professor was a weirdo bike-riding hippie. How the fuck was he going to teach me anything?" Missing class left Mikey more time for KA errands, which meant driving his SL around Charleston to pick up food or clean apartments. These runs helped him get to know the active brothers better, and in turn the older guys started to like Mikey more too. One KA told me, "We helped break Mikey out of his shell," and another said

Mikey gradually stopped bragging about getting drunk at high school parties. Rob didn't bother Mikey with too many pledge errands, but he did invite him to smoke after the pledges signed in for morning tasks at 7 Montagu. The two friends played *Super Smash Bros.* for months before Mikey learned how to knock Rob's Donkey Kong off the screen. He'd wait off to the side while the other boys fought, and while Rob wound up his Giant Punch on someone else, Mikey killed him with the charge from Samus's arm cannon.

On surprise nights of the week, the KAs held lineups. Because they didn't have an official fraternity house, the brothers gathered Mikey's pledge class in off-campus apartment living rooms, which meant moving all the sofas and laying out plastic for vomit. Pledges showed up in white T-shirts ahead of time, knowing that lineups are the kind of event where "if you're early, you're on time. If you're on time, you're late. If you're late, you're fucked." They'd stand in a circle wearing blindfolds and answer questions about things like the Greek alphabet. When Mikey's pledge brothers answered wrong they might have to drink a cup of "pledge juice"—cat food, dip spit, etc.—or do other things that might make them throw up. They might also lie blindfolded on the floor, getting doused with unknown substances that tasted like flour, or smelled like Glade air freshener, or felt like urine. In 2015, the brothers duct-taped forty-ounce bottles of malt liquor to the pledges' hands and made them chug ("Edward 40 Hands"). That same term, they made two pledge brothers shotgun Four Lokos and box each other. One boy who didn't smoke weed was deemed the "weed hazing pledge" and forced to swallow edibles. Mikey, who did smoke weed, had to wear a gas mask with a bong attached to his mouth, which the brothers filled with tobacco until his head spun. Another night he laid his elbows and toes on top of bottle caps, watching them bleed until the brothers told him he could get up. Class clowns learned not to talk back, a key part of another rule of pledgeship: "If you think you're right, you're wrong, and if you know you're wrong, you're fucked."

As a pledge, Mikey never opened his copy of *The Varlet*. He didn't join a fraternity for extra reading, and the book wasn't a major part of C of C Kappa Alpha membership training. The actives did hold weekly coat-and-tie meetings in a C of C classroom, but they never talked about Charlemagne. (During one 2015 meeting, a pledge who'd accidentally killed a brother's pet fish was forced to swallow a live goldfish.) The C of C KAs mostly used *The Varlet* as a tool at lineups, making boys repeat the Greek alphabet until they had to drink pledge juice. In my experience, this is the most common use for fraternity literature. During our first night of getting hazed in the Columbia Delta Sig basement, for instance, our pledge master handed us a century-old preamble. It began, "The Delta Sigma Phi Fraternity in Convention assembled declares and affirms the following principles: That the belief in God is essential to our welfare." When the nonreligious freshmen protested, the brothers told us we weren't actually expected to believe anything in the preamble, but if any of us didn't memorize every word, "You'll all be fucked."

It's easy to see a conflict between the high, gentlemanly ideals of fraternity literature and the low and dirty life of a fraternity pledge. *The Varlet* describes knights with feathers in their helmets, and Mikey got locked in a closet with a tobacco bong. It'd make sense if upper-class boys actually read *To Manner Born, To Manners Bred*, but instead they sample what it's like to be the help. For five months, kids who grew up with nannies and tutors learn to run errands and ghostwrite homework. For some pledges, it's the only time in their lives they'll have to actually use Windex. Taken far enough, pledging can start to look like poor-person cosplay, with rich kids acting like oppressed workers for a semester. At one top-tier Dartmouth fraternity, for instance, every pledge had to wear a ball cap, a white T-shirt, a pair of jeans, a dirty gray sweatshirt worn inside out, and beat-up "shitkicker" Timberland boots to class every day. A friend who eventually joined that fraternity told me he'd heard pledges wore that uniform because "it's the last time you'll ever have to wear a workingman's clothes."

Because every fraternity manual bans hazing of any kind, this sort of pledgeship breaks the rules of *The Varlet*, *The Phoenix* (SAE), *The Gordian Knot* (Delta Sig), *The Paedagogus* (Lambda Chi), and all the rest. But in terms of the Greek thinkers, Christian knights, and British lords that these books teach kids to emulate, the temporary degradation feels on brand. One of the first written records of hazing comes from Plato in 387 BCE, in which he describes the initiation ritual at the Academy as practical jokes that injure unruly young men. During the Middle Ages, university students went through rites of sleep deprivation and forced starvation, and they sometimes got spanked while wearing goofy costumes. In Victorian England, first-year boys at posh boarding schools had to do a year of "fagging," a round-the-clock process of running older boys' errands and listening to their verbal abuse. Although Harvard emulated fagging in its early days, hazing didn't really take off in America until after the Civil War, when men from good families returned to campus with a new appreciation for the bonds that come with struggle. And in *True Gentlemen*, John Hechinger's history of Sigma Alpha Epsilon, he describes visiting the gothic mural in the fraternity's modern headquarters and noticing that one gnome is wearing a blindfold and another gnome is paddling him.

Although he never opened his book on Middle Age chivalry and the privileges of the gentleman class, Mikey went through a newer version of the old rites of passage. To cement their status on top of the rabble, elite boys had to spend a few months suffering like peasants. In Victorian England, it meant waxing the boarding school floor like a butler before owning a country house. At Dartmouth, it might mean dressing like a construction worker before working at a private equity firm that owns construction companies. In all instances, it means getting treated like "a little bitch" before becoming the man. Perhaps for this reason, top fraternities are often known for hazing the hardest. They have the most time-intensive pledgeship on campus, and other students tell the most far-fetched stories about their lineups. (One popular myth is that an Old Row fraternity at the University of Alabama makes pledges jump off its mansion roof until they hear a bone crack.) These rumors help beef up a chapter's status—"Boys are willing to eat dip just to join their club!" etc.—but I think the pull of hazing for elite guys runs even deeper than that. For people who spend their childhoods pampered by maids and their adulthood in charge of other people, the act of submission can spice things up. When feeling powerless is a temporary game, it's mostly just a pleasure to get dominated.

In their preinitiation literature, the KA national organization tells boys to prepare for Kappa Alpha initiation with a final week of readings and a group viewing of *Braveheart*. Instead, the College of Charleston KAs did Hell Week. At many fraternities, Hell Week means living in a fraternity basement for seven days. Because the C of C KAs didn't have a house, Mikey and his pledge brothers moved into different brothers' apartments around campus. Near the end of his fall semester, Mikey arrived at 7 Montagu, turned in his phone, and got his instructions. When he wasn't in class, he belonged to the Kappa Alpha Order. He wasn't allowed to leave Rob's house for any reason, and he wasn't going to play *Smash* while he was there. When he and the other pledges got home from school, they did older boys' homework and scrubbed their floors. One of Rob's roommates made them write five-thousand-word essays on meaningless topics, but mostly they sat around, not allowed to nap or shower, passing the time before lineups.

During an early 2015 Hell Week lineup, the actives poured a half bottle of Tabasco into a liter of Dewar's scotch and locked the pledge brothers in a closet until they finished it. By then, though, the boys' alcohol tolerance was high enough that they preferred the drinking hazing to the food stuff. That same term, the pledges had to lie shoulder to shoulder on the floor, and a brother cracked an egg in the first kid's mouth and told them to pass the yolk all the way down. In 2012, they were forced to chug a few orange sodas, which was easy, and told to kill a live duck, which seemed unreasonable. When they looked into the eyes of the duck and agreed to protest, the brothers started applauding, and said, "Congratulations. It was a test. It was all about unity." The next morning they realized the orange soda had been spiked with laxatives.

During Mikey's 2013 term, Rob kept away from the worst hazing, a move that always earns love from younger kids. Even so, new faces showed up to take his place. It's common during Hell Week to meet an older fraternity guy who doesn't go to fraternity parties or chapter meetings but who seems to pay $500 a semester so he can make kids eat cat food. The Hell Week–lovers can get aggressive, and even though an active told Mikey that "if an older brother puts his hands on you, you are allowed to put your hands back on him," Mikey couldn't fight back when they forced him to sleep in the dirt underneath a brother's house for two nights. The weather got down to the forties during late fall in Charleston, and Mikey woke up both mornings feeling sick. By the time he started an overnight road trip to the KA chapters at Wofford, Clemson, the University of South Carolina, and the University of Georgia, he had a fever. After Mikey jumped into a pool at one KA house and made sandpit snow angels at another, his temperature reached 103 degrees. When he got back to Charleston covered in sand, he still couldn't shower.

After midnight on the second-to-last night of Hell Week, the actives told Mikey's pledge class to wear their Velcro shoes. After they tied blindfolds around their eyes, the underclassmen got into cars with running engines. The boys sat with their eyes closed for fifteen or twenty minutes on a drive that felt smooth. Then the ride started to throw their bodies around, and when the doors opened the pledges got out. The brothers led them through what felt like marsh up to their shins, and then to what they knew was sand. They heard waves, and the active members told the pledges to take off their blindfolds and run into the ocean. They sprinted toward the Atlantic and jumped into cold water, and when they got out the brothers' headlights were gone. As was tradition, the C of C KA pledges had to walk the four hours from the far tip of Sullivan's Island to downtown Charleston. Most years, some boys fell asleep on the walk. Mikey's year, though, a Sullivan's Island police car pulled up to investigate the two dozen kids walking at two a.m. in wet Velcro shoes. They told him, "We're a running club, sir," and he called them taxis home.

In response to a request for comment on the C of C KA pledging experiences my sources described, an attorney for the KA national organization "denounce[d], in the strongest terms, the conduct, and/or actions" that they recounted. The attorney also denied the allegations in their entirety, stating that they "do not reflect Kappa Alpha Order, the [C of C] Chapter alumni as a whole, or any of its members." He said that the alleged conduct would violate KA's bylaws prohibiting drunkenness, hazing, and any "criminal or ungentlemanly conduct," and that the national office "has neither records, documents, nor institutional memory" of any of the incidents. He added that "KAO maintains an industry-standard document retention policy. Records pertaining to this chapter and others from more than five years ago have been discarded."

By most accounts, the KAs didn't have the hardest pledgeship at the College of Charleston. That distinction belonged to the best chapters like SAE. Their hazing was different from the KAs in small ways, like meeting at six o'clock every morning instead of nine thirty, and in its totalizing nature. "We got rocked," one SAE told me. "I mean, it's deep. Like, I saw kids cry. Saw kids break down." I heard a few unbelievable stories about the C of C Sigma Alpha Epsilon Hell Week, and I tried to find someone who could confirm or deny them. Eventually I talked to another SAE who told me about a conversation he had a few years after graduation, when he'd hosted a bachelor party for his best friend from the fraternity. At the end of the night, eight guys sat around a fire, drinking and telling their favorite stories about the groom. The high school buddies told fun anecdotes, and then it was the SAE's turn. "I told a story that was really dark," he told me. "Something that [the groom] did to me in my fraternity that was, like, horrible. Everybody was like, 'What the fuck. Why is that the story you're telling us?'"

I obviously asked what that story was. He started by describing SAE Hell Week, which he said involved getting tased and running fifteen miles to take a picture with a random woman at a Waffle House. During one lineup, the future groom, who was a year older than his future groomsman, pulled his friend aside and told him, "Things are gonna get really, really fucked for y'all right now. It's gonna get really bad. But I want you to know that you can put your life in my hands, and I won't let anything go beyond the pale, no matter what." Near the end of that night, a few older SAEs asked the pledges for a hazing volunteer. The future groomsman raised his hand, and the future groom looked at him and shook his head. But the freshman kept his hand up, and the sophomore led his friend to the backyard, put a towel over his face, and waterboarded him. "One of my bigger fears is drowning," he told me. "It's scary, you know. That's a really real thing. But I'm a very good swimmer. I held my breath." The future groom poured water on the rag for thirty seconds, ninety seconds less than Khalid Sheikh Mohammed claimed to have endured at a CIA black site.

Around the fire pit at the bachelor party, the groom's buddies asked the SAE why he'd just told them that story. He answered, "Look, y'all have only had good experiences with [the groom]. You've never had what I've had with him, and you never will!"

One secret of pledgeship is that boys actually kind of love to tell each other about it. When my high school friends came home to Dallas for Thanksgiving break, we spent the long weekend competing with hazing stories. On his first night as a pledge, our Dartmouth friend had to watch a "shock and awe" talent show featuring upperclassmen drinking each other's urine and "boot"—the Dartmouth word for vomit—out of their actual boots. Another friend's SEC fraternity made their freshmen roll around on top of dead ducks, an act that came only two semesters after the chapter appeared in the local news for their "pledge goat incident." (As described by one source, the older boys assigned a pledge a live goat that he had to keep with him at all times, until an early-morning meeting, when "this one kind of psycho active just showed up with a shotgun, shot the goat, and then literally lopped off its balls, put them in an oven, cooked them, and made the pledge eat it.") Our friends at UT got tased with cattle prods and forced to eat "friendship apples," which are onions rolled in mayonnaise rolled in a can of Grizzly brand dipping tobacco. Regardless, the winner was our Duke friend, who told us a story from his Hell Week. At one point, after the pledges had to drink a kiddie pool of their own vomit, the actives lined the boys up and told "the softest" kid in the pledge class to "self-haze." Everyone assumed the boy would just put a cigar out on his own leg, but instead he took a bottle of beer, smashed it over his own head, and carved his fraternity's initials into his forearm with a shard of glass. He wore long sleeves at home for the next three years.

At the time, I was pretty embarrassed that I didn't have wilder stories from my pledgeship to share. Our Delta Sig chapter hazing was more like the C of C KA's, with a lot of forced binge drinking and a little sleep deprivation. I was glad I didn't have to swallow boot or self-haze, but I wouldn't have minded a good anecdote about friendship apples to share at home. There's social power in poorly kept secrets about funny and degrading hazing. In fact, when I called my high school friends to fact-check my memories of their stories for this book, they all made it clear that they'd do it again.

Duke Friend: People say, "I can make friends without doing that." Yeah, you can, but it doesn't make the fraternity stuff bad. It's just a different approach. It's a similar idea to the military. It builds camaraderie really, really quickly.

Dartmouth Friend: Who cares that we booted? Maybe I'm just a good example of someone who got so desensitized to not realize how absurd it is, but I'm also not quick to dismiss it. It certainly put us in a position to have more interesting memories together.

Texas Friend: Sometimes, after the older guys hazed me, they'd come and be like, "Dude, you know we fuck with you a lot because we like you the most." And I'm like, "Oh, fuck, this is fucking awesome."

Duke Friend: When we were finally done with pledgeship, that mentality was still there. And so people would just self-haze. Sophomore year we'd be late-nighting, and we'd be like, "Damn, I miss getting lined up," because there was a lot of camaraderie. So we'd line three people up in the bathtub and chew them out, make them drink something.

I asked the C of C SAE who told me the campfire story if he regretted getting hazed. He'd told me he didn't like a few things about his time in Sigma Alpha Epsilon, and I'd assumed getting waterboarded was one of them. Instead, he told me, "Hell yeah I'd do it again." When I asked him why, he said, "It's like climbing Mount Everest. It's like, why do it? It's because it's a prestigious thing. Like, why do we climb the mountain? Is it to climb to the summit and see the view? No, it's to say that you've done it. That's what being in a fraternity is like. If I tell someone 'I'm an SAE,' their response is, 'Oh, my God, he's seen some shit.'"

In its official bylaws, the Kappa Alpha Order requires its chapters to perform its secret initiation ceremony in a house of worship. Headquarters distributes a letter signed by the current executive director, Larry Stanton Wiese, for chapter presidents to give to potential church hosts. "Our members are commonly referred to as an Order of Christian Knights," it says. "Since the initiation ceremony is very religious in its basic essence, a place of worship is needed." After Mikey's Hell Week, the College of Charleston KAs met in a 160-year-old church on Ashley Avenue. The pledges put on robes, and the active members blindfolded them, which meant the boys couldn't see the stained glass around them or the hammer beam ceiling above their heads. After that, they heard the older kids recite a text that mixed Calvinist theology, three degrees of Masonic ritual, Confederate militarism, medieval romance, and what one brother called "esoteric sciences." Mikey felt a dull sword on his shoulders and tasted some wine from a special cup. Then the actives said his name and a few other things, and he went from a pledge to a brother.

At other schools, Kappa Alpha chapters had spent weeks rehearsing the ceremony and memorizing the text. They'd kept their crown and sword in a locked room and played the official Kappa Alpha CD of lute music during the ritual. But for the kind of chapter that did Hell Week, the church initiation was sometimes just a way to keep the executives at Mulberry Hill off their backs. The national organization makes every chapter reenact its official ritual, but different groups treat the ceremony with different levels of seriousness. "It was some Medieval Times bullshit," a recent KA chapter president told me. "[During the ritual], I took the CD they gave me and swapped it out with the music from *Halo*." At the end of Mikey's chapel ceremony, the brothers drove the new initiates to America Street, a heavily policed and marginalized strip of East Charleston, and told them to walk home again. The two dozen boys headed down the cracked asphalt, looking at overgrown lawns and boarded-up row houses. Without loosening their ties, Mikey and a few other KAs walked up to a group of Haitian immigrants and said, "Hey, y'all got some weed?"

CHAPTER 5

OLD SOUTH WEEKEND

The Charleston Police Department's 704-page case file on Michael Schmidt opens with a moment from Hell Week. The incident report comes hours before Mikey's KA initiation, in the middle of "Kidnap Night." During that night, the pledges had the freedom to punish whichever older kid had hazed them the worst that semester. Mikey's year, the boys voted to abduct the son of the for-profit-college CEO. When Mikey arrived at 7 Montagu from lab class, his pledge brothers had already gotten drunk and bought kidnapping supplies. After some planning, a team of freshmen ran toward his room. Other KAs slept at friends' houses during Kidnap Night, but the CEO's son apparently didn't think he'd be a target. The tallest pledge helped pin him down, and the others began to wrap him in duct tape. They bound his hands together and his legs, and kept wrapping the young heir until he was buried in tape. They dragged him outside and handed his Audi A4 keys to Mikey, who was the only pledge sober enough to drive.

When they put the CEO's son in the back of his Audi, he started to scream. While Mikey swerved around a pedestrian, he heard one of his pledge brothers punch their captive in the face. The plan was to leave him in the dunes on Sullivan's Island, but after Mikey turned on Ashley Avenue without signaling he saw police lights behind him. Mikey pulled over, and when the policeman heard a voice crying something like "Help! Help!" he called for backup. A few minutes later, a sergeant and an officer walked toward the Audi. Through the back passenger door, they saw three boys in street clothes and a fourth who'd been duct-taped and gagged. As the official Charleston PD incident report describes, the officers "advised the driver/offender (Michael Lawson Schmidt W/M) to keep [his] hands where the [patrolman] could see them. The offender abruptly stated 'Sir, this is just a joke.'"

While one officer ripped the duct tape off the CEO's son, another handcuffed Mikey. They arrested him for reckless driving and driving without a license, which he hadn't brought with him. The victim said he didn't want to press charges for kidnapping or assault, and the police gave him the keys to his Audi. The officers put Mikey in the back of their cruiser, where he sat wearing flip-flops. After they booked him at the county detention center and released him around four a.m.,

Mikey went straight to 7 Montagu to wake up Rob. He told him that one officer "was fucking asking every question [about marijuana] under the sun" and wondered if a police car had been staking out 7 Montagu. Afraid of a search warrant in the morning, Mikey gathered a few red tomato cans and moved them to a different house.

In states where marijuana remains illegal, it'd be hard to engineer a better setup for weed dealing than a college fraternity. Plenty of chapters house dozens of kids with excess funds who like to smoke. They live in groups, so you can sell in bulk, and they often come from sheltered backgrounds, so they might not know the street price of an eighth. Even if they do, they usually care more about being chill than haggling to save their parents' money. They like to stick with their own, meaning you won't face much competition from outside dealers, and they'll probably shout out your product to their friends. Also, in the unlikely case a few of them get caught smoking weed on private fraternity property, they might have a John Gioffredi–style attorney to bail them out.

As a pledge, Mikey decided to stop selling fake IDs and start dealing more weed. He'd heard that the FBI had kicked in the front door of an Atlanta ID counterfeiter, and he wanted to avoid being deemed a threat to national security. He also claimed to have watched Rob sell marijuana at a booming rate. More non-KAs visited Rob's office bedroom to make purchases each month, and Mikey noticed more tomato cans on the floor. Many fraternities have lineages of dealers, with older guys introducing younger kids to suppliers and younger kids introducing older guys to demand, but Mikey didn't need help from upperclassmen. He'd sold weed since he was fifteen, and all he had to do to get more was drive home to Atlanta and pick it up.

After he finished pledging, Mikey and a few other boys in McAlister Hall ran a freshman dorm room distribution network. When they took breaks from running heists around Los Santos in the new *Grand Theft Auto V*, they sold weed to other underclassmen. They hid vacuum-sealed containers in their backpacks, and they used their McAlister bedrooms for different parts of the supply chain. "We kinda worked it like project housing," one KA from the group told me. "There's a room you leave all the weed in, and then there's a room where you have the people come meet you at. . . . [We] never had dope in the same room as money." The KA said that he and his friends rotated between three or four rooms on different days, texting KAs and other kids in Greek life where to meet them. Other times, they ran downstairs and dropped orders through an outdoor cubbyhole facing Vanderhorst Street. "You remember *The Wire*?" he asked. "Think about the terrace stairwell where D'Angelo caught that murder. It's like McAlister, right?"

Unlike the residents of Los Santos or *The Wire*'s Franklin Terrace projects, the McAlister boys rarely faced the law. Up until Mikey's arrest for reckless driving, the only time the KAs risked police attention was when Mikey forgot to put water in his instant mac and cheese and started a microwave fire. After that, his group kept selling grams and ounces without problems. They learned that the C of C Greek world was an easy place to deal.

KA from Connecticut: There was no one in Charleston who didn't smoke weed. If you asked, "Do you wanna smoke after class?" no one said no. Guys or girls, old or young, they were just like, "Yeah, sure." Maybe it was the nice weather. Everyone was always in a good mood, good vibes.

SAE from Tennessee: They're wealthy kids with nothing to do but be gluttonous.

Lacrosse Player from Virginia: You give these affluent kids opportunities in a city like this, where there's minimal regulation, a lot of excess drugs, and a lot of people to sell them to. I can't name one kid that didn't at least try to sell pot in college.

Sigma Nu from South Carolina: People were buying a gram of pot for like twenty bucks, bro.

GDI from South Carolina: It had this explosive nature. It was like, "Okay, a kid who's master of his fraternity can take twenty pounds of weed and vape cartridges and allocate it in a week?"

Kappa Sig from South Carolina: We would go to other schools and we'd almost like brag: "You guys have no idea what's fucking going on in Charleston. You gotta get down here. It's the most decentralized network of fun you've ever seen. You can get hammered at your house, walk two blocks to a party, walk two blocks to a bar, wake up the next morning and get a five-star brunch. It's beautiful, there's three girls to every guy, and everyone is rich and willing to throw down."

✦ ✦ ✦

Looking at KA pledgeship, an outside observer might think that the KAs had taken advantage of Mikey and his classmates during recruitment. If I were a Kappa Alpha parent, I'd think that older boys had lured my son with a nice-looking fellowship and thrown him in a closet to get hazed. Actually, older Atlanta kids had warned Mikey that he'd get brutalized as a pledge, and he was still excited to join. One reason might have been the allure of hazing itself, but another was a simple cost-benefit analysis about what happens when pledgeship ends. Looking at what he'd lose as a pledge and what he'd gain as an active member, Mikey saw profit. Among other perks for College of Charleston kids, Greek life opened up that decentralized network of fun.

When Mikey and I were in school, most boys in our bubble shared a dream of what college might look like. It was an image we'd inherited from movies and our uncles. There'd be white pong balls splashing in red Solo cups, and hot girls who wanted to wrestle in mud or Jell-O. There'd be dudes who'd become our lifelong best friends, and there'd be day parties and road trips and tailgates and probably some vomit on a lawn. There would be nicknames. At the end, we'd join our buddies on a roof to pass a joint and watch the sun rise on our futures. After a few decades we'd have a reunion and agree that those were the best four or five years of our lives. If we wanted to cash in on that promise, it made sense to join a fraternity. Movies tend to get some things wrong about Greek life—too much hair gel, Abercrombie, and diversity—but in other ways a good fraternity social calendar made an eighteen-to-twenty-two-year-old boy feel like he was living Hollywood's college dream.

Once he was an active Kappa Alpha, Mikey started going out on King Street with older KAs and girls from different sororities. These nights began with an invitation to a pregame, where girls joined for beer pong in the 7 Montagu living room or shots on a row house porch. Although it was up for debate, the three best sororities at the College of Charleston were probably Alpha Delta Pi, Chi Omega, and Delta Delta Delta. "The ADPis were the goddesses in Vineyard Vines and pearls," one Tri Delt told me, "the Chi Os were local girls who loved the beach, and Tri Delt was for the chill, popular girl who was still fun." These sororities were part of a town that, at least to a certain gaze, has been known for beautiful women for a long time. Referring to a 1791 night out in Charleston, George Washington wrote in his diary: "There were at least 400 ladies—the Number and appearance of which exceeded anything of the kind I had ever seen." While stationed at the Charleston Naval Base in 1941, John F. Kennedy carried on a romance that he called "the brightest part of an extremely bright 26 years." And when *Total Frat Move*'s "Top 10 Universities with the Hottest Girls" 2015 list left out his favorite school, commentor Balls McLongfrock wrote, "Obviously none of you turds have ever stepped foot on the campus of the College of Charleston."

After pregames with sororities, Mikey could choose between a fifteen-minute walk to the bars on King Street or a four-minute ride with a pledge driver. Where they went out depended on the night: Monday was dollar drinks at the Silver Dollar bar, Tuesday was mug night at Midtown or club night at Mynt, Wednesday was the Silver Dollar or Boones, and the three-day weekend meant all of King Street plus fraternity parties, sorority mixers, and trips to the beach. Joining Kappa Alpha unlocked each of these things, and it gave Mikey a group to move with through the nightlife. King is one of America's great drinking streets, like 6th Street or Bourbon Street with slightly fewer tourists, but it's overwhelming without a guide. Lines to the door went past the sidewalk, and unless you knew the right people, it was easy to disappear in the mob of pastel. Lucky for Mikey, he had Rob.

Walking under gas lamps and into bars, Rob seemed to know a lot of other kids. He had friends from marine biology classes and student government meetings, interfraternity soccer games and weed deals. He'd also broken up with his long-distance girlfriend, and he seemed good at being single. "Robert has a gravitational pull," one KA source said. "It's not like he's even a good-looking human being, but he just gives them a natural comfort. He makes them come to him. He uses eye contact . . . and like, I don't know. He's always had a beautiful girl around."

If there was one movie that inspired the boys that semester, it was *The Wolf of Wall Street*. Martin Scorsese's film about microcap stock fraud came out that winter, and the KAs didn't see it as satire. The chapter threw a theme party based on the movie, and they made T-shirts calling themselves "Wolves of King Street," with a photo of Leonardo DiCaprio as Jordan Belfort. Other KA parties included a booze cruise where the boys threw kegs into the Atlantic and a Halloween party where they had hundreds of people in a 2,800-square-foot house. ("I think the porch shifted that night," one KA said.) As his costume, Mikey wore a Donald Trump mask from Party City and brought what he considered "the hottest date ever." During that same period, Rob and Mikey bought Illadelph bongs together, Rob's in blue and Mikey's in black. Mikey paid a little extra, somewhere around $1,400, to get the kind with a detachable beaker that he could store in the freezer.

Looking for C of C KA and SAE alumni to interview about this period, I realized that most of them were on LinkedIn, so I made a profile. I figured that sources wouldn't trust me until the account looked real, so I entered my email address and let the algorithm churn potential connections. Soon I was staring at a grid that looked like my fraternity composite: dozens of Columbia Delta Sigs, smiling at the camera in ties. I clicked Connect on thirty or forty of them, and then thirty or forty more appeared. Within about two days I was connected with about one hundred fraternity brothers, which led to more algorithm suggestions and more connections. By the end of the week LinkedIn told me I was two or three degrees of separation from most of the College of Charleston fraternity guys whose names I typed in the search bar.

Stalking my way through this network, I noticed a difference between the C of C KAs and SAEs. A few Kappa Alphas worked in banking or real estate, but others worked at local restaurants or trucking logistics firms. Some alumni lived in

Manhattan or Austin, but many had stayed in Charleston or gone back to their smaller hometowns. From the outside looking at LinkedIn, most KAs had solid careers in an otherwise disappearing middle class, but they couldn't keep up with their SAE classmates. The Sigma Alpha Epsilon alumni had spread out pretty evenly among New York, Los Angeles, Atlanta, Charleston, and elsewhere. One had started his own ecommerce business in Greenwich, and another had founded an impact capital firm in the US Virgin Islands. I started reaching out to many of these guys for interviews, and one of them added me to his industrial real estate company's mailing list.

After the real estate SAE sent an email titled "SOLD! 288.27 acres of land," I looked up his Instagram. His account was public, and his profile picture showed him standing in front of a private jet. Under that were little story highlight buttons for "Italy," "Lake Life," "Business," "Las Vegas," "Jackson Hole," "Miami," and "Drone." In one post he announced that he'd sold $19.7 million worth of property in 2020, and in another he posed in front of a big house and thanked the fellow SAE who worked as his mortgage broker. From there I scrolled through photos at Aspen costume parties, Thai coves, Manhattan nightclubs, Venetian water taxis, and more than one yacht. He captioned one photo "Yachts of fun" and another "Trust me at the top it isn't lonely." To start with his early photos and scroll through his time in Sigma Alpha Epsilon is to see a mini flipbook, where his triceps balloon and the people around him get better looking. His Thanksgiving 2012 post shows his family holding hands to pray around some mashed potatoes, and by Thanksgiving 2016 he captioned a photo "I'm thankful for private jets. . . . #barbados."

His group photos led me to other SAEs. One of them, a South Carolinian named Benjamin Nauss, described himself as an "ΣAE | Investor | Gym Addict | Former D1 Athlete." He had biceps bigger than my quads and a gold chain with a gold bullet on it. Posting from Vegas and Miami, he and his fraternity brothers seemed to subscribe to the Dan Bilzerian school of Instagram, bludgeoning viewers to submission with AR-15s and thong bikinis. At least to me, the photos said, "I have more money than you, I've slept with more women than you have, and I could also beat you up if needed."

After that, I switched to KA photos. Scrolling through, I noticed sweeter smiles and fewer thongs. Instead of power-pointing at the camera, they put their arms around each other. Their pictures made me feel less bad about myself, but I also felt less compelled to keep looking at them. They showed nice young people having a nice time together, which is less interesting than hot rich kids on boats. They seemed like just another group of boys in a random fraternity, mostly because they were. Even factoring in their weed-dealing business, the KAs had less money for parties than other chapters, and fewer sororities were interested in mixing with them. Despite their red tomato cans and *Wire*-inspired operation, Rob and Mikey had less social clout than Charleston's top dealers.

According to multiple sources close to the situation, Ben Nauss, the gym addict SAE, was a better-known force in the local marijuana business than the KAs. He'd transferred to

C of C after playing tight end at Coastal Carolina, and he drove a blacked-out Chevy Z71 pickup with an SAE sticker over the toolbox. One rival dealer called him a "big, strong dude with a lot of opinions," and he could have bench-pressed Mikey or even Rob. The second-best-known dealer in Nauss's orbit was Russell Sliker, an SAE who'd gone on Mountain Weekend 2012. His father co-owned 82 Queen, an upscale downtown restaurant famous for its award-winning she-crab soup, and he drove his Escalade with his hair slicked back. Christina Arnold, a C of C Tri Delt, told me, "He was a kid that everyone really had a crush on." Russell lived below another well-known dealer, a Sigma Nu who asked me to call him Honcho. Honcho's reputation preceded him; I'd heard of him myself years before because he'd hooked up with a friend I'd studied abroad with in South Africa. Later, while I was interviewing Christina, she told me that Honcho had hooked up with her best friend, who was in town for the summer, and then hooked up with her little sister. "His body count is in the hundreds," she told me. "I'm not gonna lie. I hooked up with him too."

Honcho got some of his marijuana from a slightly older kid named Bradley Felder. Brad could bench 405 pounds, the equivalent of Rob and Ben Nauss bundled together, and he'd played outfield for a Clemson team that'd made a nice postseason run in 2012. He'd grown up on his parents' six-hundred-acre dairy farm and ran a 6.3 second sixty-yard dash in his tryout with the Atlanta Braves, and now he sold California weed while thinking about a career in sales. He and his preposterous jawline showed up to Charleston in different rental Escalades, carrying enough for his fraternity dealers to offload six or more pounds of weed at a time. One sorority member at Clemson told me he looked like "a Ken doll on steroids," and his dealers looked up to him. After he'd drop off weed with Honcho, Honcho would try to talk to him for a bit, and Felder would say, "I'm on the road. Got to make like twenty more stops tonight, bro."

Like other fraternities at C of C, the Kappa Alpha Order threw its biggest parties away from Charleston. The KAs had a Mountain Weekend of their own, at a family camp in western North Carolina. During the spring, they also joined dozens of other fraternities and sororities from around the southeast at the Carolina Cup steeplechase horse race. The cup takes place at a track in Camden, South Carolina, developed by the owner of Jell-O. In the lots on College Park, the boys' pants were salmon or mustard colored, and their blazers were made of seersucker or patterned with American flags. The girls wore Kentucky Derby–style hats and sleeveless Lilly Pulitzer dresses. Some chapters roasted full pigs, and most competed to erect a bigger flagpole than everyone else. In the spring of 2013, *Total Frat Move* posted a picture of Ben Nauss in cobalt pants shooting a pong ball outside the SAE tent.

When Mikey arrived at the cup his freshman year, chapters from different schools had their own tents with custom-made pong tables and ice luges. Rob gave Mikey one piece of advice, which was to stay inside the KA tent and away from the police. But while Mikey and his date poured shots of liquor into each other's mouths, they got farther and farther from the pong tables. Eventually they found themselves outside the tent and handcuffed to a chain-link fence by a local policeman, who told them they'd be charged as minors in possession. Mikey and his date made out in handcuffs for the next ninety minutes, and at the end of the race the officer uncuffed them without charging them. According to that year's Kappa Alpha social chair, most boys missed the steeplechase races altogether. "The running joke, and this is still the case for me, is that the only horse you'll ever see is the cop horse."

A few weeks after the Carolina Cup, the KAs brought dates to Old South Weekend. At the College of Charleston and other schools, the party marked the peak of the KA social calendar. The C of C KAs usually chartered a bus down to Savannah, Georgia, where they'd rent a floor of a riverfront hotel and spend a good portion of their annual budget on a formal dance and other events. The KAs who'd gone to Savannah with Rob and Mikey described lobster mac and cheese at waterfront bars and booze cruises through the intracoastal waterway. Referring to the Old South of Mikey's freshman year, one source said, "First, [the hotel receptionists] were like, 'Please, do not smoke. Whatever else you do, we can handle it, but do not smoke.' But we fucking smoked that bitch. We turned that whole fourth floor into a dispensary. Then we paid for an open bar, and we all got pissed that they gave us drink tickets instead, so we started going behind the bar. People were onstage with bottles, and we got kicked out of our own formal. Shit really the entire time was on some *Wolf of Wall Street* shit."

A former KA social chair also told me about the weekend of Old South 2012, three semesters before Mikey pledged. No other KAs had told me this story, and when I asked them about it later, many said they'd never heard it before. As with most years, the KAs booked a cluster of rooms at the same hotel, and the girls hand-painted coolers of liquor for their dates. During the afternoons they drank by the pool, and at night they put on suits and dresses that fell somewhere between what they'd worn to prom and what they'd wear to weddings. While they were out on Friday, boys started getting texts that a KA who'd graduated fifteen months earlier had just overdosed in Atlanta. Some brothers raised a glass to his memory, but otherwise the weekend continued without comment. When the boys woke up hungover on Sunday, they saw texts that another recent KA, a senior who'd stopped paying dues that year, had fallen off a roof in Charleston and died around three that morning. These two accidents, the KA source told me, came four months after an active Kappa Alpha brother had died in his sleep. By April 2012, three College of Charleston Kappa Alphas had died within six months of each other, and the KA parties had gone on without them.

CHAPTER 6

DOUSING THE TREE

While I read the 704-page case file about him, I started to believe I'd never talk to Mikey Schmidt. I had spoken to a few dozen sources who had many things to say about him, but my visitation requests at Wateree River Correctional Institution were all denied. South Carolina prison administrators cited the fact that he and I didn't know each other, which left me no way to cross the seven thousand acres of Sumter County farmland that surrounded him. As a weak substitute, his friends treated me to their own version of the "Mikey voice." They'd push their mouths wide and squint their eyes, and they'd make their words half an octave higher and twice as slow. One buddy called the accent a "squirrelly whisper," but most of them described it as either

Georgia-bred or weed-infused. When they impersonated him, they made up quotes about smoking Backwoods blunts with different famous Atlanta rappers. A few sources also sent me his inmate photo, which showed his wavy flow shaved to a nub.

Then one of Mikey's friends texted me: "(803) ★★★-★★★★. This number is Mikey btw." When I called, a man with a baritone answered, and then he handed the phone to someone else. The second voice sounded like Mikey's friends' impersonations. Even in a 130-year-old prison with no air-conditioning and a horsefly infestation, Mikey seemed more laid-back than I did. After I stupidly asked, "How's it going?" Mikey responded, "Well, other than the fact that I'm in prison, everything else is mighty fine. How about yourself?" I made my introduction, and he told me that if he hung up all of a sudden, it was because guards were passing by his cell.

Before we got started, Mikey established the walls around what we could talk about. "I'm sure you're interested in the connection with the music industry and all that, but there are certain things where you just can't go down that road, if you understand." I told him I did. I asked him how he'd smuggled a cell phone into Wateree, and he said that eighteen of his twenty-eight barracks mates owned contraband phones as well. He told me that some phones came in through the dairy and cattle operations that served as inmates' labor camps, and others came from kitchen workers or even guards. Mikey had paid $1,000 for an LG Journey, which connected him to the outside world and allowed him to use mobile payment apps like Venmo and Cash App. "Everything costs ten times as much in here," he said. "Cigarettes are twenty bucks a cigarette. A pound of weed is ten thousand dollars." Later, he coughed and added, "Anyone will tell you, I don't really partake in any other substances, but I'm a weed head. In fact, I'm smoking weed right now."

During our first calls, Mikey shared his theories about who killed Patrick Moffly. We also talked about the informants who'd put Mikey in jail, and he wondered out loud if he could trust me after being "kind of traumatized by phone calls." He warned me to look wide while investigating his story. "Honestly, Charleston has some weird culture that I can't even explain. Secret societies, the judges—all that stuff is intertwined. It's almost as if Charleston is run by a shadow organization." He understandably refused to answer anything that might hurt his chances in a potential retrial, but the only time he got defensive was when I told him I'd heard SAE was the best fraternity at the College of Charleston. "You remember GreekRank.com?"—a site where internet users voted on the status of different Greek chapters. "My fall semester, we were voted most athletic, best-looking, best on campus. . . ." When I pushed back that anyone could take GreekRank.com's anonymous polls, he said, "Look, SAE was so organized and had all this fucking support and everything. . . . But KA was the *Animal House* fraternity. We'll be on the top of Stars [the King Street rooftop bar and grill], and you'll probably be carrying most of us out in handcuffs."

Besides that moment, I was the one trying to impress him. I mentioned that I'd been in a fraternity and let my vowels ring out extra southern. While I did that, Mikey kept his usual casual tone. When he walked through his case file by memory and analyzed the South Carolina justice system with precision, his voice sounded like it was describing the water hazards on a nice par 4.

It was after a few calls that I finally asked Mikey about the Kappa Alpha brothers who'd died in 2011 and 2012. He said, "One of them fell off a roof, right? One of them was heroin. There were more kids who died."

In 280 words, Hawkins Wilber's obituary describes a great suburban boyhood. He excelled at lacrosse, football, and basketball at Atlanta's Lovett School, helped his Little League team win the Georgia state baseball championship, and served as parliamentarian and sergeant at arms for the KAs in Charleston. He'd backpacked through Italy and the Ecuadorian rainforest before starting a career in real estate. In his obituary photo, Hawkins sits in front of a fraternity-composite-style backdrop, his dimples stretching over a regimental stripe necktie. The blue of his eyes picks up the camera flash, and his hair looks wet from the shower. The obituary doesn't mention how Hawkins died, but his father wasn't afraid to talk about it. "Hawkins is a great poster child for this. He was tall and athletic and very photogenic," Joe Wilber told me. "My sister is a medical director for Kaiser Permanente, and when they did a big work session on drug abuse, she showed a picture of him. You look and think, 'That's the all-American kid.' You know? 'I wish my kid would grow up to be him.'"

Near the end of Hawkins's junior year at the College of Charleston, his younger brother told their father that Hawkins was addicted to Oxycodone. Joe drove up to South Carolina and asked his son how the dependence had started. "He was very open about it," Joe said. "He said, 'Dad, we would go to fraternity parties and get hungover a lot. But if you took Xanax, instead of drinking ten beers, you could drink two. The Xanax made you feel good all night, and you'd wake up the next morning feeling okay." He told his father that alprazolam pills were cheap and easy to access. "And that's how he got started on it. In hindsight I think he had a personality that was subject to addiction, and he inherited that from his father and his mother, so you can't blame him for it. But he went from Xanax to Oxycodone."

At the end of the semester, Hawkins's parents moved him home and helped him through his opioid withdrawals, and they eventually sent him back to Charleston to finish school. As a senior he started taking heroin, which he later told his father was cheaper than Oxycodone, but he finished at C of C after his mother came to live with him. "The day he graduated we sent him to a rehab center in Tucson, Arizona, for thirty days. . . . [Then] we spent the next eighteen months going through a living hell trying to keep him alive. He and I got an apartment together, and he came to work with me every day. He wasn't an employee, we called him an intern, but he had an adult job. And he got dressed and had a regular schedule. And the thought was that we would try to get him into the real world. But anyway, the bottom line is it was a nightmare. He couldn't get off it. And he would go through periods of depression, related to the drug use, and, you know, one afternoon, we found him in the garage apartment."

Hawkins's father told me he had no interest in blaming the College of Charleston for the overdose. "The school, KA, it wasn't their fault," he said. "It was Hawkins's. He's responsible for his actions." He wanted to tell his son's story with the hope of warning boys like Hawkins about opiates and Xanax, which to him "is the definition of a gateway drug. . . . The story really is to me is that these kids go off, and they think Xanax is some kind of play toy. It's like having a couple beers. 'Well, I'll just have a Xanax instead.' And what's so shocking to me is that the dealers are students."

Hawkins's KA brother Spencer Pitts died two days after Hawkins did. When Spencer's father, John, arrived in Charleston on the Sunday of Old South Weekend, he went to the town house on Corinne Street where Spencer had fallen at 3:15 that morning. He walked past the second-floor kitchen and the third-floor bedrooms to the hot tub on the deck outside. From there, he went up a three-step ladder toward the roof where Spencer had slipped. It was a metal roof with a gradual pitch, only thirty feet above the street. After a baseball game and a night out, Spencer had gone up on his friend's roof to watch the stars, and on the way down he'd lost his footing and slid on his stomach. The next afternoon, John could see the streaks in the metal where Spencer's fingers had tried to grab on to the roof.

Like Joe Wilber, John Pitts didn't hesitate when I asked to interview him about losing his son. "I don't mind being reminded of Spencer one bit," he said. "It gives me another excuse to talk about him." But in addition to being a grieving father, John is a longtime publishing executive, and he knew how his son's story could be misconstrued in print. After Spencer died on April 15, the local newspapers highlighted that he came from Greenwich and excelled at skiing, golf, and tennis. Many of them mentioned that the house on Corinne Street had been cluttered with beer and liquor bottles. Some outlets included the fact that Spencer had interned at FrontPoint Partners, a Connecticut hedge fund that was cofounded by Spencer's uncle and profiled in Michael Lewis's *The Big Short*. In the photos they ran, Spencer had gold hair and eyes that looked like fjords. "I don't think saying he's this 'well-liked kid from Greenwich' is going to earn him much sympathy," John told me. "In this climate, they're going to think he blew it."

As his father describes him, though, Spencer can't be boxed in by the phrase "a well-liked kid from Greenwich." He was an autodidact who asked for physics books and cheese for Christmas. He struggled when his parents' divorce took him from Connecticut to Florida to California and New York. "He was sweet in a real, genuine way that people picked up on," John said. "Children in particular were drawn to him. He was just a good soul. He didn't speak ill of people." After he died, more than six hundred people joined the Spencer Gladding Pitts memorial Facebook page, writing things like, "You were by far the smartest person I've ever met, and the most fun to talk to." They called him by his nicknames—Spoodle, Sven, Spence, Meerkat, Gladdings, Gatsby—and shared photos from Little Compton, Rhode Island, and the Carolina Cup. John posts often, especially on birthdays, holidays, and the fifteenth day of the month. On December 15, 2019, he wrote:

Hi Spence, the [Christmas] tree is up and you are front and center as always. I've said it before—I would have no qualms dousing this poor tree in an accelerant and torching it if it would bring you back. Is it possible that you are forever in oblivion? That these celebrations of earthly milestones mean nothing to you? Probably. I can only hope that I know pretty much nothing. I do know that we miss you and love you beyond measure. Love, Dad.

Each time a recent brother died, the C of C KAs mourned in increasingly familiar ways. To remember Hawkins, Spencer, and Ryan Grand, a KA senior from Atlanta who'd died in his King Street apartment on November 15, they threw parties where they gathered to make toasts and cry. They took pictures with the dogwood tree that Spencer's family planted in the Cistern Yard, and they made donations to the Ryan Grand Scholarship Fund at Saint Anne's Day School in Atlanta. They wore bright colors to Spencer's service in Little Compton and joined five hundred people at Hawkins's memorial at the Carter Center. For each death, the KA national organization also provides the text for an official Kappa Alpha "Chapter of Sorrow." The ritual calls for baskets of crimson roses, a reading from Ecclesiastes, and a dedication to "a good man, brave knight, and brother faithful until death."

These tragedies didn't give administrators reason to investigate the College of Charleston KAs. Hawkins had died after he'd graduated, Spencer had died after he'd stopped paying KA dues, and investigators never linked Ryan's death to either his school or his fraternity.* In addition, the three boys had died away from College of Charleston or Kappa Alpha–affiliated property. Still, after mourning three brothers in 128 days, another C of C KA stood up at a fraternity meeting and campaigned against what he saw as a broader problem. He asked the younger guys why they took so much Xanax, which he'd seen each year of college but which now seemed to dominate their social world. Alprazolam wasn't just part of Hawkins's addiction story, he said; it was also the cause of other tragedies in Greek life. "I wanted to campaign against Xanax, because we were having so many incidents with accidents and deaths," he said. "It ended with a lot of people agreeing but not wanting to do anything about it."

Rob arrived in Charleston the semester of the Old South Weekend deaths, and Mikey showed up a year later. During that time, it got easier to see two separate forces pressing on fraternity houses. The first was the "climate" that John Pitts alluded to, the fact that our culture didn't talk about bros the same way anymore. When Rob, Mikey, and I were growing up in the 2000s, America had loved movies about wolf packs of men who broke things and slept with beautiful, forgiving women. Hollywood had released new *Animal House*–inspired

---

* Beyond announcing that they had no suspicion of foul play, Charleston officials never publicized Ryan Grand's cause of death. I was unable to make contact with his family.

comedies every year, starting with *American Pie* and running toward films by Todd Phillips's crew (*Old School* and *The Hangover*), Will Ferrell's and Adam McKay's boys (*Anchorman, Step Brothers, Talladega Nights*), Judd Apatow's posse (*The 40-Year-Old Virgin, Knocked Up, Superbad*), plus the Ben Stiller/Owen Wilson/Vince Vaughan/Jack Black collective (*Zoolander, Wedding Crashers, Tropic Thunder*), otherwise known as the "Frat Pack."

Mikey got to Charleston after *The Hangover Part III* came out, though, and in some pockets the "all-male wolf pack" was starting to mean something different. That September, for instance, *The Cut* published an article titled "How Do You Change a Bro-Dominated Culture?" The writer, Ann Friedman, described how "mainstream news has been dominated lately by stories lamenting 'bro culture'—a term that used to be found solely on feminist blogs." To Friedman's eye, more people were lamenting the kind of guy who dominated tech, finance, the government, and even parts of academia. If an *Old School* viewer saw a bro as something like a fun-loving alpha who liked to party with his boys, Friedman described an opposing view: "'Bro' once meant something specific: a self-absorbed young white guy in board shorts with a taste for cheap beer. But it's become a shorthand for the sort of privileged ignorance that thrives in groups dominated by wealthy, white, straight men."

Mikey and Rob didn't read *The Cut*. And now that they were C of C KAs, they didn't have to think about how people who couldn't get into KA parties saw them. Instead, it was easier to notice the other force changing the world of fraternity kids, because it usually came from the inside.

I came to college knowing very little about Xanax. When my friends and I were in high school, we heard about the dangers of smoking "dope" (marijuana) and thought of Xanax as the thing parents took when they flew. I didn't know that it could be used as a fun drug until a spirit party in twelfth grade, when I watched a defender on the lacrosse team grin and fall into a bush. I knew a few kids who'd been prescribed alprazolam for their anxiety disorders, but even then I didn't know what a pill looked like until my first year of college. Usually, it's a white 2 mg rectangle, perforated into four 0.5 mg doses. It's colorless, odorless, and not much bigger than a Tic Tac. The first time I saw one, my pledge brother, a city kid from an Upper East Side day school, called it a "bar" because of its shape. He broke off two quarter bars, which he called "QBs," and took them with a Natural Light. I didn't see him until the next morning, when I asked how his night went and he said he couldn't remember.

For the rest of freshman year, though, my friends saw Xanax as less of a pregame drug and more of a hangover cure. During our first semester, most of us went through the Sunday Scaries for the first time, feeling the weekend's comedown and the next week's deadlines blend into a kind of panic attack cocktail. A scientist might explain the Scaries as alcohol withdrawal and generalized anxiety lowering gamma-aminobutyric acid (GABA) receptors and turning up the electrical activity among the brain's neurotransmitters. The British novelist Kingsley Amis described them as a "compound of depression, sadness, anxiety, self-hatred, sense of failure and fear for the future," which leads you to believe you are bad at your job and that your loved ones are "leagued in a conspiracy of barely maintained silence about what a shit you are." Older generations have tried to fight this despair by attending church or drinking more, but some of my friends knocked it out with a few QBs of Xanax and ten straight hours of NFL football.

When I asked kids at the College of Charleston about their first time trying Xanax, many of them talked about Sunday mornings after four or five nights out. An alumnus of the C of C Cougar lacrosse team told me, "When it started, at least for my friend group, it was 'Hey, we're hungover as fuck, we feel like shit, what's really gonna make this day better?' Just like a quarter Xanax bar and NFL Sundays." Taking a QB and watching Terry Bradshaw straighten his double windsor knot, the C of C kids felt the ice picks in their heads start to thaw. America's best-selling benzodiazepine (a class of depressants that also includes Valium and Klonopin), Xanax increases the presence of GABA, which blocks signals among neurons. By boosting GABA levels, a QB turns down the electrical activity in the brain and depresses the nervous system, slowing the breath, lowering the blood pressure, and calming the heart rate. By the time Erin Andrews smiled into her fuzzy microphone on the sidelines, the C of C boys felt a full-body warmth. Alprazolam was originally designed for panic attacks and seizures, and it works with potency and speed. Within an hour on the first try, one 0.5 mg quarter bar gives the sensation described by one

C of C KA as "you just feel like you've melted into whatever chair you're sitting in."

For people who experience some level of anxiety every day, it's hard to overemphasize how good that melting feels. When I tried a half bar of Xanax in college, it was the fastest I'd heard the buzzing in my head disappear. It turned off a fan that'd been running in my brain since childhood and revealed another level of silence. Benzodiazepines don't flood the head with euphoria like other drugs, but they might erase anxiety better than any other depressant, stimulant, psychedelic, opioid, or dissociative. This is a great thing on Sundays, and for many College of Charleston guys I talked to, it was helpful on other days of the week too. Boys took QBs on nights before tests when they couldn't sleep, on mornings after break-ups with their high school girlfriends, and before parties when they wanted to feel chill. "There's like a high-pressure scene in Charleston of being cool, of being rich, of putting on a lot of show. It takes a toll on your psyche," Honcho, the Sigma Nu lothario, told me. "And Xanax was almost like a cheat code, you know? Very easily, you could just be a loose goose."

Before Mikey, Rob, and I were underclassmen, nearly all alprazolam bars on campuses were genuine name-brand Xanax tablets. If kids wanted to buy alprazolam, they either needed a doctor's prescription or a dealer who had backdoor access to the Pfizer supply chain. The first route wasn't impossible: in 2012, Rob's freshman year, American doctors wrote over forty-nine million scripts for alprazolam, making it the second-most-prescribed psychoactive drug in the country, after hy-drocodone. The dealer route could bring more pills than a pharmacist would be willing to sell, but you had to get lucky to find someone who'd flip prescription pills under the counter. For instance, one Alabama SAE I interviewed happened to meet an alprazolam thief at a Widespread Panic concert. "We tripped acid together—I took a ten strip with this kid—and I disappeared for a weekend with him," he said. After their trip, the SAE learned that the Panic fan had a brother who worked at a pharmaceutical lab and stole alprazolam pills in bulk. "I pulled together like ten drug dealers I knew—DEKEs, SAEs, Kappa Sigs—and I'm like, 'Hey, you want to buy five thousand bars for ten grand? Two bucks a pop.' And they're like, 'Are they real? Fuck yeah.'" The SAE bought fifty thousand Xanax bars at forty cents a pill, and he drove them back to Tuscaloo-sa's Old Row in trash bags.

By the time we got to college, easier supply chains started to open up. Mikey's freshman year, the best-known Xanax sup-plier in Charleston was a Mount Pleasant local whom I'll call Johnny Drama. Johnny was known for his black market al-prazolam and his sense of style. ("You can ask anybody," he told me. "I like fashion. If my Air Max Nineties were red and black, I'm wearing a black Polo with the red horse. And the socks gotta match the Polo.") For a guy who hung out with SAEs and described his Land Rover as "sexy," Johnny was very good with computers. He liked to hack other peoples' iPhones, and he found his first alprazolam supply through a Pakistani ecommerce portal. Without a prescription or working knowledge of Urdu, he ordered "ONAX" bars that came to South Carolina via US Mail. "We had to go to the post office to pick it up," one of his accomplices told me, "and it's in a burlap sack. It's got a tracking number, and the name is written in Sankrit [*sic*]." Thanks to Google translate, Johnny Drama had a quality stream of pharmaceutical alprazolam to sell. "They were legitimate," he told me. "I would always test them out and stuff and I'd be like 'Wow, this is crazy.'"

It was around this time that Mikey first tried benzodiazepines. He was in his bedroom in McAlister Hall, pregaming for a sorority mixer in his suit and tie. After a few hours of drinking and smoking with other KAs, one of his pledge brothers opened a box of SweeTarts. Inside were normal-looking Tarts in their five Easter colors. The KA told Mikey that they'd been dipped in liquid alprazolam that he'd bought online. Because he'd had bad childhood reactions to the stimulant Focalin (used to treat ADHD), Mikey didn't take prescription pills, but because he'd already been drinking and smoking, and maybe because these pills looked like actual candy, he took a red one out of the box. He swallowed it, and after more pregaming the active ingredient started to kick in. "So boom," he told me from his prison cell phone, "I ripped my bong, and I was about to go to the mixer and all I know is I laid my head down, and I woke up and it was Sunday. I didn't remember anything—I just was so confused. . . . I had a smoking hot date, too. She had gone without me."

Mikey didn't take any more benzodiazepines during his freshman year. He went out on King Street with Rob and stole armored cars in *GTA V*. He sold weed in McAlister, drank on Folly Beach, loaded up his $1,400 Illadelph bong, and texted pledges to bring him food. Whatever he was doing, though, he wasn't going to school. After he'd left the lecture at which his professor complained about Charleston's lack of protected bike lanes, he'd started skipping other classes too. He knew he wanted to get some sort of business degree, but he wasn't sure what he was passionate about, and he knew it didn't involve an introductory liberal arts education. He struggled to focus on getting organized and watched his 2.4 GPA slide further down. "Mikey didn't have any motivation to study, whereas Rob did," one KA told me. While Rob made the National Honor Society for the second year, Mikey dropped out of the college and moved back to Dunwoody, Georgia, with his mom.

Not long after our phone calls started, I lost my ability to speak to Mikey. Whenever I tried his LG Journey, the call went straight to a message saying, "We're sorry, you have reached a number that has been disconnected or is no longer in service." My texts came back with a red exclamation mark, and the friend who gave me his number hadn't talked to him either. At some point in the fall of 2020, I checked South Carolina's Incarcerated Inmate Search database, which showed the photo of him with his shaved head. Under "Disciplinary Sanctions," it listed two counts of marijuana use and one count of cell phone possession.

CHAPTER 7

QB SNEAK

While Rob and other KAs drove back to Charleston for rush parties at the end of summer break, Mikey sat in his childhood bedroom. From a cul-de-sac twenty miles north of Atlanta, he watched Snapchats of other kids on Folly Beach. He was too far from C of C to see what was happening on Yik Yak, a geolocation-exclusive app that'd become Greek life's favorite new way of talking to itself. At home, his stepdad told him, "Thirty thousand dollars a year and you didn't even go to class." While his college friends were hazing new pledges, Mikey was going to dinner with his mother, who hates drugs even more than other southern mothers. According to Mikey, she looked across the table at his red eyes and scolded him: "You're loaded, aren't you? What's wrong, puff puff, no pass?"

Before the guards at Wateree had confiscated his phone, I'd asked Mikey about his family life in Dunwoody. He'd told me that his mom was a vice president at a market research firm, and that she was a "literal saint who worked so hard to give me whatever I wanted." Mikey's stepfather grew up in a double-wide trailer and now ran an advertising division for a local TV network, and Mikey saw him as his "straightlaced polar opposite." Mikey's mother's parents lived down the street, and his grandfather Frank had spent four decades climbing to the executive class in IBM's office products division. When I asked Mikey what his birth father did, he said "drugs."

Mikey then shared two memories of his father from the four years before he left him and his mother in Dunwoody. In the first, three-year-old Mikey napped on a table at a bar while adults talked to his dad. In the second, Mikey and his father drove north on Highway 400 when a police car turned on its sirens. Before his dad pulled over, he said something like, "Son, control your breath. You can't be nervous. A lot of what will happen to you gets decided in the first twenty seconds. You gotta smile, make direct eye contact, offer a feeling of safety." His father left home soon after that, and Mikey hardly spoke until his fourth birthday. His mom worried that the problem was cognitive, but later Mikey said he'd been so upset at being lied to that he'd decided not to talk. When Mikey's grandparents told him "Your dad is on a work trip," he knew they were leaving things out.

When Mikey began speaking, he started acting out. In his own words, he was a "hellion" until third grade, when a school administrator gave his mom the choice between holding Mikey back or prescribing him ADHD medication. Mikey went on Focalin XR, an extended release stimulant that made his mouth dry. He made the middle school dean's list, but the improved focus didn't keep him from punching a kid in the face during a church league basketball game. Even so, his grandfather Frank watched Mikey's games from the bleachers, and when they got home he taught his grandson how to throw a baseball and swing a driver. Mikey saw Frank as his surrogate father, and with each year he thought less about his birth dad. "There's really just not that much to talk about. It's just one of those disaster stories," he told me. "I definitely couldn't give less of a fuck about my dad. Honestly, if he died right now, I wouldn't have any emotion, any feeling. I only love my mom. All he really is, is a sperm donor."

At home, Mikey played with the family dogs, two Havanese and a mutt named Bandit. Sometimes he walked them to visit his Granny and his grandfather Frank. On weekdays he took classes at Georgia State's Perimeter College, a community college with more than eighteen thousand students, and he started meeting a Mount Vernon high school cheerleader named Alexis for lunch at Five Guys. At night he fought with his mom and stepdad about using his car. They told Mikey he needed a job if he wanted to live with them, and he asked his connections for suggestions. Before long he discovered two links to the Tongue and Groove, the best nightclub in Buckhead, the neighborhood known as "Beverly Hills of the South."

Mikey's KA brother's father co-owned the T&G, and Mikey's neighbor in Dunwoody owned the valet company that worked the lot outside.

Even with that inside track, though, Mikey had to take an exam to park cars at the Tongue and Groove. First he ran shuttle drills in the parking lot and drove a stick shift through its gears. After that, his potential boss handed Mikey a cup for a drug test. Once he realized management wasn't actually going to watch him pee, Mikey took the cup into the bathroom and filled it with water. When he passed, his boss gave him what Mikey described as a "bellhop-looking-ass uniform" and stood him out on Main Street. While he waited on the first night, the lights at the corporate office died across the street, and a few cars exited the LongHorn Steakhouse around the corner. Mikey would see many Atlantas during his time at the Tongue and Groove—the club had nights for EDM lovers, Top 40 fans, and bachata dancers—but the day he started was a Monday, which meant it was hip-hop night.

From his valet booth, Mikey saw Ferraris and Dodge Chargers with thirty-eight-inch rims pull up to the T&G. On Mondays, butterfly doors might reveal people Mikey recognized, like 2 Chainz or T.I., or anonymous guys in just-as-expensive shoes. Mikey imagined those guests were "dope boys," the drug traffickers who he believed ran Atlanta. While Mikey parked their cars, the bouncers let them cut the line, and managers walked them to private tables by the stage. After they ordered Grey Goose or Krug Grande Cuvée, a line of bottle girls carried in their drinks. The sparklers on their bottles shot toward the ceiling, bright enough that guests on both levels could see them. After that, the subwoofers played Future or Young Thug, the dancers took selfies with a neon sign that read, MIRROR, MIRROR ON THE WALL, WHO'S THE DOPEST OF THEM ALL?, and hundreds of beautiful people throbbed under golden light bulbs that spelled ATLANTA.

Of course, Mikey didn't get to see any of that. He was outside parking cars. And besides the rare Lamborghini worth taking photos in, he usually drove regular sedans owned by nonfamous people. "I was watching all these fucking losers come out of this club and throw five-dollar bills at me like I'm a stripper," he said. "I was fighting them, all types of shit . . . Even the manager was taking an onslaught from everyone, getting talked to like a dog. He didn't have a boss mentality, and I couldn't do it." After Mikey had been there a few weeks, he told management, "Listen, fuck this, I'm quitting."

On those early phone calls, Mikey and I had started to talk more about Robert Liljeberg, the main reason he'd joined KA and the person who'd ushered him into college nightlife. When they went out on King Street, Mikey had watched his friend climb through the C of C social world so casually that other people didn't notice. Rob could be laid back to the point of seeming quiet, but he had a special ability to "tune into other peoples' frequencies" and discover the things they wanted to talk about. This trait made him an attentive listener around sorority parents, a premed jock in class, and a chilled-out pot dealer at KA afterparties. It was a nice magic trick to watch, and it was even more fun to take part in it. "We were best friends from day one," Mikey said. "When I say that me and Rob were connected at the hip, me and that fucker we were really connected at the hip."

This friendship made it even harder for Mikey to sit at home in Dunwoody. While he parked cars at the Tongue and Groove, his best friend killed it in Charleston. As a junior, Rob dominated interfraternity soccer and did well in pickup football. According to one source involved in his business, he scaled up his weed sales with mail orders from a woman in California. He attended every Kappa Alpha meeting, lifted weights at the George Street Fitness Center, and drank Coronas at Midtown with Chi Omegas. His performance in marine biology and history classes put him in the National Honor Society for the third straight year, and he planned to spend his summer researching coral reef growth in Bali. He published essays in the *Odyssey Online* about ecology and sustainability, writing things like, "If man is the parasite that has caused this turmoil upon itself and upon the planet, how long will Mother Earth allow him to rule the land?" He eventually won a place in the student senate, which took only nine members per class, and the Student Organization Review Board, which chose which new student clubs got to join the C of C community.

By 2014, the College of Charleston was as politically active as it'd been since the 1960s. After the South Carolina state legislature threatened to slash the college's funding for assigning the graphic novel *Fun Home* by Alison Bechdel, which representative Garry Smith believed promoted "the gay and lesbian lifestyle," student activists marched on campus and hosted special productions of the story's Off-Broadway adaptation. The same semester, students joined professors and NAACP members to protest the news that trustees were considering South Carolina lieutenant governor Glenn McConnell to be the college's next president. McConnell was a C of C alumnus, a proven fund-raiser, and by some metrics the most powerful man in the state legislature. He also owned an old-time memorabilia store filled with Confederate flags and once posed for cameras wearing Civil War regalia next to two Black reenactors who seemed to be dressed as slaves. As a response, the faculty announced a vote of no confidence, and the national media reported on students holding signs saying THIS IS 2014, NOT 1814.

Rob had a few reasons to stay away from these protests. Greek life was a conservative bubble on an increasingly liberal campus, and McConnell had been a Pi Kapp at C of C. In addition, two of McConnell's potential allies on the Board of Trustees were former College of Charleston KAs. Out of sight from the rest of campus, a group of Kappa Alphas flew a Confederate battle flag in their living room, and an SAE date painted the stars and bars on a Mountain Weekend cooler next to the *Total Frat Move* logo. According to one brother, Rob and his friends continued to lift their beers for a toast that some KAs did on both sides of the Mason-Dixon: "One, two, three, Robert E. Lee! Three, two, one, South shoulda won!"

Even factoring in his social climb, it'd be a mistake to confuse Rob for one of the dominant guys in Greek life, kids who came from real money. While Jake Rockefeller (C of C class of 2015) docked his family boat at Charleston's 1,530-foot Mega Dock and invited pledges on board, Rob wore hand-me-down shirts and lived off peanut butter sandwiches. While Jake's roommate, Craig Rothschild (C of C class of 2016), flew private with his dad and Venmo'd girls for "being hot," Rob drove his twenty-year-old car home to Troy, Alabama. When I asked one of Rob's ultra-high-net-worth roommates at 7 Montagu to describe his friend, he called him "Average Rob." He wasn't a legendary figure in the way of some SAEs or Pikes, and although his KA brothers told me that he made enough money selling weed to smoke for free, his profits were still marginal compared with the college's biggest dealers.

Ben Nauss, the SAE bodybuilder, for instance, wore a Rolex and ordered double-decker oyster towers at the Ordinary on King Street. During Christmas break, he posted an Instagram of him and other SAEs holding Solo cups on a private jet. Working on an even larger scale, Brad Felder, the former Clemson baseball star, owned a $45,000 Audemars Piguet and carried his money in a Louis Vuitton duffel bag. When he landed at the Las Vegas airport that October, agents discovered $120,000 of cash in his bag, which he allowed them to confiscate before he flew back east. That same year, Johnny Drama sold 250,000 bars for seventy cents a pill in a single deal, and he used the proceeds to buy a 42-foot Sportfisher boat in cash. "The boat was called the *Hurricane*," he told me. "It was a party machine. . . . This was a little after the *Wolf of Wall Street* came out, and people would say, 'Oh, look, it's the Wolf of King Street.'"

While Rob stuck to marijuana, these other dealers had found a new way to buy large amounts of Xanax on the internet. Instead of navigating Pakistani pharmaceutical portals, they now only had to use the dark web. A bundle of hidden internet sites accessible only through encrypted browsers, the dark web is hard to explain but easy to use. As a friend who sold alprazolam from an SAE house told me, "You download a special internet browser called the Onion. It's like Firefox or something, but it's even slower than Firefox. To protect your privacy, it sends your requests through Norway and New Zealand and these other places. You look up the dark web URL for Silk Road or another site, copy and paste the URL into The Onion Router (TOR), and the front page will sell you black tar heroin and other things that are usually just the punch lines to jokes." Googling the "DarkNetMarkets" subreddit, boys could easily find lists of hidden Onion URLs. Pasting those links into their encrypted browsers, the Charleston dealers could access Silk Road or Agora, online marketplaces that were kind of like Amazon for mail-order felonies. Typing "Xanax" or "alprazolam" into the search bar led to product descriptions, photos, even user reviews. There were different prices, quantities, and types—2 mg "bars," 0.5 mg "footballs," 3 mg "Green Hulks"—and after they entered their address and paid, usually via Bitcoin, the pills came through the mail.

It's hard to overestimate how much the dark web changed how college kids sell drugs at school. For decades, any student who wanted to deal coke or weed had to join a supply chain that most likely began with a cartel or a gang. This sometimes involved the great white parent nightmare of a young Sigma Chi driving to "the hood" to find a Black or Hispanic trafficking plug. Starting in the 2010s, though, that same boy could buy Xanax without leaving the safety of campus Wi-Fi. Johnny Drama, Brad Felder, and my SAE friend who explained the dark web to me all got their wholesale alprazolam from a dark web vendor named Xanax King, and they never had to meet him. Instead, my friend's smaller orders went straight to the student mail center hidden in Rob Schneider DVD sleeves, and Johnny Drama and Brad Felder had hundreds of thousands of Xanax pills shipped in USPS boxes to their doors.

Ben Nauss never mastered the dark web, but he received Xanax from someone who did. One of his sources for bars was a twenty-two-year-old named Zackery Kligman. Zack was a longboarder from Myrtle Beach who liked what one source called "trippy electronic music." He weighed 130 pounds, mostly knees and elbows, and his father co-owned Klig's Kites, Myrtle Beach's longest-running gag gift shop. On a given day at the local Broadway at the Beach strip mall, his father wore plastic gums and disco ball earrings, mooning customers with fake plastic cheeks. Nothing about Zack said "Charleston SAE," but guys like Ben came to him for Silk Road alprazolam and high-THC weed. Moving from Myrtle Beach to Charleston, Kligman had reportedly customized his black Cadillac CTS with a hidden hydraulic compartment under his seat.

Rob didn't take bars himself, but he had good reasons to distribute them. As these other kids showed, dark web Xanax was safe to buy, easy to hide, and probably not too bad to get arrested with. Unlike weed, bars were lightweight and odor-free. They were Schedule IV drugs, and South Carolina didn't have a trafficking-level alprazolam charge on its books. The Charleston police showed little interest in rounding up college boys selling otherwise-legal pills, and the courts didn't assign mandatory minimum sentences for benzodiazepine distribution. For a C of C kid from a certain background, Xanax offered a low-risk, high-leverage way to earn clout and money.

If Rob hadn't made the decision to start selling dark web alprazolam, it's unlikely he would have met Zack Kligman. Zack, who wasn't a C of C student, didn't socialize with student government types, and Rob didn't mix with hippies. According to Charleston police documents, though, the two boys met through a kid in Rob's lab class. Rob agreed to buy "sticks" for between seventy and eighty cents each, which he could distribute for a more than 300 percent profit.

While Xanax became easier to access, more C of C students realized that the same attributes that make it effective against panic attacks make it fun to take at parties. Given how quickly and potently benzodiazepines work on neural pathways and the nervous system, they mix well with other drugs. Charleston students learned that a stick of Xanax is a versatile little arithmetic sign, multiplying the force of downers, halving the edge off of uppers, and subtracting from the next day's hangover before it starts. "Sometimes people would take Xanax just to take Xanax," one Kappa Sig told me, "but usually it was just part of a vibe. It was a sidecar to another experience."

What the Kappa Sig called "sidecar-ing"—combining two or more drugs to get an effect that one drug can't provide by itself—scientists call "polypharmacy." In college I thought this technique was so common that it wouldn't have occurred to me there was a special word for it. But when I interviewed Dr. Anna Lembke, who runs the Stanford Addiction Medicine Dual Diagnosis Clinic and coauthored "Our Other Prescription Drug Problem" about benzodiazepines, she told me that polypharmacy is a generational phenomenon. "Ten, fifteen, twenty years ago, people usually had one drug of choice," she said. "Either it was alcohol, or it was meth, or it was opioids, and they kind of stuck to that. Now that's very uncommon. What we see now, especially among millennials, is cocktails."

In social situations, I've rarely seen someone take Xanax by itself, but I've watched plenty of kids use it to supplement whatever else they're taking. According to a 2018 article in the *Journal of Clinical Medicine*, nearly 80 percent of recreational benzodiazepine use comes as part of a wider polypharmacy mix. You can combine a QB of Xanax with weed and increase the high, blend it with cocaine and ease the paranoia, take it on an acid comedown and fall asleep, or use it with opiates and deepen the euphoria. In my experience, the most popular mix for fraternity kids is Xanax and alcohol. Both drugs work on the body and the mind in similar ways, depressing the nervous system and boosting GABA neurotransmitters, and together they amplify each other. The synergy is almost exponential: a milligram of alprazolam and three beers can make you act and feel like you've had seven or eight drinks.

These different blends often worked together at once. This dynamic was best described to me by a former C of C lacrosse team Xanax dealer. For our interview, I met him for a drink at a biergarten downtown. Because he'd come straight from work, he wore a suit and carried a leather notebook. When I asked him how his friends used Xanax bars, he smiled and said, "So I'll give you a Saturday in my world senior year. I wake up, and I'm waking up late because I went to sleep late. So it's ten, eleven, maybe noon. I'm horribly hungover. I wake up, look at my phone, okay, cool, there's a day party in two hours at my buddy's place. So I wake up, and I hop in the shower, and I start drinking beer. Right? I'm, like, drinking beer in the shower, and my buddy comes out, and he's like, 'Oh my God, dude, this hangover, horrible, take a QB,' whatever, whatever. We each take a QB, and then you're like drinking or whatever. 'Okay, it's time to go to the party.' Right? So you do a bunch of lines of cocaine. And then before you've realized it, you've had multiple drinks of alcohol, you've put Xanax in your system, and now you've put cocaine in your system. And throw weed in there, of course. You're smoking weed all day. So then you get to the darty, an hour and a half passes, you keep drinking, you're rip-shit wasted, and you're like, 'Aah, waah, I'm slowing down, I'm slowing down.' So you do more cocaine, right? And then you're like, 'Oh, God, I'm sweating, I'm paranoid now.' So then another bar of Xanax. Before you realize it, you're multiple drugs deep, just trying to balance-act this whole thing. It becomes another day in the life."

Like other guys I'd interviewed, the lacrosse player had first tried Xanax on hungover NFL Sundays and then discovered it as a fun drug. Around sophomore year, he also started to watch his friends prank each other by dropping quarter bars into drinks. Many guys call this maneuver a "QB sneak." Friends would slip a quarter bar of nearly flavorless alprazolam into each other's beers, and everyone would get three times drunker than planned. "It became almost like a roofie drug that you wanted to be a part of," he told me. "I can remember a good buddy of mine, we would do a pregame mix with a half bottle of gin, two liters of Mountain Dew, and a bar of Xanax. It would disintegrate together, and we'd play pong and drink that. You add a little cocaine to that, and it's next level."

After I turned off my recorder, the source asked if I would give him fifteen more minutes of my time. I said sure, and he pulled out his leather notebook and asked if I had a financial planning adviser. I said no, and he told me about his employer, a Fortune 500 life securities company. He finished his beer and pitched me on why he'd be a good steward for my financial planning and life insurance too.

At the end of every fall semester at the College of Charleston, the Kappa Alphas met to vote on their next executive board. "E-board" voting looks similar at fraternity chapters around the country, with members sitting on grimy couches to watch sophomores make low-energy speeches. It's the kind of event that means a lot to the brothers running for office and not that much to everyone else, and when I asked Kappa Alphas about Rob's presidential speech, most of them said they didn't remember it. One source told me that the previous president had done a "shit job with finances," spending 85 percent of the budget on Old South Weekend in Savannah, and Rob was known for being good with spreadsheets, but otherwise he couldn't remember Rob's pitch. Another KA thought he might have run against Rob himself, but he couldn't recall. A third brother with a better memory told me Rob had kept his remarks simple: "He was wearing this fucking ugly-ass rugby shirt with some khakis and some boots, just looking goofy as shit. I was like, 'This guy's a complete fucking weirdo.' But he stood up in front of everyone, and he was like, 'Yo, I'm Rob. Everyone knows me, I think. There's a lot of things I wanna change about the culture around here, the way that we spend and use our money. . . . I wanna add an extra day on Mountain Weekend.' It was a unanimous vote."

Although other brothers told me the vote wasn't actually unanimous, every source agreed that Rob won the 2014 KA election by a nice majority. After arriving from Elmhurst College with a long-distance girlfriend and a lot of merit badges, he became what the Kappa Alpha Order called a "Number I." Number I's had the logistical responsibilities of a fraternity president and the spiritual responsibility of a leader of an order of knights. Every other E-board member reported to him, putting Rob in charge of chapter recruitment, pledgeship, party planning, finances, and risk management. He would preside over chapter meetings, set chapter laws, and, if needed, remove lower-ranking officers and discipline his brothers. *The Varlet* writes, "The powers of Number I are extensive and this is due to his responsibilities. . . . He is commanded by the Knight Commander to prevent or stop hazing, follow our policies, and uphold our laws."

Mikey didn't end up quitting his job at the Tongue and Groove. Even if he didn't get along with the customers in Hyundais, he needed work, and he liked to bond with the higher-end patrons. After a few repeat visits, the wealthier clientele would shout "Little Mikey!" on their way into the club, and he'd flash his smile and compliment their girlfriends. Recognizing this dynamic, his boss assigned him to the T&G's VIP parking spots. When a Bentley or Lamborghini drove up to the valet booth, Mikey would duck his head into the window and say, "It's one hundred dollars if you want to be parked up front, or the next guy is gonna come up and take your spot. What you want to do?"

Mikey still earned only a few dollars per car, and he looked for ways to supplement his income. After a few weeks of parking in the VIP spots, he started dropping sample bags of weed or other drugs in patrons' leather cup holders. When some customers walked to their cars, Mikey handed them their keys and said things like, "You got a beautiful girlfriend, but I know you need some help. Try this." Some VIPs started asking for Mikey's number, and others told their friends that the valet boy who looked like he was ten years old sold good molly.

On nights when he wasn't parking cars, Mikey kept taking the Mount Vernon high school senior, Alexis, out to eat. He didn't know it, but she'd had a crush on him since cheerleading on the sidelines of Mikey's JV basketball games. (When I asked Alexis why so many women are drawn to him, she said, "I have absolutely no idea. I've questioned it myself.") They Snapchatted during school, and he took her to dinner in the suburbs and to haunted houses for Halloween. After enough dates, he talked a little about his family situation, and Alexis opened up too. A few years earlier, her father, an artisan who installed venetian plastering in Atlanta mansions, had been working on a three-story living room ceiling when the scaffolding had buckled and he fell. His insurance had covered his employees but not him, and his shattered legs left him unable to work. Alexis told me this loss made her nonjudgmental of anyone who struggled to pay bills, and she never made her new boyfriend feel unsuccessful for working valet.

Still, other people reminded Mikey of his place. One night at the Tongue and Groove that winter, Mikey saw a white Range Rover swerve past the valet booth and park near the VIP spots without asking. Before Mikey could stop the car, a large figure in khakis opened the door. Mikey recognized him as Wilson Warren, a T&G regular who hung out with Justin Bieber and T.I. People called him "Biscuit," probably because he was doughy and white, but one source told me he walked into the Tongue and Groove with the confidence of "Jesus Christ on a spaceship." Biscuit had pregamed before driving that night. When Mikey told him it'd cost $100 for a VIP parking spot, Biscuit pulled out a pistol and said, "Fucking park it."

Mikey looked at the gun. Another valet driver who knew Wilson said, "Jesus, Biscuit, come on." After more silence,

Mikey's boss told him to park the car, and Mikey nodded. He kept the peace and got inside the Range Rover, but after he parked it he looked for a way to retaliate. He dug around the center console and found a vial of pills, which he put inside his uniform pocket. At the end of the night, when Mikey gave Biscuit his keys, Mikey said, "I stole your Xanax," and Biscuit laughed.

The next morning, Biscuit got Mikey's number and called him: "Yo, you really took my shit." Mikey responded, "Yeah, I took your shit. Also, if you wanna shop, this is what I've got." Biscuit wasn't looking to buy anything, but he appreciated Mikey's cheek. "I've known Mikey since my dumb ass showed up pretty fucking hammered and pulled a gun on him," Biscuit told me years later. "At this point it feels like we're more like brothers."

CHAPTER 8

BLACKOUT PUNCH

Looking at his photos online, I couldn't understand how Wilson "Biscuit" Warren fit into Atlanta's music circles. When he flipped off the camera next to Young Thug or held money to his ear with Gunna, smiled with Jimmy Iovine or laughed with T.I., he seemed like he'd walked in from an SEC tailgate. His second chin looked especially in need of shaving, and he wore the same type of gingham button-downs as his little brother, who was a Georgia SAE, and his father, who consulted on David Perdue's 2020 senate campaign. But even though Wilson himself moonlighted as Perdue's social media consultant, he also somehow dominated hip-hop night at the Tongue and Groove.

When I asked Biscuit how he did so well in the music business, he said, "It's in part because I look so unthreatening." One source did compare Wilson to a man-size hamster, but everyone I asked said there was more to Biscuit under his cuddliness. When he was fifteen, Wilson informally recruited high school players for the Georgia Tech football team, a move he says he parlayed into sideline tickets. When he was sixteen, he talked Atlanta's Opera nightclub into replacing its gay night with a teen night, promising a higher turnout and lower overhead. Two thousand teens came to the first show. "These kids were used to lame high school dances in the gym with parents checking their breath for alcohol," he told me. "This was a finger bang sesh." Biscuit said that Scooter Braun, then a fledgling impresario, began to use teen night to promote his up-and-coming acts, including "I Love College" singer Asher Roth and a fourteen-year-old Justin Bieber. After both shows attracted thousands of screaming teens, Scooter Braun asked Wilson to work for him, and Biscuit and Justin Bieber became friends.

In 2009, Bieber was still a prepubescent Ontarian in a town full of strangers. He'd gotten a few million YouTube views for his Chris Brown and Justin Timberlake covers, and he'd just moved from Canada to Atlanta to work with Braun. He wasn't world famous yet, and he started to invite Biscuit over for sleepovers. (Biscuit's mom would ask, "Why are you spending the night at a kid's?") Soon Biscuit left Atlanta for Justin Bieber's My World tour. He was Justin's day-to-day assistant, a position that involved answering the phone and "keeping people from getting in trouble." The tour grossed $53 million, and Wilson's social world grew to the point where he once had to apologize to Will and Jada Pinkett Smith for yelling at their television during the Florida-Georgia game. After he came home from the tour, Biscuit felt ready to take on a few different businesses, including a concert promotion company and a private jet brokerage firm. Some jobs worked better than others, but the constant was his relationships with famous people. He became a recurring character at Atlanta nightclubs, and he kept running into Mikey in the Tongue and Groove valet line after Mikey stole his pills (which Biscuit remembers as Vyvanse, not Xanax). "We would chat while I waited on my car, and we vibed really well," Biscuit told me. "Mikey was telling me about his ambitions, and I was like, 'Well, I need an extra hand right now, if you wanna come be my little right hand man for a bit.' He told me, 'Fuck yeah.'"

Mikey still worked nights at the Tongue and Groove, but he spent his days with Biscuit. He rode down Peachtree Street in Biscuit's supercharged Range Rover, watching his new mentor spew and charm into the phone. Wilson was working on a few different ventures, including a new business called FratShows.com, which brought famous rappers to southern Greek mansions. Biscuit had been hired by Daniel Kuniansky, a former Indiana University Alpha Epsilon Pi whose music career began when he booked Bubba Sparxxx to play his fraternity soon after "Ms. New Booty" came out. To help grow the business, Biscuit and Mikey talked fraternities into booking rap acts, and Biscuit talked rappers into playing fraternity houses. The startup competed with a new wave of brands, like I'm Shmacked and *Barstool Sports*' Blackout Tour, that all threw campus parties and posted YouTube videos showing just how wild "college millennials" could get.

FratShows.com specialized in trap music, a type of drum-heavy rap named after trap houses where drugs are cooked or sold. Fraternity guys loved trap artists like Juicy J and Migos, but the Platonic ideal of FratShows acts might have been Waka Flocka Flame. A mentee of Gucci Mane, Waka Flocka had helped define the trap sound—*Pitchfork* called his first album "a furious torrent of gangsta rap id"—but by 2014 he'd started to mix trap music with Greek life's other favorite genre of that era, big-room EDM. At fraternities in Texas or Florida, he'd rap over synthesizers and fog cannons, headbanging his dreads and throwing birthday cakes off the stage. When he played the University of Oklahoma SAE "Jungle Party," he sprayed champagne on boys and girls in camo fatigues, and when he played an Alabama fraternity living room, a girl kicked in a window with her bare foot and opened up an artery. After shows he'd stay and drink at fraternity houses. (I remember opening Snapchat during college and wondering why my friends had selfies with Waka Flocka Flame.)

When Waka looked down nearly a foot below him and met Mikey Schmidt for the first time, Mikey must have looked like every other kid at FratShow afterparties. After Mikey left C of C he still wore Southern Tide visors and golf shirts, and he'd kept his swoopy haircut. But, at least according to Biscuit, Mikey separated himself from other kids right away. "When you're a gang member or a rapper, you don't like meeting new people," Biscuit said. "And you fucking hate a coked-up frat boy coming up talking a thousand words a minute about how much he fucking loves your new music video. Mikey wasn't like that. He knew when to shut up and when to talk, and most people don't have a clue when to do that." Biscuit told me that Mikey's relationship with Waka built slowly, but Mikey impressed Waka's friends by carrying good weed and rolling great Backwoods blunts. "Mikey and Waka's brother would just sit around and smoke and giggle," Biscuit said. "Smoke and giggle."

While Mikey worked for Biscuit in Atlanta, the Charleston Xanax dealer Johnny Drama was learning to make even more money selling bars. "I went to Miami and blew ten thousand dollars on a Sunday," he told me. "There are different tiers of VIP at [the Miami Beach nightclub] LIV, and I paid to get up in the section with Lil Wayne. I ended up chilling with Rick Ross and Wale and all these people. The girls that were with us were like, 'Oh my God.'" Back in Charleston, he docked the *Hurricane*, the 42-foot Sportfisher he called a party machine, in the local Mega Dock and threw boat parties on weekends.

For Cinco de Mayo that year, Johnny stuffed forty friends on the *Hurricane* and took them to Morris Island, where they drank all afternoon on a sandbar. Then he cruised home and went out on King Street, and when he got home to Saint Philip Street he ordered a late-night Jimmy John's delivery. A few minutes later he heard a knock on the door and opened it expecting his sandwich but instead felt a pistol whip his face. Two men in ski masks dragged him into his apartment and tied him to a chair, where blood ran down his forehead from a gash that he was too drunk to really feel. The men searched the house like they knew where things usually were, and after they found only $200 they put a Glock to his temple and asked, "Where is the money?" While he stuttered, he heard someone knock again, and the two men opened the door and started to beat the Jimmy John's delivery man. Once they'd stomped on the delivery worker enough times that Johnny knew he'd have to get facial reconstruction surgery, they took the $200 and Johnny's gun and disappeared.

Without really thinking through the consequences, Johnny Drama decided to call 911. When the police arrived, they searched his apartment and found 180 benzodiazepine pills and four ounces of weed. After some interrogation, he gave them the key to a bank deposit box containing $44,000 in cash. He received five years of probation, which, combined with the fact that the police never found his assailants, convinced him to retire from selling Xanax. The supply hole left by his departure grew considerably larger two and a half weeks later, when federal authorities seized the dark web dealer known as the Xanax King in Oakland. In a sting totally unrelated to Johnny's, the King and eight associates were indicted for shipping hundreds of thousands of alprazolam pills. These two losses—one local, one global—left a Xanax vacuum in Charleston. It was a hole that perhaps only Zackery Kligman had the capacity to fill.

During this period, most boys who worked with Zack didn't understand the extent of his operations. Even though some other dealers called him the "Charleston Kingpin," he didn't usually act like it. "If I saw him walking down the street in his dirty skater shoes, I wouldn't be like 'drug dealer, dope boy, he's got a shit ton of money,'" a C of C SAE told me. Drinking his Pacifico at a bar off of Mount Pleasant's Shem Creek, a Clemson Phi Delt dealer looked me up and down and said, "He was, like, soft spoken, not a party animal. He looked like you." When I tried to respond that I was almost a foot taller than Zack, the Phi Delt said, "Yeah, but just innocent, sweet. But then I remember one time he came over with an envelope full of cocaine that he got in the mail, all in one brick. I was like, 'Wait, Z., are you in this shit too?' And he was like, 'Ha-ha-ha buddy! I bet you wish you knew!'"

Later, a different source passed me a few hundred pages of law enforcement documents on Kligman. In August 2011, when Zack was nineteen, a Charleston County Sheriff's lieutenant saw Zack's Cadillac swerve between lanes on Highway 17 North. When Zack rolled down his window, the lieutenant was "immediately overwhelmed by the odor of raw marijuana," and watched Zack's hands "shaking uncontrollably while attempting to retrieve his information." Noticing that Zack's "carotid artery was visibly pulsating," the lieutenant placed him on the ground and walked to the back of the Cadillac. After he opened the trunk and found a jar of weed, five bags of molly powder, a book of drug ledgers, and a pack of LSD gummies that Zack begged the lieutenant not to touch, Zack fell backward and started weeping. "I am so fucked," he said. "I am going to jail for a long time." For reasons that weren't elaborated in the documents, though, Zack's charges were dismissed before he went to trial. Then, in 2012, Georgia policemen arrested Zack near the CounterPoint Music Festival, which brought DJs like Skrillex and Bassnectar to the Chattahoochee River. He was charged with trafficking MDMA and possession of LSD, marijuana, and ketamine, all with the intent to distribute. One year later, according to the *Post and Courier*, Zack was arrested again, this time in Myrtle Beach, and charged with the manufacturing and possession of flunitrazepam, which can be used as a date-rape drug. For reasons that also didn't make it into the files, each of these charges was also dismissed before it went to trial. When Zack established his business in Charleston around the summer of 2013, he'd never been convicted of a crime.

According to police and DEA documents, Zack's scope expanded when he left Myrtle Beach. As his business grew, he used U-Haul trucks to deliver thirty to fifty pounds of marijuana to Charleston at a time, stuffing bundles inside furniture and paying an elderly man to drive them cross-country from Oregon. Starting work around three p.m. because he liked to "party all night," Zack used his Cadillac to make deliveries in specific batches and geographic loops around the Low Country. He installed a safe under his house and keypads and cameras for the rooms inside, and he kept ledgers in a journal by hand. In addition to the pot from Oregon, he reportedly ordered MDMA from the Netherlands, ketamine from a local supplier, cocaine from Atlanta and Miami, and LSD from a place that the Charleston PD informants couldn't remember. According to police interviews, though, Zack's "thing" is Xanax. After

Johnny Drama's mugging and the Xanax King's arrest, Zack claimed to be Charleston's main source for bars.

My sources had different names for the group of college kids who sold Xanax for Zack. One interviewee called them "the Island Boys," another "the Grateful Dead Family," and a third, for some reason, "the Cannabana Bandits." But really, Zack's drug operation was less of an organized ring and more of a Mary Kay–style multilevel-marketing network. At least in Charleston, what had started as a decentralized economy morphed into a sales pyramid with Kligman on top. Zack bought hundreds of thousands of bars at thirty to sixty cents apiece from an undisclosed source and sold them by the thousands for around a dollar a pill to wholesale dealers. These boys would sell the pills by the hundreds for three to five dollars each to other guys, who'd flip them in small batches to students for as much as they could charge. Zack's dealers included at least two College of Charleston SAEs (Ben Nauss and Russell Sliker), two Citadel cadets, and three upperclassmen living on 97 Smith Street, but the list involved dozens of names. According to the Charleston PD interviews in the files, though, of all the kids who bought Zack's pills in bulk, no one sold more than Robert Liljeberg.

As the C of C KAs' Number I, Rob led weekly chapter meetings. He also brought back the local Parents Weekend tradition. Using it as a fundraising vehicle and a social outing, he invited over one hundred guests to a brother's grandparents' house in the suburbs. Rob's mother and his father, who'd found new success as an orthopedic surgeon at the Troy Regional Medical Center, came in from Alabama. They woke up early to cook a Cajun-style shrimp and crawfish boil, dumping the shellfish out for families to eat with their hands. Digging through corn and potatoes, Rob showed northern parents how to crack open mudbugs and suck out the juice. When he finished, he could talk about his premed classes or bemoan LSU's mediocre 2014 season, or he could describe the ways he'd changed the order. As president, Rob had beefed up the chapter's finances, giving it enough money for good parties besides Old South Weekend. He'd actively sought out higher-quality kids to rush, and on his own résumé he described his role as "economic management of the organization, to include evaluation, prioritization and development of an action plan to improve the organization's recruiting and public image."

Like a few other campus dealers, Rob bought ten thousand Xanax pills at a time from Zackery Kligman. Faster than other boys, Rob broke these deliveries into pieces and offloaded them without leaving his room. He sometimes emptied out bags of popcorn or potato chips and refilled them with Zack's product, and then he closed the bags with a manual heat-sealer. From there he sold thousand-pill orders of alprazolam to KA brothers and other customers, who sold smaller amounts to guys who sold them in turn at off-campus houses and King Street bars. Other times Rob paid his KA drivers to move the pills around, carrying them in Cape Cod chip bags or other heat-sealed packaging. The younger guys dropped bundles around Charleston, and according to several sources they took bulk orders to fraternities at UNC Chapel Hill and USC Columbia. As the business grew, they also worked with Mikey in Atlanta.

After enough deals outside the Tongue and Groove and inside fraternity parties, Mikey moved out of his mom's house. He rented an apartment at the Cyan on Peachtree, a glass tower of bachelors looming above a Del Frisco's steakhouse. It was the kind of amenity-full condo popping up from West LA to the Boston Seaport. Mikey bought a circular white sofa and barely used his stainless steel kitchen. Biscuit sometimes came over around two p.m., making music business calls while Mikey met with customers. The door always seemed to be opening or closing with pickups and drop-offs, and when Mikey let Rob know about the money he was making, Rob sent drivers to Georgia with Xanax for Mikey to sell. Less than a year after he'd left the Kappa Alpha Order, Mikey returned to the bubble. When pledges came to Atlanta he took a lacrosse stick and made them dodge tomatoes in his yard. After Mikey beat them in *NBA2K* and punished them by making them eat onions like they were apples, the underclassmen drove him east for KA parties or Mountain Weekend. When he returned he dealt the Charleston Xanax to customers in Atlanta, UGA, and Ole Miss. He managed to sell the pills faster than he even sold weed or molly, and Rob's supply pyramid began offloading ten thousand Xanax bars a week.

Soon Mikey quit his job at the Tongue and Groove. This move freed up time for deals at the Cyan and trips up I-20 to visit Rob.

When Mikey arrived in Charleston, the Kappa Alpha Order he saw looked different from the one he'd left. Walking next to upperclassman Rob, Mikey entered parties with bigger boats and fuller triceps and girls from better sororities. More people wanted to go on KA's Mountain Weekend at Camp Wayfarer in North Carolina, and Rob had started dating a Chi O who was the cover model for *Swig* magazine's "Hottest Bartender in Charleston" issue. KAs were listening to more Bassnectar than Alan Jackson, and when Rob and Mikey got kicked out of the Stars rooftop on King Street for being too drunk, Mikey pulled out $25,000 in cash and offered to rent the place for the night instead. (The Stars manager recalls declining his offer.) Even though an anonymous hater posted "Every guy in KA is short" on Yik Yak every day at four p.m., the post usually got as many downvotes as upvotes.

Mikey also saw more Xanax than he had before. Some guys took bars before class or stumbled into palm trees at night, and at one house party, one barred-out freshman girl climbed onto the roof and threatened to jump for fun. (She didn't.) Sometimes Mikey joined in on the belligerence, and one night he stole a Citadel cadet's cap on King Street and sprinted back to Rob's house. The cadets need their full uniforms to reenter their military college gates each night, and Rob scolded Mikey for risking police attention at 7 Montagu. Another night, while Mikey and a half dozen other KAs walked up King Street, an SAE came up and punched Mikey's pledge brother in the testicles. The KAs mobbed the SAE brother, and according to one KA who was there, "We beat the shit out of him in the middle of the street." After the KAs took shelter in a house on Morris Street, the SAEs "pulled up strong. It was like six of us versus ten steroided-out motherfuckers. We wound that shit up . . . It was a real brawl."

On nights like these, more kids were blacking out on Xanax and alcohol. Although some of their parents would misunderstand the term, "blacking out" doesn't mean passing out, but walking around while parts of your brain go dark. When two Xanax bars and six Keystone Lights enter the central nervous system, the pathways that turn short-term memories into long-term memories get severed, leaving no way of storing what's happening for the morning. A blackout kid might be able to spill his beer on a security guard or take his date upstairs, but those moments won't be recorded, because the camera in his brain is already off. To be clear, getting to that point was by no means the aim for every boy every night. Still, at least for kids in socially dominant fraternities, blacking out was a more acceptable choice than staying in.

C of C KA: I remember asking younger guys in the fraternity, "What's the fucking point of blacking out? You don't remember any of it." And one of them said, "Well that's exactly the point: to not remember anything."

Duke KA: It's cool to not remember. It's cool to be like, "Bro, what happened?"

C of C KA: It was hilarious to black out and be like, "I can't believe I hooked up with that chick, but we won't tell anybody."

C of C Kappa Sig: I loved it because I could take a half bar and get to the point where I wanted to be, which was a total loss of inhibition, a loss of memory. I'm not worried if I dance next to this girl and look like a fucking idiot, because I'm blacked the fuck out, you know?

Clemson Phi Delt: It blocks the sensor in your brain that makes you think, "Oh, should I talk to this girl?" You take a bar, and you're like, "What's up mamma? I am the *dawg.* I don't give a fuck!"

UT Sig Ep: It's almost a sign of prestige. While everyone else is refining their lives to get ready for the professional world, the fuck boys can go hard. It's the whole notion of like, "I'm connected to enough people that I can be a cocksucker, and I'm still going to be taken care of."

C of C Alumna from Myrtle Beach: After my freshman year, I was talking to some random people on the beach, and I was like, "My favorite thing about Charleston is you can black out and always make it home."

Because Xanax and alcohol lead to easy blackouts, I wondered if any C of C boys used bars as date-rape pills. The guys I interviewed denied it, and one C of C KA told me about his other technique for attracting women: "Imagine we walk into a steakhouse, right? And there's two beautiful women at the bar. Before we sit down, I'm going to use eye contact to tell what's going on. Then when we sit next to them, I'm immediately going to start talking shit to both of them. Their chipped nail, the scuff on their shoe, whatever small detail, I'm just gonna go ahead and attack that." (When I asked if he'd learned his "negging" technique from the pickup artist book *The Game*, he denied it.) "And not only that, I don't really do too much talking. I speak more through body language. [I communicate that] I don't give a fuck."

When I pressed other Charleston fraternity guys about it, though, they said they'd heard that other C of C chapters made Xanax punch at parties. Apparently, these other fraternities poured water into Kool-Aid powder, adding bottles of vodka or Everclear and sprinkling crushed-up alprazolam in the mix. Because the hosts didn't write "contains benzodiazepines" on their coolers, some female guests woke up the next morning surprised that they didn't remember the night before. But if fraternity sources told me that other guys put alprazolam in the jungle juice, they all insisted that they'd never seen it happen themselves. They attributed the drugging to other fraternities and told me that their chapter was above it. "We never did that," a KA told me. "One, because we didn't want to do that with women; and two, because we didn't want to waste the Xanax."

Regardless, several College of Charleston women told me they'd seen fraternity boys spiking their punch. "Yep, yes, that happened for sure," Tri Delt Christina Arnold told me. Before one lower-tier fraternity party, a boy whom Christina had known since high school let her watch his friends mix bars into their juice. While they dropped alprazolam into the mix, he told her, "We usually never do this." In addition, another C of C alumna told me that she'd blacked out at several Kappa Alpha parties after drinking their Kool-Aid. During one house party, she brought her Tervis tumbler and specifically asked for the Xanax punch, and a brother led her up a thin stairway, past a bathroom clogged with hair, and into a bedroom with a Coleman cooler on the floor. The boys didn't have a serving ladle, so she dipped her Tervis into the warm red slosh. "It was the kind of juice that would stain your clothes," she said. "Like if you spill the KA juice on a nice cashmere, that thing's gone."

When I asked the KA national organization about Xanax-spiked punch, its attorney stated that it had never received reports of the conduct and denied the allegations. When I asked the Kappa Alpha who'd told me about picking up beautiful women at steakhouses if his brothers ever spiked their punch, he said, "They would do it. Put ten bars in there, shake the fucking cooler, see where the night ends up. . . . Although none of it was me."

When I'd learned about Xanax spiking, I'd assumed that boys at parties handed out juice to girls and drank beer themselves. But according to each source I talked to about it, the punch-makers usually drank their own Kool-Aid. This meant that they roofied their victims and themselves too. After two Solo cups of his own juice, a boy wouldn't be able to remember having sex, and he might not even be able to perform. I asked the C of C alumna about the logic of drinking your own spiked punch, and she told me that shared incapacitation was the point. "For guys, blacking out means there's no pressure," she said. "Then girls won't say, 'He tried to sleep with me, but he has a whack dick and couldn't get hard.' It's just like, 'Oh, he was on Xanax.'" Armed with this excuse, boys got the social prestige of getting laid without any of the actual pressures of having sex. The next day, a kid could tell his brothers that he woke up next to a Chi O and leave out everything that happened beforehand. "Sometimes, I waited until sunrise for their dick to start working, and they'd start talking about their feelings," the alumna told me. "They'd be like, 'My mom this and my mom that, and my dad and my brother and whatever.' And I'm like, 'I'm not even adding to the conversation. I'm literally a free therapist.'"

Elsewhere in America, students and adults were talking about college sexual assault in new ways. In certain online pockets, opening Twitter in 2014 meant reading about Emma Sulkowicz's "Carry That Weight" mattress protest or the wave of Title IX sexual violence complaints that rose exponentially from the year before. A lot of this talk revolved around fraternities, from Brock Turner's rape of Chanel Miller after a Stanford KA party to *Rolling Stone*'s fabricated "Rape on Campus" story about UVA Phi Kappa Psi. Comparing themselves with these headlines about night stalking and gang rape, the guys who made Xanax punch ignored their own questions of consent. Boys still put alprazolam in jungle juice and shared girls' nudes on GroupMe, and bar-dropping someone didn't usually bring many social consequences. Christina Arnold told me that at a Tri Delt party, her date, a Sigma Chi, gave her a glass of Bombay gin that he'd dropped a Xanax inside. "I had one drink and I was done. I was puking at my own date party, and then I woke up in my roommate's bed." She warned her friends not to go on dates with that particular Sigma Chi, but she didn't press charges or tell the school. "You get so scared to accuse people," Christina said. "You don't want to be 'that girl'. . . . But it was such a common occurrence. . . . I knew going into pretty much every party that I would go to that it was a thing." Later, when Christina confronted the Sigma Chi, he didn't deny that he'd dropped Xanax into the gin. Instead, he told her, "Yeah, like, I think you drank my drink."

CHAPTER 9

PURE WATER

Each year during Christmas break, the KA national organization hosts something called the Number I's Leadership Institute (NLI). If a Kappa Alpha chapter president doesn't attend, the knight commander will remove him from office. If a boy needs to miss the conference for a death in the family, he has to send an obituary clipping as proof. When Rob Liljeberg walked into the NLI in 2014, he carried a suitcase full of "KA casual" clothes: khaki pants, button-downs, dress socks. He arrived at the Caraway Conference Center, a Southern Baptist event space in the central North Carolina pine forest. When he walked inside, he shook hands with his contemporaries and joined the name tag line. After he posed for a composite photo with 130 or so other chapter presidents,

Rob sat down for what another KA Number I told me was four days of "torture. . . . It's just a bunch of white college guys sitting around asking, 'When the fuck is this going to be over?'"

Every morning at seven thirty, the KA Number I's reported for fourteen hours of talks, meals, and breakout sessions. The Caraway Conference Center has little cell service on the premises and no tobacco or alcohol for one thousand acres, and Rob had no choice but to listen to a PR expert from Dallas give a talk titled "You Are ALWAYS on the Record." During the lectures, Rob sat at the end of a row and untucked his shirt. He looked at a whiteboard where someone wrote "winning = emotional intelligence" and went to an event described as "How to Give and Take Criticism like a Man." During one speech, he listened to the former knight commander, J. Michael Duncan, give him the "tools to run a chapter," bringing to bear his experience as a senior special agent with the Bureau of Alcohol, Tobacco, Firearms, and Explosives.

Rob and the other boys couldn't leave the woods until they also listened to talks about risk management. In the late 1980s, when the National Association of Insurance Commissioners declared fraternities only slightly less risky than asbestos-removal companies, Kappa Alpha and ten other major frats had created the Fraternity Insurance Purchasing Group, Inc. (FIPG). The FIPG published a "risk management policy," a long set of best practices that frats could adopt to more easily obtain insurance for claims of wrongful death, sexual assault, personal injury, etc. But as Rob and the others learned, the FIPG risk management policy was even harder to follow than

normal laws. To get coverage after a tragedy at a party, fraternity members would have had to prove they had followed the
FIPG's official BYOB policy, used sober monitors, ID checks,
drug bans, hazing prohibitions, drink limits, and other restric-
tions. "I remember thinking, 'We break every single one of
these rules,'" a former Number I at a large state university told
me. "If someone actually complied with them, it would be the
lamest fucking party in the history of the world."

After hours of listening to the FIPG's insurance language,
the boys of KA looked dead behind the eyes. Instead of watching college football bowl season with their friends, they had
to read legal-minded documents in a Southern Baptist conference center. Without enough Wi-Fi to text Mikey or his
other friends, all Rob could do was sit there. After a few more
sessions of boredom, the national leaders opened up the "fun"
part of the weekend. In an event called "The Power of Ritual,"
they invited boys who'd memorized the Kappa Alpha initiation text up onto the stage. There, they performed its secret
mix of old southern romance, New Testament ethics, and the
knightly chivalry of medieval times.

Long before Biscuit took him to Magic City for dinner, Mikey
knew it was America's most important strip club. He'd heard
it mentioned in YouTube interviews with his heroes, like the
rapper Jeezy and the narcotics trafficker Big Meech. To outsid-
ers Magic City was a windowless building next to a Greyhound
station, but Mikey saw it as the place where Atlanta's econo-
mies proved themselves to each other. Rappers like Future and

Migos had started their climb to success by getting Magic girls to dance to their songs, and the region's biggest dealers let the city know they'd made it by throwing their money onstage. Michael Jordan once visited during the daytime, and Drake once sent an armored truck to the front door. Biscuit, for his part, said he didn't usually go to Black strip clubs, but he liked Magic City because he loved their wings.

When Mikey walked inside on his first night, pink and purple lights hit his eyes. New songs by 2 Chainz and T.I. came out of the subwoofer, and men fanned stacks of bills toward the ceiling. Instead of approaching the performers onstage, Mikey ordered chicken wings. They were in fact really good, small enough to grab with two fingers, with a light crunch wrapped around a few perfect bites of juice. Mikey tucked into crinkle-cut fries and watched women with bodies very different from the ones he'd seen in Charleston climb poles and give dances. He kept his distance from the stage, but the more he drank the more he wanted to give a "Magic City shower." The idea was to rain so much money on the dancers that other patrons would ask, "Who is that?" From there, the rappers and traffickers in the room would know Mikey was an earner and maybe want to meet him. As he'd heard someone say about Magic City, "If you throw that money, it comes back." After more drinks, Mikey took out rubber-banded rolls of cash from his pockets and threw them into the air. He released money above his head—one source told me it was tens of thousands of dollars—and watched it make a green carpet on the floor. One woman danced under Mikey's currency, and Mikey looked out at the crowd. But in the sensory overload of lights and bodies around them, no one noticed.

Still, Mikey was earning too much for his failed money shower to hurt him financially. As his business grew, he'd bought an Infiniti G35 and an old BMW 335i drop top and blacked out their windows. He kept some stacks of money on hand at his Cyan apartment and stored others at his grandparents' house in the Dunwoody suburbs. Once he'd confirmed that Frank was playing online poker in the basement, Mikey would run and hide cash under the guest room mattress. Sometimes he'd look out the window and see Frank in the backyard, puffing his inhaler and shooting BBs at squirrels. After he'd visit with his grandfather, Mikey would make various pickups around Atlanta, receiving Xanax from Charleston, ecstasy from his friend Flip, and weed from nearly a dozen different sources. Then he'd return to the Cyan, where a few bulk sales to smaller dealers could empty him out for the day. These calls and meetings would leave him free for his favorite part of the night, which was visiting the studio with Biscuit.

When he wasn't taking calls from his Range Rover, Biscuit worked from an office inside the studio where the 808 Mafia made records. Named after the drum machine that has propelled rap music for the last forty years, the 808 Mafia helped Atlanta trap dominate the sound of twenty-first-century pop. As a production and songwriting collective, they'd started making beats for Waka Flocka Flame and went on to produce for Future, Drake, and other artists whose songs traveled from Magic City to fraternity parties. Because he knew Biscuit, Mikey got to sit on the sofa and watch the 808 team collaborate. With success they'd grown to dozens of members, and while producers like Southside and TM88 programmed their hi-hats and clipped their kick drums, artists like Xanny Tomy and Nechie came in with their girlfriends and entourages. At first they ignored Biscuit's preppy friend, but some of them eventually glanced at the five-foot-seven kid with bangs who rolled Backwoods blunts and left in a blacked-out BMW.

After the studio, Mikey usually went out with Biscuit. For dinner they liked Chops for steak or 10 Degrees South for upscale South African fusion. After that they might head to the Tongue and Groove and finish the night at Tattletale, which one of their friends described to me as a "white strip club." One night Mikey went to another gentlemen's club with one of the bigger ecstasy distributors in the South, and while there he reportedly shared a wooden burial coffin full of liquor with the former Clemson baseball star Brad Felder. Brad was as big and loud as Mikey was quiet and little, but when a spotlight passed by Brad's rose gold Yacht-Master, Mikey told his fellow dealer, "Nice watch, bro." Another night Mikey carried a brown paper bag with $50,000 in cash inside it to 10 Degrees South. After Mikey pulled out a few thousand to pay for a few bottles of cult Napa wine, Biscuit said, "Dude, let's go to the strip clubs." Mikey grabbed his paper bag. "So we went to this one place called Mardi Gras," Biscuit told me. "[After spending] ten grand there, we were anointed holy knights of the fucking crusaders. And then we went to Tattletale, which is my favorite.

It's actually very nice. We spent about thirty-five thousand of that money in a matter of about six hours."

When he woke up in the mornings, Mikey sometimes drove to the studio and made work calls from the sofa. After coordinating pickups and drop-offs, he'd bet on games of *NBA2K* with Waka Flocka Flame's brother. Mikey was about as good at *2K* as he was at *FIFA*, and according to Biscuit "Mikey took [Waka's brother's] money like it was his job." Sometimes Waka came into the studio himself, and producers swiveled their chairs and hangers-on laughed at maybe-jokes. Mikey was a big Waka fan at the time, but he stayed on the couch and didn't try to impress him. Perhaps for this reason, Waka appeared to like Mikey. The six-foot-four rapper apparently called him "Lil Mikey," and one day he gave him a sweatshirt promoting his label, Brick Squad Monopoly. Once it was socially acceptable to take out his phone, Mikey texted Rob, "He is so nice. [The sweatshirt] says bricksquad on it. your gonna have to get ya grams up if ya want one of these he says," adding six crying-laughing emojis. Rob responded, "Haha fuck you gimme a sweatshirt."

In early 2014, Waka and his entourage scheduled another tour with FratShows.com. They planned to hop around the South, with stops at Kentucky and Auburn and elsewhere. Thanks to his success at SAE Jungle the year before, he'd also scheduled a return to University of Oklahoma Sigma Alpha Epsilon in April. Waka's tour plans changed on Monday, March 9, when he saw a video from the OU SAEs' weekend. It was a nine-second clip from the boys' chartered bus ride to an

SAE Founder's Day celebration at the Oklahoma City Golf & Country Club. In the video, two brothers in tuxedos stand up and lead the party bus in a nursery rhyme: *There will never be a n——SAE [clap, clap], / there will never be a n——SAE [clap clap], / You can hang him from a tree, / but he'll never sign with me, / There will never be a n——SAE [clap, clap].*

Waka canceled his show. When a CNN anchor asked him about his decision, he said, "I performed for those kids. They made me feel like a brother. Just to see what a person do behind closed doors . . . I wasn't angry. I was just disgusted." In response, *Morning Joe*'s Mika Brzezinski suggested that the SAEs had learned to use the N-word by listening to Waka's songs. Smiling in front of three American flags, she added, "He shouldn't be disgusted with them; he should be disgusted with himself." While Waka responded, "This isn't about rap; this is about what happened on that bus," a team of University of Oklahoma investigators looked into the origins of the song. After interviewing 160 sources, they announced that the OU chapter hadn't learned the SAE lynching jingle from rap music. As the Sigma Alpha Epsilon executive director would later confirm, the OU kids first heard the chant on the SAE annual summer leadership cruise.

The two boys in the OU SAE video, Levi Pettit and Parker Rice, grew up near my house in Dallas. We lived in what some people call "the Bubble," a stretch of oak trees and McMansions that starts in Highland Park and runs up through Preston Hollow. When the OU video became global news and protesters marched outside the Rice family home, Bubble people reacted in a few different ways. A small fraction agreed with the comedian Will Ferrell, who said the video was "a real argument for getting rid of the [fraternity] system altogether." A smaller fraction thought the boys had nothing to apologize for. But for the many of us who grew up learning not to say the "N-word" but who also had deep ties to Greek life, the video stirred up an uncomfortable mix of feelings. Even if they don't sing it out loud, plenty of elite chapters share the OU SAE admissions policy.

Up until the 1950s, most major American fraternities had official "whites only" rules, and some, like SAE and Phi Delt, had "Aryan" blood requirements. National organizations changed these bylaws by the Eisenhower years, but it's a badly kept secret that some chapters still enforce them seven decades later. Even now, if you go to the right fraternity parties on Alabama's Jefferson Avenue, or UT's West Campus, or Ole Miss Fraternity Row, the only nonwhite people you'll find are visiting athletes or security guards. By sophomore year, boys who grew up playing sports and going to class with Black friends start to hang out more or less exclusively with other white kids who drive Chevy Tahoes. Some end up attending theme parties like "border patrol" or ironic MLK Day celebrations with fried chicken and malt liquor, and other guys with no prior known views on the Civil War start to love the "Robert E. Lee, South shoulda won" chant. At C of C, when I asked a Black fraternity member why he didn't rush the Kappa Alpha Order, he said, "I heard they were a 'predominately southern' fraternity and just ran. . . . I think I speak for other nonwhite Greek life members in this, all five of us."

In early 1904, when the Kappa Alpha Order opened its chapter at the College of Charleston, the *Kappa Alpha Journal* alumni magazine ran a picture of the new brothers. In their racial makeup and general vibe, they looked a lot like 2015 C of C KAs. In the 1904 picture, the tall, good-looking one swept his hair to the right, the short, wealthy-looking one tucked his bangs into a center part, and the athletic-looking one spread his feet into a power stance. Crossing his legs in the front row was a thirty-year-old KA alumnus who'd come to initiate the new Charleston chapter. He was the Reverend Henry Judah Mikell, an Episcopalian pastor and KA evangelist who helped boys form KA colonies around the South. The Reverend Mikell went on to serve as the bishop of Atlanta and the knight commander of the Kappa Alpha Order, and today the KA website calls him "an influential role model for many KAs." Looking through other *Kappa Alpha Journal* issues for information about him, I found an alumni banquet speech he'd given called "The Kappa Alpha Sentiment" in 1917. Reverend Mikell began the speech by reading a few poems, and then he preached the order's origin story:

> *The conditions which obtained in the South after the Civil War brought about the rise of two unique institutions: The Ku Klux Klan and the Kappa Alpha Order—K.K. and K.A. The times were out of joint, the former slaves threatened to be the*

masters. Our fathers had to devise something which would make their outward life livable, which would make their hard situation tolerable, and so the Ku Klux was instituted by which they preserved the mastery over the outward circumstances of their life. But there was something deeper to be done. The nobler spirits of the South felt that they must have some institution which would help them to preserve the mastery over themselves, which should inculcate in their young men such high ideals, such instincts of chivalry, that in a brutish time they might beat down their own brutishness, and in a lawless time they might be unto themselves a higher law. And so the Kappa Alpha Order was founded.

I kept reading *Kappa Alpha Journals*. In a 1920 issue, the *Journal*'s editor wrote that KA brothers have "doubtlessly added to the Klan's effectiveness" and claimed the KKK "strove to do by the employment of intelligent force what Kappa Alpha set itself to do by means of the example of a noble idealism." In 1921, next to an announcement that Kappa Alpha alumnus J. Edgar Hoover would serve as vice president of the KA board, the *Journal* quoted a *Washington Times* article that suggested the Ku Klux Klan had been founded by "members of the Kappa Alpha and the Sigma Alpha Epsilon fraternities." In 1922, the magazine ran an original prose poem titled "The Birth of an Order" about the Reconstruction era, when "lovely women shrank from the ambitious gaze of scalawags and negro men" until KA "lifted bleeding Dixie to her feet." The *Journal* didn't usually write about movies, but it did run a positive review of *The Birth of a Nation*, which was based on *The Clansman: An Historical Romance of the Ku Klux Klan* by Kappa Alpha alumnus Thomas Dixon Jr. In the article, the *Journal* wrote: "[The Klan's] members wore upon the breast the circled cross of the Kappa Alpha Order. And the Klan served by militant warlike means, those same ideals which our Order was organized to cherish."

These quotes weren't hard to find. A lot of them are on the Kappa Alpha Order Wikipedia page. In the footnotes, there's also a link to KA's 1891 self-published history, which describes the order's early mission: "Southern in its loves, it took Jackson and Lee as its favorite types of the perfect Knight. Caucasian in its sympathies, it excluded the African from membership." Really, for much of the first fifty years of its life, the Kappa Alpha Order told anyone who would listen that it shared the same goals as the Ku Klux Klan. Rising from the ashes of the Confederacy, both organizations saw themselves as white knights who defended pure womanhood and kept the old slaves down. Instead of using public violence, though, the KAs hoped to achieve those goals by indoctrinating the region's elite boys. One hundred years later, the KKK makes people think of trailer parks and *Chappelle's Show*, and the Kappa Alpha Order maintains chapters on more than 120 college campuses.

Of course, Kappa Alpha's leaders don't identify with the Klan anymore. The order removed the phrase "Aryan" blood from their mission statement by the 1950s, and the national organization hired a director of community engagement who is Black in 2020. College freshmen seldom think about a fraternity's origin story when they rush, and they don't usually research its history when they pledge. The order has rebranded itself as a moral compass for today's gentlemen, and many of its chapters do have Black members. Still, for half a century, the Kappa Alpha Order wanted to mold students into crusaders for the Lost Cause of the Confederacy, and that campaign has had a momentum of its own.

Next to its lessons on Charlemagne, *The Varlet* still teaches boys that KA's knights rose after the Civil War to defend women's purity. Before it describes Kappa Alpha's risk management policy, the book still calls Robert E. Lee KA's spiritual founder. For most of the twentieth century, Kappa Alpha brothers still wore Confederate battle uniforms to their Old South formals, escorting dates dressed like plantation belles. (The 1981 Tulane yearbook, for example, shows Robert Liljeberg II's KA brothers in their Old South grays.) The order banned the costumes in 2010, but they continued to appear at different chapters until at least 2018, when the eventual winner of *The Bachelor* was photographed wearing a *Gone with the Wind*–type gown at Georgia College & State University. And even after two Ole Miss KAs were suspended from the fraternity for posting a picture of themselves holding assault rifles next to a bullet-riddled Emmett Till memorial in 2019, the KA national organization continued to meet on Robert E. Lee's birthday to toast him with glasses of "pure" water. The words they recite were written by former KA knight commander John Temple Graves, who is quoted in Rob's and Mikey's edition of *The Varlet*, and who is most famous today for a 1903 speech he gave defending lynching as the most effective way to prevent rape. (In their review of Graves's speech, the *Kappa Alpha Journal* at the time called it "a most powerful address on the subject of lynching and the race problem.") And in 2020, when I asked Rob's Kappa Alpha housemate what his brothers had said about allowing Black members in their chapter, he told me, "There was talk of it, and guys would be like, 'There's never been a Black member, and it's not gonna fucking happen today.'" (The KA national organization did not respond when asked if the C of C chapter ever had a Black member.)

Even though some KAs wanted me to know they had Black friends back home and played pickup basketball with Black guys in Charleston all the time, the housemate told me that other "guys would be jokingly racist. . . . You know, just, 'Like no chance we're having that in our fraternity. This is KA!'"

At the end of summer break 2015, Mikey Schmidt moved back to Charleston. He drove east on I-20 in his silver BMW convertible and stepped into downtown wearing Gucci slippers. He rented an apartment at 930 NoMo, an amenity-stocked condo with a pool like the Cyan's. He told his mom, whom he hadn't seen much since he moved out of her house, that he'd enrolled at Trident Technical College. His plan was to split time between Charleston and Atlanta, where he'd kept his condo, going out on King Street with Rob and in Peachtree with Biscuit. In the back of his car, he'd installed a JBL subwoofer as a place to hide his pills. The speaker took up most of his trunk, and when he drove around his girlfriend, Alexis, he'd make the subwoofer rattle until she lifted off her seat and bumped her head on the roof.

On Montagu Street, the KAs welcomed Mikey back into their social calendar. They threw him into darties and postgames, and Rob showed him the local Xanax business up close. After his marine biology summer in Bali, Rob, now a senior, had transitioned from KA's Number I to its philanthropy chair, and he'd moved in with his girlfriend, the Chi O who'd been named one of Charleston's hottest bartenders. He sold alprazolam pills at an impressive clip, but the bars were starting to look and feel different. As the Xanax multilevel marketing economy expanded, kids saw more pills that didn't say XANAX on them. Some bars had GG249 printed into the cellulose, and others were blank. They were chalkier than name-brand pills, sometimes to the point where they crumbled in the bag, and they carried powder residue that made it hard to know the strength of a dose. If the pills sat outside for too long they'd start to melt, and even when stored correctly the active ingredients sometimes concentrated in one part of the pill or the other. Regardless, these bars usually did the same things to the brain as psychiatrist-prescribed benzodiazepines, and unlike the Pfizer product, the off-brand units seemed to flow through town in an endless stream. With Zackery Kligman offloading these pills in bulk and guys like Rob distributing ten thousand of them a week, Mikey saw up close that more boys were earning money selling bars.

C of C Lacrosse Player: Shoot forward to my senior year, and the streets were running with it.

C of C Sigma Nu: You could buy a thousand for fifty cents a pop, and if you sold someone twenty, you'd give it to them at four dollars apiece. There's a ton of kids that want it, so, you know, you can make thousands of dollars in a day.

C of C Lacrosse Player: Kids would deal in nice houses on Calhoun, during sports practice, on the way to class.

C of C GDI: You could go and sit at a bar and wait until your pockets were full of money instead of the pills that you brought in.

Kligman C of C Xanax Client: It was like the containers that southern women sell, the plasticware. It just gets handed down and down and down and someone is at the bottom.

C of C SAE: A pyramid scheme.

C of C Sigma Nu: Everyone's making their cut off of the person who's buying five at a time, or whatever. You know, it's kind of like a nice little Ponzi scheme.

C of C KA: One time as a pledge I went to fold laundry for [a midlevel fraternity Xanax dealer.] Under his bed was an M4 assault rifle, and above his bed was a copy of *How to Win Friends and Influence People*.

C of C Sigma Nu: Any time you're successful with any business, it's very cool. You're playing the game, and you're winning. And you just had to hold on to a bag for a certain amount of time and then sell it to someone else.

Alabama SAE: It's like guys who put real estate deals together, connecting the buyer and the seller. You didn't put in any of your own money, but you're the maker.

C of C Lacrosse Player: If you could take all the guys that were involved in this and make their experience legal, then suddenly you've got a bunch of kids with sales experience, inventory experience, pricing strategy experience. When you get to a certain level, it is a business.

Clemson Phi Delt: We did this thing I called the Triangle Trade. It's named after the Transatlantic slave trade, where you'd pick up rum here, trade the rum for slaves, take the slaves abroad, trade the slaves for crops, come back, and trade the crops for rum. So I would get [Xanax] sticks, and then I'd go in the hood with guns out, and I'd be like, "Here's ten thousand bars," and they'd give me an ounce of blow for every thousand bars. And once I had the coke, which is the sketchy part, I could go and trade an ounce of really, really nice cheese for a pound of weed. It's basically a 4X arbitrage. So for me, I can either work at a restaurant and make a thousand dollars a month, or I can make a thousand dollars in a few hours and be the fucking man.

CHAPTER 10

UNCLE'S COKE

Although KA nationals allow only four-year students with nonfailing GPAs into the order, Mikey Schmidt joined the informal tradition of community college fraternity kids. He wasn't enrolled in the College of Charleston, but he attended C of C KA meetings and parties and even hazed C of C KA pledges. When I asked younger brothers about Mikey's return to Charleston, one of them said, "Here's a fun story: I'm sure you've heard of seven Montagu by now. One night when I was pledge class president, I got a call at two a.m. to get over there." While he and other freshmen arrived and lined up against the wall, the older KAs did lines of cocaine off a coffee table and yelled at the pledges for scratching a member's car. This was standard pledgeship fare—inventing a crime as an excuse for a lineup—and the freshmen knew they had to stand there only until someone let them go back to bed. They waited while the actives did more lines on the glass table, and then Mikey Schmidt opened the front door. "He just came in, big dick, straight from the bars," the pledge said. Mikey looked up at the freshmen and asked, "Which of you pledges did it?" and when no one answered, he said, "I'm gonna go to my car and get my gun." Mikey left the house, and one pledge responded, "If he gets a gun I'm fucking leaving." The freshmen stood on the living room wall and wondered if the older guy had been joking. After a bit, Mikey came back in without a gun. "That was the first time I met Mikey."

For some KAs, these kinds of nights only added to their sense of Mikey as a legendary character. Younger brothers threw him stacks of bills during chapter meetings, and other boys said he played Xbox with Waka Flocka Flame. His girlfriend, Alexis, had left for college and agreed to try an open relationship, and he took dates to The Vendue hotel roof for truffle fries before leaving the next day for parties at Ole Miss. During one of Mikey's Charleston visits, he introduced the C of C guys to Biscuit, who dropped casual stories about hanging out with Dave Grohl and Atlanta Falcons players. (Biscuit was less impressed with the KAs: "Those guys had a combined IQ of five," he said. "After dinner they'd be like, 'Let me rip a heater . . . Time for a postgame!' and I wanted to go to the fucking beach and bury my head in the sand.") In a given week, Mikey drove to Georgia in his BMW convertible only to return in a silver Infiniti G35.

Compared to Mikey, Rob worked to hide his position on the Greek life drug trafficking pyramid. He still wore sweatpants and hoodies, and he either drove his 1990s Mercedes or his mom's 2002 Toyota Tacoma pickup. While Mikey ordered steak and lobster entrees during the same dinner and finished neither, Rob kept eating peanut butter sandwiches and mooching his housemates' beer. Because Rob sold Xanax wholesale to other dealers, he was able to offload his pills without most people realizing he'd ever been involved. When he did spend money, it was in the ways of the South's idle rich, at events like Mardi Gras balls or philanthropic golf tournaments. "Rob ended his college experience living like a king, but he wasn't flashy," a younger KA told me. "He had a hot girlfriend, he lived in a nice house. He was quietly the man."

As Rob got closer to graduating, he and Mikey found a new income stream outside of weed and Xanax. Since freshman year they'd watched kids' benzo use go from chilling out on Sundays to blacking out on King Street, and now more customers wanted another ingredient to keep going at night. While bars and alcohol depressed their nervous systems, they needed something to keep them awake.

C of C Lacrosse Player: With enough Xanax and alcohol, you black out instantly. You're like not even a person. But cocaine keeps you functioning.

UT Sig Ep: My buddies and I called Xanax and cocaine the "rich white man's speedball."

C of C Lacrosse Player: Mixing cocaine and alcohol and Xanax, you get these crazy zombies of destruction.

Clemson Phi Delt: You feel like fucking Godzilla. You fear nothing, and you're numb to any kind of anxiety or second thought, or whatever.

Johnny Drama: It was just the lifestyle. You go out, you take bars, you do coke.

C of C Lacrosse Player: Imagine a kid with all the energy in the world but none of the cognitive ability to understand whether what he's doing is right or wrong.

Alabama SAE: I would tell people, "I'm the biggest bar-tard in Tuscaloosa." And people would be like, "You're so full of shit." And it's so dumb, but I would take a handful of bars and blow a half gram line of coke right in their face just to be like, "Go fuck yourself."

While they watched their friends' cocaine use go from key bumps in bathrooms to gator-tail lines on coffee tables, Rob and Mikey recognized a hole in the market. More of their peers wanted coke, but unlike with Xanax, most boys were still too afraid to sell it. Few Xanax dealers had access to the other ingredient in the "rich white man's speedball," mostly because the cocaine trade was controlled by organized crime in a way that alprazolam sales were not. Several fraternity members told me they'd bought random grams from gang-affiliated dealers on King Street, but they would've preferred to get coke by the ounce from friends inside their bubble. Mikey had no problem becoming that source. He already knew how to transport and sell narcotics, and he knew someone in Atlanta who could get him pure cocaine at wholesale prices. He started driving bricks of powder into Charleston for Rob to sell, and when their customers asked where it came from, Mikey said that "Uncle" gave it to him.

For many KAs, Mikey's "Uncle" source became part of his lore. Some boys said that Uncle worked with Mexican cartels, and others somehow believed he'd flown planes for Pablo Escobar in the 1980s. When I asked Mikey where he got that nickname, he said, "'Uncle' is a really good throw-off, you know what I'm saying? 'Let's serve a search warrant at Unc's house.' Also, I call everyone 'Uncle.' Anyone older than me is Uncle." When I pressed him on Uncle's real identity, he told me, "I don't even really want to talk about it. Those are the people that cut your fucking head off."

The only Uncle sketches I could find came from police files and an Atlanta source. The Charleston PD report describes him as a skinny man with dark hair who lived in a gated community. The file also claims that he looked twenty-six years old even though he was forty-two. One Georgia trafficker who'd worked with Uncle corroborated that description, telling me he was a middle-aged white man who spoke fluent Spanish and looked like a "frat kid." The source added that Uncle had cartel contacts in Atlanta, Houston, and "over the border" built on relationships that went back decades. "You know how Verizon has grandfathered people into their unlimited plan?" he said. "They damn near grandfathered his ass in. He has the best prices I've ever seen in my life." According to the trafficker,

Mikey impressed Uncle, whoever he was, with his prior success and his obvious hunger, and eventually the older man offered to supply him.

Like his heroes in *The Wire*, Mikey liked to use burner phones, but unlike Stringer or Marlo he also had a reputation for breaking them. He'd get out of the car with a phone on his lap or leave a gas station with a phone on his car roof, and then he'd have to drive to Best Buy to get another. Regardless, Uncle gave his suppliers a second phone that they weren't allowed to lose. Mikey could use it only for calls between them, and it rang at unexpected times with directions for meetings around greater Atlanta. Uncle taught his customers simple transportation methods, like hiding a brick of cocaine at the bottom of a Publix grocery bag and dropping it in the unlocked car next to his own, but mostly he left them in charge of their own business. "[The cartel method] is to have one person who does the logistics, and a lot of the other people are just buyers," the trafficker who worked with Uncle told me. "Once they get the dope to your door for three seconds, it's on you." After pickups, Mikey would apparently take the cocaine to the Cyan to test its purity. If he liked the quality but wanted to stretch the quantity, he sometimes added white Inositol powder, which natural health stores sell as a vitamin B8 supplement believed to stimulate dopamine. From there he weighed the powder on a scale and divided it into ounces, preparing it for two or three destinations.

A large amount of Mikey's weed, cocaine, and pills went to fraternity houses around the southeast. Sometimes his Greek life customers drove to the Cyan or downtown Charleston to pick up from him, and other times Mikey sent his product out on interstate driving loops. When a chapter hosted a fun party like the Georgia SAE Shower Cap, Mikey drove the loop himself, and other times he let boys drive without him. A few times a month, he or his couriers left during rush hour for Athens, where they made stops at the University of Georgia's SAE, KA, Chi Phi, and Beta houses, and then they drove up to the University of South Carolina in Columbia to meet Kappa Sigs, SAEs, and KAs. Sometimes Mikey or his drivers drove back through Clemson, and other times they went all the way to Oxford, Mississippi, where they could stand in mansion backyards and sell in bulk. "At Ole Miss there's three to four hundred kids in a fraternity," a C of C KA dealer told me. "We walk in and they know we're coming, and each kid gets a gram to an eight ball, some even more. You can offload at least a quarter pound at a time." In addition to the cocaine, marijuana, and Xanax bars, Mikey sold "Donald Trump roll pills" of MDMA shaped like the head of the soon-to-be presidential candidate. He smuggled all these drugs in a used Toyota Prius with a BABY ON BOARD sticker on the rear window, a method he'd learned from watching *Weeds*.

When Mikey finished these loops, he returned to the 808 Mafia studio in Atlanta. He kept listening to recording sessions from the couch until he felt comfortable enough to give notes. Ever since Mikey's sixth-grade teacher had sent him home for wearing Jeezy's "Snowman" T-shirt to class, Mikey had been unknowingly preparing for his time at Silent Sound Studios.

Listening to new artists like NBA YoungBoy or Gunna, Mikey could hear the music's references and influences. "He gave input on tracks that turned out to be very good songs, and it gave you an idea that he's in tune with the culture," Demario Smith, who worked A&R for the 808 Mafia, told me. Eventually, the guys from the studio invited Mikey to visit their neighborhood off Old National Highway. Mikey knew that the residents of Shady Park were called "Shady Babies," and when he entered the neighborhood he saw Italian cars parked in front of Section 8 housing. "Mikey came over with the homeboys to Xanny Tomy's mom's house," Demario said. "This is a different setting from the studio, you know, this is where we're from. But he was cool. Nobody was messing with him." After that, Mikey started going out at night with the studio crew. "Mikey liked to turn up," Demario said. "He liked getting fucked up and turnt up with the girls."

A few weeks after spring break in 2015, Waka Flocka Flame's Turn Up Godz tour came to Charleston's Music Farm. Onstage, Waka played an EDM remix of "Hard in da Paint" while kids lifted hands for the builds and pumped fists for the drops. The eight-hundred-person crowd included Waka's mix of rap fans, brostep fans, and Greek life members, including a good amount of KAs. The Kappa Alphas heard that Mikey was backstage, and they debated whether to invite Waka to their postgame or not. Mikey's world was overlapping with the rappers in new ways, with FratShows' founder Daniel Kuniansky managing Waka's transition toward dance music and Biscuit helping convince Waka to endorse David Perdue for US

Senate. The KAs wondered if Waka's and Mikey's connection stretched toward Mikey's usual line of work. A few months earlier, when Waka Flocka Flame rapped on "Techno" that "my plug is a white boy / we selling kush, not white, boy," some guys at the College of Charleston swore it was a reference to Mikey Schmidt.

I never found out if Mikey sold anything to the 808 Mafia. He refused to discuss it on our calls, and state and federal investigators decided not to investigate it later on. Instead, they focused on the third destination in Mikey's network. Besides his deals in Atlanta and his trips to fraternities around the southeast, Mikey delivered bulk orders of cocaine to Robert Liljeberg. He smuggled Uncle's supply to C of C, and Rob resold it to his friends and to Zackery Kligman. While Rob made these deals, Kligman sold him Xanax, which Rob broke up and sold wholesale to Mikey and others. The resulting corkboard involved many names and strings, but at its simplest it looked like this: Rob sold Mikey's cocaine to Zack and Zack's Xanax to Mikey. This move allowed Rob to offload a good amount of coke without exposing himself to many customers, and it gave Mikey and Rob cheap access to alprazolam as more boys competed to sell it. During the summer break of 2015, Rob sent Mikey a screenshot of a text from an unknown number that read, "Sticks are being made. Should be here soon." In the screenshot, Rob wrote back, "Worddd."

When Zackery Kligman told his customers that sticks were being made, he usually didn't describe how much work it took to manufacture your own Xanax bars. Each time he dropped off an envelope of chalky benzos and rode away on his longboard, he was making a hard process look casual. Zack's customers knew him as a guy who slept past lunch and "partied all night," but he and his colleagues spent vast amounts of effort running a clandestine alprazolam manufacturing lab. They'd realized they'd make more money if they manufactured their pills themselves, and now they used black market chemicals and industrial methods to make counterfeit Xanax at scale. Before any C of C student took a GG249 bar to chill out or black out, Zack and his superiors had guided the pill on a long, strange supply chain.

Each GG249 tablet started as raw alprazolam powder in a black-market Chinese factory. Connected to East Asian manufacturers by a dark web user in Quebec, Zack's boss ordered over nine pounds of powder at a time. It arrived in North America inside printer cartridges labeled with Mandarin characters. Each cartridge was paid for in Bitcoin and shipped to one of a few destinations around the Low Country, where the organization unpacked it and drove it to a pop-up laboratory. A good alprazolam manufacturing site is hard to find—it needs to be quiet and unassuming, but not so nice that you don't mind wrecking it with benzodiazepine dust—but luckily a member of their operation had a friend who worked for a beach house rental company. The team found vacation homes in Isle of Palms or Sullivan's Island, where they'd listen to Jet Skis running through the marshes and get alprazolam powder ready for their industrial press.

The beach house pill press, a TDP 5, weighed more than 275 pounds and also came from mainland China via the dark web. It was a Willy Wonka–like collection of wheels and levers powered by an electric motor attached to a drive belt. Running the TDP 5 required an engineer's facility with mechanics and a chemist's skill with toxic blends, and in this case the whole operation was coordinated by a thirty-three-year-old former University of South Carolina fraternity member named Eric Hughes. In 2013, under the username "Casey Jones," Eric had been the first citizen in American history to have his Bitcoin seized by the DEA, and now he sold counterfeit Xanax on the dark web under the name "Genius Bar." Pouring roughly 3,966 grams of Prosolv binding agent and 34 grams of alprazolam powder into a plastic tote, Eric mixed the materials using a concrete auger bit, and then he funneled his blend into the press.

Once Eric and his colleagues poured their mix into the funnel and pressed the big green button on the TDP 5, the motor rattled and the belt started to turn 1,400 times a minute. Each time it stamped another bit of dough into a perforated GG249 rectangle, it made a loud thump. Because the machine kicked up white powder while it ran, Eric covered the whole operation in a tent, but the team still spent hours scrubbing carpets, dusting air-conditioning vents, and going over the floor with a thousand-dollar vacuum to suck up benzodiazepine dust. If boys let enough dust get on their skin or in their lungs, they'd get "perma-barred," entering a daylong Xanax blackout. Still, Eric's crew found the manufacturing process worth these troubles. The TDP 5 could punch out 4,800 Xanax tablets an hour, and when they ran their operation correctly, the beach house crew made 500,000 pills a month.

Filling orders, Eric and his workers sometimes counted out pills individually, but generally they shoveled the tablets onto a scale and counted them by weight. After dropping a few tablets from three feet above the ground to test their brittleness, they poured them into mylar bags and took them to a room full of USPS boxes and shipping supplies. There, they boxed up their Genius Bar shipments and printed labels for destinations across the continental United States. They paid a man named Willie to drive around Georgia and South Carolina, dropping a few dark web orders at each USPS collection box. Few if any packages were ever confiscated—one DEA agent told me that the overburdened US Postal Service is the largest drug trafficker in the world—but even in the case of botched deliveries the overall numbers worked in the boys' favor. The alprazolam powder that came inside printer cartridges cost somewhere between $4,000 and $5,000 per kilogram. One kilogram created about 500,000 Xanax tablets, which the beach house organization sold for sixty cents a pill. This way, they profited around $59 for every $1 they spent on powder. The organization had other expenses, like TDP 5 parts and beach house vacuums, but the DIY benzodiazepine economy still carried strong margins. In 2017, Eric Hughes sent a friend a screenshot of his Bitcoin wallet showing $1.2 million in one account. (If Eric held on to it, that much BTC was worth more than $60 million at its 2022 peak.)

In addition to the Genius Bar mail orders, the beach house team delivered pills by hand around the southeast, and their organization had representatives at Ole Miss and the University of South Carolina. More than those destinations, though, the pills traveled to Charleston in the back of Zackery Kligman's Cadillac. He flooded the Low Country with GG249 Xanax tablets, keeping the pills in the safe he'd drilled underneath his house downtown. He sold the homemade tablets to guys like Rob, often requiring no down payment. In a process called "fronting," C of C wholesale dealers were happy to sell pills on consignment, trusting that the collective peer pressure of Greek life would force debtors to pay up at some point. The debtors then fronted the bars to other kids at slightly higher prices.

At a few points in this extended supply chain, boys ran into actual drug world violence. At a row house on Coming Street, a group of C of C students, some of whom worked with Eric and Zack, got robbed at gunpoint by their nonstudent customers. According to one of the victims, after one boy took a tequila bottle and smashed it on an intruder's head while the other intruder fled, a Charleston policeman told the students, "Boys, let's keep that shit in the ghetto." And at the "Mustard Mansion" apartments on Smith Street, while three boys who sold Zack's bars played Xbox, a woman in a hoodie and two men with knives smashed open the front door, looking for pills or money they did not find. With these nights in mind, Kligman started looking for a place away from home to store his GG249 tablets. Driving on the antebellum streets beneath campus, he searched for a genteel-looking "stash house." As a rule, the homes in downtown Charleston get more expensive the farther south you drive, and Zack eventually found a guest house at 43 Gadsden Street. The structure was hidden by a main house and a BMW in the front yard, and it sat across the street from the $5.6 million Gaillard-Bennett House, built in 1800 by the British consul as "one of Charleston's most elaborately embellished Federal mansions."

Zack knew better than to rent a stash house under his own name, so he paid a College of Charleston senior $600 a month plus expenses to sign the lease. The student had been one of the victims of the robbery at the Mustard Mansion, and now he lived on 97 Smith Street with four other boys, a few of whom sold Zack's Xanax. Although he believed Zack was a "try-hard," he told me he worked for Zack so he could afford the C of C nightlife. ("Everybody's loaded, and I'm not," he said. "I had to make up appearances.") Because the guest house sat behind an elevated front porch hidden by magnolia leaves, Zack called it the "Treehouse." He installed a safe and some firearms, and he refused to take anyone to see it unless they agreed to wear a blindfold on the drive. According to a police informant with the codename "Buddha," Zack stocked the Treehouse with up to twenty pounds of marijuana and nearly a million alprazolam pills at a time, plus cocaine that came from Atlanta.

Even after his failed money shower, Mikey kept coming back to Magic City. His friend Xanny Tomy was dating a Magic dancer, and the guys from the studio introduced Mikey to the women who worked there. When a dancer named Krystal ran her acrylic nails through Mikey's bangs, he asked her, "What would you do if someone came up and did that to your hair?" She responded, "Oh my God, I'm so sorry," but from then on everyone rubbed his head. Just as at the Tongue and Groove valet line, "Lil Mikey" became a mascot at Magic City, but this time Mikey got to see the inside of the club from the start. He befriended the dancers and learned a few of their real names, and one night the 808 Mafia guys paid the women to take him up onstage. While Mikey sat by a pole and dancers moved around his face, his friends from the studio yelled, "Suck Lil Mikey's dick!" They threw more money onto the stage, and Mikey shouted, "Biscuit, what the fuck are they doing?" Biscuit responded, "I don't know, it's initiation, Mikey, enjoy it."

At some point Rob came to visit Atlanta. When he returned to Charleston, he talked a lot about Waka Flocka Flame. Rob told the KAs that Mikey's rap friends ordered them Uber Blacks to strip clubs, where they made business deals and were the only white guys in the building. During one of these nights, Rob and Mikey apparently saw T.I. get up to use the bathroom surrounded by armed guards. The T.I. strip club night became part of Rob's legend with the KAs, and he found ways to drop it into conversations with younger kids he'd only recently met. On the other hand, he didn't tell many people besides Mikey that he'd met a girl on Atlanta Tinder. Before his next trip to Georgia, he texted Mikey:

Rob Liljeberg: Might have to hit up that black chick for another bj
Rob Liljeberg: JK I already did

Mikey Schmidt: Hahahahahahahahahahahahahahahaha ⬤⬤⬤⬤◥
Mikey Schmidt: You should see how ghetto you can get with her like ayy mama send me a poster pic of that pussy
Rob Liljeberg: She's like not black though
Rob Liljeberg: Has a nice apartment by herself and plays on the golf team
Mikey Schmidt: Four!
Rob Liljeberg: Into her Anus

As he got closer to graduation, Rob coordinated deliveries by phone from the middle of Mardi Gras, and he shaved his curls into a high-and-tight. His C of C girlfriend posted an Instagram of the haircut, with Rob holding a red Solo cup in blue pants and a white button-down that highlighted the twenty-five pounds of muscle he'd gained since freshman year. As a senior, he hung out with the SAE chapter president, and he started selling to Sigma Alpha Epsilon dealers. This arrangement meant that Rob and Mikey sat above the Sigma Alpha Epsilons in the College of Charleston narcotics economy. As Mikey texted Rob, "Lol they work for us indirectly, pussys." While Rob drove around with the SAEs, other fraternity kids assumed he came from money. Several C of C students told me his parents were very rich doctors, and one SAE dealer showed an odd understanding of the Liljebergs' Catholic roots: "He was so wealthy. Oh my God. Super wealthy Jewish family."

During his last year of college, Mikey bought a Porsche 911 and paid something like $70,000 in rent. That same semester, his grandfather Frank found cash under his guest room mattress and told his grandson, "Listen, if you get in trouble doing what you're doing, we can't save you." Mikey played ignorant and drove back to Charleston. When he got to C of C, he stored money under his new girlfriend's bed. He'd gotten upset at Alexis for posting an Instagram with a guy at her new school, and now they'd officially broken up. Besides the mattress, Mikey also stored his things in a safe at 7 Montagu. Around campus, rival dealers did the same, buying safes and drilling them into the floors of their off-campus houses. They filled them with money, weed, cocaine, and pills, but also with more surprising items, like one SAE dealer's collection of syringes and anabolic steroids, or Zackery Kligman's Mossberg 715T assault rifle with a Tac-D grenade launcher.

Away from their safes, the boys sold Xanax and compared their Rolexes and Gucci sleds. They outspent each other on bottle service at the nightclubs Trio and Mynt, and Zack Kligman bought a large depiction of the Monopoly man painted by a C of C girl who also modeled for Nike. Bros fluffed themselves up for and against each other, and their ongoing party kept them cloistered from nearly everyone else. Even in the spring of 2015, when news trucks came to town to cover the killing of a Black motorist named Walter Scott by a North Charleston police officer and the massacre of nine Bible study members at Mother Emanuel African Methodist Episcopal Church, C of C Greek life remained untouched. When I asked an SAE what his friends did the weekend after the Mother Emanuel killings, he said, "Things just aren't going to stop. If we don't throw a party, everyone's just gonna drink in their own rooms. As insensitive as it sounds, it's still Friday."

Heading into 2016, though, the outside world did start to press on the bubble in one small way. After arresting a Citadel student who dealt LSD and chalky pseudo-Xanax, the local police asked the dealer about his supply chain. He told them, and they started investigating Zackery Kligman. In December 2015, operatives disguised as electrical workers climbed up a utility pole and installed a hidden camera overlooking the guest house at 43 Gadsden Street. By New Year's, the Charleston Police Department took a picture every time a black Cadillac parked by the Treehouse porch.

CHAPTER 11

PATRICK

When I first interviewed Patrick Moffly's family in 2019, I visited their sixty-five-acre horse farm on Paradise Island, South Carolina. Forty minutes from downtown Charleston, their house sits between an equestrian jumping course and the Wando River. During my first visit, I met Patrick's father, David, a former College of Charleston varsity sailor who builds homes for billionaires and families "down to their last five hundred million," and Patrick's mother, Elizabeth, a C of C alumnus who's run for Congress and served on the Charleston County school board. Two years later, I came back to interview David and Elizabeth and their two daughters, Sarah and Bridget, over dinner and a swim in their pool. In between, I talked to as many people who knew Patrick Moffly as I could, trying to get a sense of his boyhood and young adulthood in addition to his death.

David Moffly: Before we moved out here, we had a house in Charleston Harbor, across the water from Fort Sumter.

Elizabeth Moffly: In the Old Village.

David Moffly: We lived across the street from a historic graveyard. It's split; one side is Black, and the other side's white. Between Greenwich and Simmons Streets.

Elizabeth Moffly: Actually, when Patrick was little, he had the ability to see dead people. He'd get me by the hand and take me to the graveyard and say, "Mom, come see my friends."

And I would look at his expression, because he was always dumbfounded when they weren't there anymore.

He just had this special spiritual thing about him, and it actually scared him. Even to the day he died, he slept with the lights on.

From David Moffly's Funeral Eulogy for Patrick: He was always a risk-taker and had no fear. As a child we called him Reckless Rick. He was always getting banged up.

Elizabeth Moffly: He was klutzy. You know, he'd get in our boat and immediately fall down.

David Moffly: The problem wasn't so much that he was clumsy but that he moved too fast at everything he did. He was just always moving.

William Sawyer (childhood friend): The first time I hung out with him, we were skateboarding behind a church in the Old Village. He was a beginner, but he was trying to ollie down a concrete stair set with a very short landing. He kept throwing his body down the stairs and falling and falling and falling very hard.

Austin Moreland (childhood friend): He'd just hurl his body into things that you wouldn't think beginners would try.

William Sawyer: He was also a little chubbier, which obviously makes it a little hard to balance.

David Moffly: He didn't start out chubby, but in fifth grade he got sick and doctors put him on steroids.

Skylar King (childhood friend): Fat Pat. . . . He was the class clown, funny, wild.

Elizabeth Moffly: When Patrick was in middle school, he had this shitty history teacher who blamed everything on the kids. Patrick came home and made him a fake Myspace that made him out to be a Nazi.

David Moffly: It went viral. He also made a website, "GoBack ToOhio.com," with an interactive map of how to get from Charleston to Ohio.

Elizabeth Moffly: I was campaigning for state superintendent at the time, and the school called me and said I had to come pick up my son. Well I'm out of town, so I got the ACLU involved. It happened off school property, so it should have been a civil suit from the teacher, not the school district disciplining a student. [The ACLU] wrote this stern letter to the school: "You will return his record back to the way it was."

Austin Moreland: The first memory I had with him was the summer before ninth grade, drinking Crown Royal and chasing it with milk under his parents' house. We were into stupid, mischievous "kids being kids" stuff back then.

David Moffly: He got in a few fights, messed around with smoking a little weed.

Elizabeth Moffly: He also had anxiety. We worked with him for years trying to find a doctor that he could communicate with, but he'd get frustrated.

David Moffly: They'd give him medication and he'd say, "It makes me feel dead. I don't wanna take it anymore."

Elizabeth Moffly: Then he broke into a drug dealer's house and stole his pot.

David Moffly: He and another kid kicked in the dealer's door and stole his stash. The guy was going to kill him, and Patrick was scared shitless. He slept with my pistol grip shotgun and a baseball bat.

Bridget Moffly (sister): He was getting phone calls threatening the family.

David Moffly: I said, "Patrick, we are going to go buy this guy off. It's the only way out." We agreed to meet him in front of Causey's Barber Shop in broad daylight. I told Patrick, "The money's going to be in a magazine, and you're going to give him that fucking magazine." The guy had a wife and kids, worked in a kitchen in a restaurant. He sat down and gave Patrick a fatherly discussion. "What the fuck is wrong with you? We are friends, why would you do that to me?"

Elizabeth Moffly: Pretty much right after that, Patrick told me, "I've got to get out of here. I can't stay here." I offered to pull him out of high school and send him to Costa Rica for a semester of Outward Bound.

For the next three months, sixteen-year-old Patrick hiked through the Costa Rica rainforest and surfed on the coast. Using his mosquito net as a blanket and a machete as his spoon, he did so well that his Outward Bound counselors offered him a job as a white-water rafting guide, which he turned down. When he returned to Paradise Island for online homeschooling that fall, he looked like a surfer, and he no longer went by Fat Pat.

Elizabeth Moffly: By sixteen, Patrick was Mr. Slim.

Austin Moreland: He'd lost weight, had cool long hair, was all in shape and stuff. And that's probably what kicked everything off.

Johnny Drama (high school friend and later rival): I remember all the girls would be like, "Oh my God, he's so cute, and he's so different." He just had such a swagger about him.

Skylar King: When we were sophomores and juniors, he'd pull up to the Wando [High School] parking lot and text everyone, "Run out to the BMW. I am bailing you guys out."

Austin Moreland: He would drop people off at school and then pick them up. It was almost like he was waiting for you on the outside.

Skylar King: The BMW was sick as shit. It was a 750 V12, and it had bulletproof windows. He'd pass people a hammer, and be like, "Yo, I bet you can't bust out this window." Some guys went as hard as they could at it, and it never chipped, never cracked, never dented.

Johnny Drama: After school I'd drive to their farm on Paradise Island to ride in his golf cart and listen to Andre Nickatina.

Austin Moreland: Obviously his family comes from money, so there's toys and dirt bikes and golf carts and boats. It was Candy Land.

PATRICK

Caroline Cordina (high school friend and neighbor): It's like a playground really. I would go over there and suddenly we're skateboarding or paddleboarding or wakeboarding.

Austin Moreland: I have plenty of memories of feeding the horses Oreos at two a.m. and trying to ride them bareback through the pastures.

William Sawyer: We'd surf, skate, fish, get in the boat, ride horses, or look for alligators.

Austin Moreland: We wanted to catch this thirteen-foot alligator that lived in their pond, so we shot one of his chickens and tied it to a string on a hook. We never got the big gator, but we caught two babies with a cast net.

Skylar King: He kept the gators in a baby pool in his closet for nine months. One day a gator got out and went downstairs to tan in their sunroom, and his dad was like, "PATRICK! ARE YOU FUCKING KIDDING ME!!" There was no, "Why is there an alligator in the house?" He knew why there was an alligator in the house.

Austin Moreland: You know the Mofflys. They're really cool people. They're awesome people. But it was always, "How can we avoid David seeing this?"

Johnny Drama: Patrick would take a gravity bong hit in the house, and his dad would go, "You have fucking fifty acres of fucking land and you want to smoke in my fucking house? Get the fuck out!" And they would go on like that.

Austin Moreland: One time David saw an extension cord running from the barn. He followed it into the woods and realized

Patrick was growing pot out there. He unhooked all the water pipes Patrick set up for irrigation.

David Moffly: You can't even imagine how many parties I've had to break up out here.

Although he didn't go to class during the week, Patrick was a major part of Wando High School nightlife.

Johnny Drama: Patrick was the soul of the party, man. . . . He was the "I Don't Give a Fuck" God.

William Sawyer: When the cops broke up this one party in high school, he ran up a tree. They shined a light on him and told him to come down, and he whispered, "There's no one up here."

Skylar King: He was an absolute rock star. He walks into a party, and people literally stop talking.

Austin Moreland: For a flat-footed five-six troll he was a fucking ladies' man.

Johnny Drama: One night in high school we were on a second-story balcony downtown, and Patrick sees this really cute girl walking on the street. He jumps off the balcony, shatters his ankle, and gets her number.

Caroline Cordina: Gosh, his confidence, his personality, were just so different. He wasn't like every other rich guy in Charleston. Money didn't show on him.

Johnny Drama: He always wore a Cookie Monster T-shirt and board shorts, like he was ready to wakeboard at any time.

From David Moffly's Funeral Eulogy for Patrick: Patch was popular amongst his peers and had many friends. He was friends with old people and young people, rich people and poor people, white people and Black people, preppy people and people who dressed like bums. He did not know a stranger.

David Moffly: One Halloween he asked if he could have friends over. "It's just gonna be thirty people, Dad." Three to four hundred people show up, maybe more.

Caroline Cordina: Everyone I could have possibly known in my grade and the grade above me was out there.

David Moffly: We have two acres of gravel parking lot, and it's wall to wall with people. Fucking kegs fucking everywhere. Elizabeth is running for Congress or some shit like that. I'm like, "This is fucking bad."

Austin Moreland: Did you see the movie *Project X*?

David Moffly: Two girls come in dressed as blue Smurfs, right? After about five minutes I realize they're buck-ass naked; they're just painted blue. The cops were in the driveway, and I'm thinking, "I gotta shut this down."

Austin Moreland: People are out in the pastures fucking around with horses, getting lost in the woods. Guys started pelting this one poor kid's car with rocks.

Skylar King: They just picked up rocks and started hucking them at this Jeep until there were no windows and the body was destroyed.

David Moffly: I pull my backhoe into the middle of the crowd and whistle everybody up. "Cops are in the driveway. You need to get the fuck out of here!" Patrick's like, "Dad, Dad, Dad, calm down, calm down. We're forming a train." He had the cars lined up, and when he gave the symbol, everybody left at once. It was just one rush, *shoo, shoo, shoo, shoo, shoo*. Patrick said, "The cops can't fucking pull everybody over," and sure enough they only stopped a handful. I thought to myself, "That was pretty fucking smart."

After these kinds of nights, Patrick usually got in trouble with the local police or his parents. David and Elizabeth hired one of Charleston's best lawyers to keep some offenses off his record, and then they made him work chores on the farm. While Patrick mended fences or unloaded bricks for construction, he turned off his phone. According to his friends, he'd feel low for weeks and then reemerge.

Skylar King: He'd fall off the face of the map for days, weeks, but then he'd be like, "What's up, you ugly fucker, you trying to go on the boat today? Yee *yee*! I'll buy the beer and the gas."

Johnny Drama: I wouldn't see him for weeks, and he'd be like, "Yo man," like I saw him yesterday.

High School Friend 1: It was kind of a bipolar swing. . . . He'd be lighting up cigarettes in bars, skateboarding all fucked up with eyes closed and getting nailed by cars. There was a feeling of, "I can get away with anything. Andy Savage is my lawyer. I got the guy who sued Big Tobacco, baby. I can fucking do anything I want."

Patrick Moffly's One-Star Facebook Review of the Mount Pleasant Police Department: Mt pleasant police department is a joke. It is an organization with nothing better to do other than harass teenage kids and write [minor-in-possession charges] and simple poss, and [it] handles most encounters poorly, but with that said there is still a number of great officers on their force, just a large sum with nothing to do.

High School Friend 1: Patrick got out of everything. . . . But even though he's from a very affluent family, I think it almost kind of created a complex. "I'm not just a rich kid, and I'll still fight you right now."

Johnny Drama: I've seen him one-hit KO somebody. The guy swung, Patrick was nimble and dodged the punch, and while the guy had his arms down, Patrick hit him. The guy's eye socket was fucked.

David Moffly: One New Year's we had a big bonfire out here, and some older kids showed up and started picking fights. Patrick went up to them, these two big guys, and told them that if they were gonna fight they couldn't be here. They chopped him in the throat. Patrick jumped on this guy and knocked all of his fucking teeth out, every one of them.

Skylar King: He had huge hands, because he'd broken them so many times fighting. They were like swollen grapefruits.

Johnny Drama: He started hanging out with this crew of twenty-five-year-old guys who let him into their friend group for being a badass. That's where he did his first line of coke. He told me, "Oh dude, it's like Adderall, but you take one hit and you don't have any feelings."

High School Friend 1: The first time I saw Xanax it was with him. We had to go to the post office to pick it up, which is the sketchiest thing, but he was like, "No one can touch me." And

God, dude, we would just get fucked up, man. Chugging liquor, popping Xans, weed, party drugs, I mean, you name it. It was just around us.

High School Friend 2: The first time I took Xanax was downtown with Patrick. We went out with our fake IDs, and Patrick kept stealing rubber bar mats off bars. When the cops saw us I ran, and Patrick started running with the bar mats stuffed in his pants. The K-9s found me hiding in a car three hours later, and I had on khaki shorts—no shoes, no shirt—with blood and dirt everywhere. I don't really remember much of this, obviously, because of fucking Xanax.

November 2011 Charleston Police Report: R/O notes that Offender was unable to provide him with his date of birth or address.

Patrick turned eighteen in 2010, and while his friends left for college, he went on a multiyear walkabout. He surfed in Nicaragua, snowboarded the Swiss Alps, and worked for a bar crawl company in Barcelona, where he got in two fistfights with Romani travelers and appeared shirtless in La Vanguardia *newspaper. In 2015, after working in Charleston restaurants and taking classes at Trident Technical College, he enrolled in the College of Charleston. Introduced by a mutual Barcelona friend, he moved in with four C of C upperclassmen on 97 Smith Street, a 165-year-old house one block from campus.*

97 Smith Housemate 1: We were looking for a fifth roommate, and initially the vibe was good, because you could tell he was genuine, and he came from a good family. I know he dabbled with drugs, but I think pretty much all of us did here and there.

C of C Tri Delt: The boys at 97 Smith didn't look shady. They looked like regular white kids, kind of preppy, very "college." They lived in another cute little Charleston house.

97 Smith Housemate 2: We weren't in a fraternity, but we had friends in KA, Sigma Chi, Kappa Sig.

William Sawyer: You know, Patrick kind of had another group of friends there for the last couple of years—his College of Charleston friends.

97 Smith Housemate 2: We drank every day but Wednesday, because Wednesday was the Silver Dollar, which was sketchy. It was all like freshman girls and a bunch of huge black dudes texting each other from across the bar. But Tuesday was Midtown, Thursday was Boones, Friday and Saturday was either Midtown or Warehouse. Sundays our buddy, who was a bartender at News, would close down early for us. We'd all come in, toss him fifteen bucks, and get an open bar.

97 Smith Housemate 1: We definitely like snorted some blow and obviously took Xanax. . . . I would sell some here and there, but it was more of that party-culture vibe.

97 Smith Housemate 2: Patrick drank Mount Gay and Coke, Bud Heavies, and Natural Lights, which I called "Nostalgia Lights" because they reminded me of high school. He was always spilling things, so eventually I started calling him "Spilly," and it just stuck like gum.

Skylar King: He was "Spilly" for the last nine months of his life.

97 Smith Housemate 2: He saw himself as a surfer outlaw. He was always watching this movie about the Bra Boys, who basically were an Australian gang of surfers who just partied and beat people up.

Caroline Cordina: I'd come over in between classes, and he was either playing *Call of Duty* or watching drug trafficking movies. He used to watch surf videos, but in the end he always wanted to show me YouTube videos of what the cartels did to people.

Summer McNairy (C of C friend): When he moved into that house on Smith Street, that's when stuff started to get bad.

Caroline Cordina: He'd have a bunch of Xanax all over the living room in little bags, and cocaine on the table. He'd offer me, and I'm like, "I'm good. I'm good."

Sarah Moffly (sister): I met Zack Kligman a few times at that house. He'd come in, and everyone would get semiquiet. Patrick would be like, "I'm going to go do a deal upstairs with him. You can stay down here and hang out." I'd continue watching TV, and after he'd come back down and leave, Patrick would be like, "Did you see his car?! He has a sick car."

When Patrick moved into 97 Smith, he learned that a few of his housemates were part of Zack Kligman's alprazolam distribution network. One had signed the lease for Zack's "Treehouse," and another had helped operate the beach house pill press. Several of them sold Kligman's Xanax on campus. Patrick, who already dealt weed, joined their group.

David Moffly: Patrick was apparently very good at the whole packaging program. After they pressed the pills, Patrick would go into a room with the hair net, Tyvek suit, rubber gloves.

He'd empty out Starburst and Skittles bags, put the pills in there, and reseal and package them.

Sarah Moffly: I was at 97 Smith almost every day, and that's what Patrick was doing at his desk. He'd put the candy bags into gift boxes and send them to Columbia and Atlanta. I was like, "This is really sketchy, Patrick."

Victoria Collins (C of C girlfriend): He hung a surfboard on wires from his bedroom ceiling, and he started keeping bags of Xanax up there.

Elizabeth Moffly: He also kept getting "burner phones," even though we paid for his regular phone.

C of C KA: One time I went to his house on Smith Street to buy something, and I saw another buddy outside. I was like, "Oh fuck, what are you doing here, man?" He said, "Same thing you are." I knew Spilly had bars, blow, molly.

C of C Accomplice: None of [the dealing] ever felt weird, you know? Any aspect of it. None of it felt weird because you were dealing with the boys.

Johnny Drama: I liked to get bottle service at bars—that was my thing—and Patrick and the 97 Smith guys started getting it too. If he was with Kligman, I would say, "Yo, what's up?" and he would kind of just nod at me. I don't know if it was the Xanax loosening him up or if he was just riding on a power trip, but he was on his John Gotti. He thought he was a Teflon Don.

Caroline Cordina: I started hearing rumors about him having $30,000 worth of drugs in his house. . . . I remember talking to him, like, "You have a great life. Why are you even doing this? You've got plenty of money."

William Sawyer: Patrick would say, "I'm going to get rich or die trying." He said that all the time.

Bridget Moffly: It was, "I'm going to make money the fast way, and then I'm going to get out. I'm going to make my parents proud that I'm making it on my own."

David Moffly: "Make my parents proud: I am a drug dealer."

Josh Bowman (friend): He made a lot of money when he went out. Eighty percent of those kids downtown were doing Xanax, so it was like nonstop traffic, you know? But while all that money came in, he fell in fucking pills. Oh my God. That shit is addictive.

In October 2015, Patrick borrowed a cigarette from twenty-nine-year-old Josh Bowman outside the Silver Dollar bar. When they went back inside, Patrick bought Josh a shot and gave him his phone number. In December, Patrick learned Josh was living on different friends' sofas, and he offered Josh a pallet next to his bed on 97 Smith. Josh had gotten arrested that fall with between 10 and 28 grams of cocaine, and although the charges were later dropped, he was still struggling. Patrick told him, "We'll get you on your feet, dude, and we're gonna have fun while you're doing it." After that, Patrick folded Josh into a C of C social world that was usually closed to temporarily homeless Black couch surfers. Because Patrick had stopped going to class, they skated during the day and sold Xanax at night. On King Street, after Patrick told girls, "Hello, beautiful," and added numbers to the 3,100-plus contacts on his phone, Josh watched him eat as much as 10 mg of pressed alprazolam at a time.

Josh Bowman: He'd take like five bars, dude, and switch up into a whole different person. Just completely blacked out.

PATRICK

Victoria Collins: When I first started dating him I didn't really know the extent of it, but toward the end, it just kind of seemed like he was always barred out.

Caroline Cordina: He'd sound normal on the phone, and then I'd get over there and he'd be in that zombie state. Slurring his words, drinking in the middle of the school day.

Victoria Collins: He'd get really clumsy and repeat the same questions, or he would randomly fall asleep.

Josh Bowman: He'd usually start around two o'clock, then he'd start mixing drugs, man.

Housemate 1: He was pretty much always doing blow, at least towards the end.

Josh Bowman: We'd have late-night talks in his room. He just wanted to get better.

Housemate 1: I tried to understand what fueled his addiction. His dad's super successful, obviously, and Patrick felt pressure because he wasn't really going anywhere. But I just remember he would, like, cry and stuff, you know?

Josh Bowman: He'd cry, man, so many times. He felt like he was a loser. And I told him like, "Man, you got school, you're letting this shit pull you away, man. And it's going to do that."

Skylar King: Patrick's the man, the man, the man, the man, and then he's like, "I don't know what I'm doing with my life. I'm a fucking loser." It'd get dark.

High School/College Friend: He would go into a fucking sad spiral for like three or four days until he bounced himself out of it. To keep himself from going back down, he would snort a fat line, eat a Xan, and start drinking rum at like eleven a.m., because he knew he was about to get into a depressive state again. He'd self-medicate.

Charleston PD Homicide File: [Redacted] advised me that Moffly had been depressed recently . . . and had begun hanging out with sketchy people.

High School/College Friend: He started hanging out with more street guys at the Silver Dollar bar. Not "crackhead" sketchy. Like, "I'll fucking crush you like a can" sketchy.

Housemate 2: Jordan Piacente came around fairly often.

Summer McNairy: She wasn't like most of the girls Patrick would hang out with, who had nice things and nice clothes and always tried to look our best.

Sarah Moffly: Patrick saved her name as "Spicy" on his phone.

DEA Interview with Jordan Piacente: PIACENTE stated on multiple occasions MOFFLY "gave" her (PIACENTE) Xanax bars.

Victoria Collins: One day I went during my lunch break to Patrick's house, and as soon as I walked in, his roommates were like, "Hey, come sit down, let's talk." I even thought, "Why do they not want me to go upstairs?" Then I went up and saw Patrick and Jordan in bed together smoking weed, and she was wearing his Cookie Monster T-shirt.

Charleston PD Homicide File: Ms. Collins said they broke up because she caught Mr. Moffly cheating on her with [fellow C of C student] Jordan.

Victoria Collins: After work I sent him this really long text message. I think the cops have it. I don't remember what I said exactly, but basically it was that his friends were going to be his downfall. I said, "They don't want the best for you," and I mean, it was pretty obvious.

In November 2015, Patrick drove a few kilograms of cocaine to the fraternity lots at a University of South Carolina Gamecocks tailgate. When he arrived, he reportedly met with two other boys from Zack Kligman's network and carried a backpack around the parking lot. Patrick's childhood friend Austin Moreland, who happened to be there selling chicken sandwiches from his Charleston Bird food truck, watched Patrick take the backpack into the food line and talk to a few policemen. Three hours later he saw Patrick handcuffed to a four-wheeler by a Sigma Nu's pickup truck, where he'd been arrested for trafficking 13 ounces of cocaine.

David Moffly: We hadn't heard from him in a while, and he called us. "So, just so you know, I'm in jail in Columbia." He told me not to call a lawyer. Then we found out his bail was $75,000.

Sarah Moffly: Patrick told me what happened later. He was sitting in a pickup truck, scaling coke out for somebody on the center console.

David Moffly: Selling to frat rats in the fucking parking lot.

Sarah Moffly: His friends were supposed to be keeping watch, but he looks up and they've all just scattered and ran. Patrick tried to clean the center console off, but the cops had already gotten him.

David Moffly: The two policemen from the chicken truck line were the ones who arrested him. Later one of them called me and said, "You know, your son was the most kind, polite kid. I really hated to arrest him. And honestly, if it goes to trial, I'm going to say nice things about him."

Sarah Moffly: The friends Patrick was working with got away [with the backpack] to another area.

David Moffly: According to Patrick, they ran off with several kilos. I think one guy took the drugs and the money to Ole Miss, paid off Kligman, and kept the difference.

Sarah Moffly: They were supposed to bail him out, but they didn't.

David Moffly: I'm fucking pissed, for starters, but I'm not gonna leave my kid to fucking rot in fucking jail.

Elizabeth Moffly: It was three o'clock in the morning, and I'm like, "We need to go to Columbia now."

David Moffly: Patrick told me not to hire a lawyer because Kligman was gonna hire a lawyer. Kligman likes to control the defense and keep you under control and on the team and not become a rat. But I called Andy Savage and said, "We need your clone in Columbia," and he said, "You need my buddy Jack Swerling."

Elizabeth Moffly: Patrick was just barely over the limit for distribution, but it was over the limit.

David Moffly: He was looking at fifteen years.

Elizabeth Moffly: I thought it was thirty?

David Moffly: Fifteen to thirty. Regardless, Jack said that Patrick was going to do some time. He promised little, but apparently he's a guy that delivers big.

Sarah Moffly: But Patrick was pissed at them.

PATRICK

David Moffly: He was upset at me for getting a lawyer. He was like, "Dad, you really fucked me up, because now Zack Kligman is going to think I'm a rat."

Elizabeth Moffly: His trial was coming up in April.

David Moffly: I wanted to take him to rehab, and he begged me the whole way home not to take him. Fucking biggest mistake I ever made.

Thanks to legal aid from Jack Swerling, Patrick was able to leave South Carolina for a family New Year's trip to Lima and Machu Picchu. During their hike through the Andes he talked to his mom about seeing a therapist, and during a party at a youth hostel he shaved his head at the bar. When he landed back in Charleston in January 2016, he decided not to return to 97 Smith Street or C of C. While he waited for his trial, he remained on Paradise Island and turned off his phone.

David Moffly: When he was out here, he was mowing the lawn, not answering the phone. He didn't have people come out.

Elizabeth Moffly: Just watching TV. He was antisocial, not talking to us, not talking to anybody.

Andy Savage (defense attorney): He went through a terrible depression crisis.

High School/College Friend: He got to the point where no amount of Xanax could stop his waves of anxiety.

Elizabeth Moffly: He said he'd kill himself before he'd go to jail.

Bridget Moffly: He started crying and told me that.

David Moffly: Patrick said that Kligman was worried that Patrick would put Kligman in jail. And Patrick said, "Dad, you don't understand about this guy. If he thinks you're doing something wrong, he'll get you fucked up."

Charleston PD Homicide File: [After] Patrick was arrested on cocaine charges in Columbia, SC, Zack "cut him off" as a precaution.

David Moffly: After a month, I sent him back downtown, because the roommates were crying and whining about $100 worth of utility bills. I said, "Patrick, you can't stiff your fucking roommates. They fucking need the money; they're college kids. Here's a check, go fucking pay your roommates."

High School/College Friend: I drove out to pick him up. That night before we drove back, we got real barred out, drank his parents' booze, swam in the pool, went out in the boat, and then threeway'd my girlfriend on his bed. He was, like, trying to hold my hands and shit, and I was like, "Am I gay now?"

Patrick returned to campus on Thursday, March 3, 2016. His plan was to give his roommates the utilities check and leave town Saturday for a family spring break trip to Vail, Colorado.

High School/College Friend: On the drive back downtown, he was like, "I'm going to face the fact I owe my roommates rent, and the whole Zack thing, and I'm going to get this all sorted out, and don't you worry," and blah blah blah. . . . He had this plan he called "the Big Dirty," where he'd make $50,000 off one last deal and use it to fly to Brazil on a private jet. After a year down there, he was going to hit up his parents and be, like, "Hey, Mom and Dad, will you buy me a hostel?"

Elizabeth Moffly: That could be. It sounds like a Patrick plan.

High School/College Friend: After I dropped him off, he went skating at Bob's Bowl.

Sarah Moffly: He called me from the skate park to say he broke his arm. He was like, "What do I do? It hurts so bad, and Mom and Dad are going to be so mad." We were supposed to go skiing, and now he couldn't go.

Victoria Collins: He texted me, "I'm in the hospital. I think I broke my arm. My friends just dropped me off and left, and I don't have anyone here." My mom was in town, and she said, "You should go."

Charleston PD Homicide File: Ms. Collins went to MUSC [Medical University of South Carolina] to visit Mr. Moffly at 1930 hours.

Victoria Collins: We hung out while they put a temporary cast on him. He told me he felt like he had no friends, no one who was even there with him. He said he regretted everything and wanted to work it out, and I told him that it was going to take time.

Charleston PD Homicide File: They went to Mr. Moffly's house afterward, got some food from Norm's across the street.

Victoria Collins: I brought him back to his house, and we hung out for a little bit. He was definitely lonely. He was just like, "I'm not accomplishing anything," and he really felt like he was letting his parents down. I remember him mentioning that a lot. I had an exam the next day, and he kept asking me over and over again to stay. And I was like, "I really need to study for this exam, but I can see you tomorrow." I guess Jordan came over after I left.

DEA Interview with Jordan Piacente: According to PIACENTE, MOFFLY had "a few" grams of cocaine and "a lot" of Xanax tablets that were "crushed up" with him. PIACENTE said she snorted a portion of the crushed up Xanax tablets MOFFLY brought. . . . PIACENTE admitted she was with MOFFLY all night.

When Patrick woke up the next morning, he called his father and told him he was feeling better. He went downstairs to watch The Wire *and invited his friend Caroline Cordina over to shoot paintballs after class. Around lunch he offered Josh Bowman a ride from Hardee's burgers in Mount Pleasant, but first he had to "make this play real quick." At three p.m. he laid nine ziplock bags of pills under his "Don't Tread on Me" Gadsden and opened Snapchat.*

Charleston PD Homicide File: At 1502 hrs, Moffly sent a "snap" to multiple people. This "snap" was screen captured by user "Xo.summerlove." She described the "snap" as a video Patrick sent of himself doing cocaine with a dollar bill on a mirror. She stated that she saw several plastic bags full of white pills in the background of the video and was able to "screenshot" the video and capture the last second of it.

Summer McNairy: I knew that basically any Xanax downtown at the time was coming from Kligman, and that's kind of why I screenshotted it. I was like, "Okay, not cool."

Charleston PD Homicide File: The photo, which showed nine plastic bags full of white pills on what appears to be Mr. Moffly's bedroom desk, was captioned, "Maybe im the plug?" . . . Plug is common street slang for drug dealer, drug source, or supplier.

PATRICK

Josh Bowman: I sat at the Hardee's burgers for like thirty minutes, calling Patrick, blowing up everybody on that side, and nobody's answering. I ended up walking the Ravenel Bridge. I walked over the river and all the way to the house, man, and as soon as I got on Calhoun I see the fucking yellow tape and go "Oh my God."

From David Moffly's Funeral Eulogy for Patrick: Patrick's mother got a call from the Chaplain at MUSC that he had been shot, was in surgery, was in critical condition, and that we needed to come right away. She said, "No, that's not right. He had a broken arm, not a gunshot." The chaplain said, "No, the broken arm was last night. Tonight he has been shot."

CHAPTER 12

COUNT CRAZY

Even though they chose a nice beach town for their college years, C of C students love to visit other coasts for spring break. On Friday, March 4, the first day of their 2016 break, Patrick Moffly's 97 Smith housemates got ready to fly to Puerto Rico while a group of SAEs booked moped rentals in Nassau. Separate groups of Tri Delts and ADPis headed to Saint Martin and Sint Maarten, and one Pike took his food blog to Lisbon. While some younger KAs drove south to Gulf Shores, Alabama, Mikey Schmidt prepared to leave for Fort Lauderdale, where he'd been invited to stay at a beach house owned by one of his Kappa Alpha brother's parents.

Mikey spent the afternoon smoking a blunt on his new C of C girlfriend's front porch. Sitting on the corner of

Vanderhorst and Smith Streets, he wore a backward Atlanta Braves hat and no shirt. Stepping into the grass in flip-flops, he saw a few police cruisers turning left with their blue lights on. Twenty minutes later, Rob called his phone and said, "Somebody got gunned the fuck down on Smith Street." When Rob hung up, Mikey kept smoking on the porch. A few minutes later Mikey heard that the boy who'd been shot was named Pat, and he called his friend Pat to ask, "Are you all right? Did you get shot?" Mikey's Pat, who was also very high, responded, "What the fuck are you talking about? Stop calling me with that crazy shit."

Although the local news ran several articles about the son of a school board member dying in a neighborhood "where you never hear about gunshots," Patrick Moffly's death left most of the College of Charleston bubble undisturbed. Many students had already left town for spring break when news of the March 4 killing ran in the next day's *Post and Courier*, and even Patrick's own housemates flew to Puerto Rico the next day. After he got to Florida, Mikey texted Rob for advice on bamboo sunglasses that came in "Dapper Gold" and "OG Black." In Charleston, Rob focused on his post–C of C ambitions. He'd finished his credits for a biology major and a history minor the previous semester, and he made a résumé describing himself as a "recent graduate searching to enhance my strong research, analytical, and communication skills by gaining experience." On the last Sunday of break, after considering his strengths, he texted Mikey, "I think I'm gonna go to law school."

Although he'd already come back from Florida, Mikey

didn't respond to Rob's text. While he'd been day-drinking in Charleston that afternoon, his mom had called to say "you need to come home." His grandfather Frank was in the hospital for chronic obstructive pulmonary disease (COPD), and after promising an early release the doctors had realized his condition was deteriorating. When his mother hung up, Mikey sprinted to his Infiniti G35, and on some stretches of the three-hundred-mile drive he hit 130 miles an hour. "When I made it to the room he was just sitting there like a body I didn't know," Mikey said later. "He was glazed over like a ghost." Leaving the hospital, he responded to Rob's law school text.

Mikey Schmidt: My grandfather died

Rob Liljeberg: Damn man I'm so sorry. You need anything?

Mikey Schmidt: I drove 130 mph the whole way and missed him

Rob Liljeberg: That last second stuff is tough. He knows who you are and how much you cared for him. God takes care of his own.

Rob Liljeberg: I'll be there tomorrow and we'll sit down and figure out what we gotta do to help this be a natural healing for you.

Rob Liljeberg: Try to stay from drugs and alcohol even weed if possible

Mikey Schmidt: His last words to me were get clean it will be your biggest downfall

Mikey Schmidt: I'm fucking losing it

Rob Liljeberg: Well get there. Shit happens for a reason maybe he's saving you

A few months earlier, Mikey had let himself cry in front of Frank. On a Thursday morning in Buckhead, he'd gotten a call from the girlfriend of his friend Flip saying that the police were at her apartment. Mikey had assumed they'd come to serve a warrant for Xanax or cocaine, but in fact Flip had taken a counterfeit Roxicodone pill and overdosed on fentanyl. When Mikey saw Frank he'd hugged him, and after he'd buried his head in his grandfather's shirt he'd started whooping crying. Frank had a cold streak—one of Mikey's uncles described him as a man who'd drown a baby duck if he needed to—but that day, after Flip's death at the age of nineteen, Frank held his grandson while tears ran down the lobsters on his golf shirt. Before he let go, Frank told Mikey that life might only get harder from there.

After Frank died, Rob rescheduled a job interview so he could travel to Dunwoody to be with Mikey. He was the only KA to make the trip. He offered to play *Smash* with him, and he suggested Mikey try to sit in a steam room to "feel like the badness in the world is literally being sucked out of you." Over text, Mikey said that he was struggling, and Rob told him, "I know it's tough but Rob is here for you when it counts." Mikey wrote back, "Yes well on a side note I'm a million dollar nigga so let's invest."

During their last year of college, Rob's and Mikey's earnings reached a point where they needed to launder their money. The space under Mikey's grandmother's mattress wasn't a long-term option, and there was a limit to what he could spend on cars.

Looking for other strategies, the boys apparently ran profits through the C of C Kappa Alpha books. According to a member of their KA operation, they exaggerated the costs of parties and invented donations from alumni, making it look like alprazolam profits came from their order slush fund. Even so, new money came in so fast that they needed other places to store it. While the boys talked about startup investments and real estate opportunities, their cash and Venmo surpluses kept growing. Before Mikey could legally drink and Rob could rent a car, they'd stumbled into an ideal wealth-creation system, an item with limited supply and sticky demand. As they knew by now, Xanax is great at creating repeat users.

Even compared with the other drugs the KAs sold, alprazolam bars are hard to quit. Xanax turns down the electricity in the brain to an almost unreachable level of quiet, but six or so hours later the calm recedes and the noise rushes back. This fresh chaos calls for another QB, and when the body develops an alprazolam tolerance it requires a higher dose to get the same cure. Although Xanax is incredibly effective against panic attacks and seizures, it's therefore a pretty disastrous way to treat daily anxiety. Instead, eating bars every day can just open up more need. A Royal College of Psychiatrists study found that daily benzo use for six weeks resulted in dependency for four of every ten users. Once the body has become dependent, quitting can trigger devastating chemical withdrawals.

When Patrick Moffly tried to stop taking Xanax after his trafficking arrest in Columbia, he entered a month of withdrawals. Because his brain needed its daily GABA boost, it created an electrical storm of neurological activity that put him at risk of a seizure. (Benzodiazepines are one of two substances for which withdrawals can kill users; the other is alcohol.) At his family's hotel room in Peru, he threatened to jump out of a seventh-story window unless his father bought him a skateboard, and when he returned to their farm he cycled among depression, panic attacks, and delirium. As one of his good friends who saw Patrick's attempt at sobriety and eventually developed his own Xanax dependency told me, "Once you start withdrawing, the fear comes, and it comes stronger than before," he said. "It alters the chemicals in your brain, and you're hiding out at your parents' house on some paranoid shit. You're thinking the fucking feds are coming to blow down your door, or the Mexican mafia, or whatever illogical thoughts you have. And you convince yourself, 'I'm just taking medicine.'"

When one of my childhood friends tried to quit alprazolam after a semester of taking ten dark web bars a day, he checked himself into an emergency room near his college dorm. His hypertension, combined with a panic attack, made him think he was dying of a stroke. After a doctor said they'd have to taper him off Xanax to avoid a seizure, he poured eight packets of salt into a water bottle with the hope that his altered blood levels would convince the hospital to give him a higher dose. After those withdrawals, he struggled to quit Xanax for the next four years. After Patrick Moffly's month at home on Paradise Island, he returned to the College of Charleston on March 3 and started taking GG249 pills again. During his March 4 autopsy, the coroner found alprazolam in his bloodstream.

By the 2015–2016 school year, Rob's and Mikey's KA dealers had watched some of their own customers try and fail to quit Xanax. Various student users stayed in their off-campus bedrooms, and others, including one KA, dropped out of school and entered rehab. When some fraternity traffickers cut off their benzo-dependent friends, others stepped in to profit from the growing demand. "Kids would come through my buddy's house [to buy Xanax], and they're just a fucking wreck," Honcho, the C of C Sigma Nu dealer, told me. "And after they'd leave, we'd all gather round to powwow, talk shit, and be like, 'Yeah, we really should stop selling to them.' But then the moral compass would reset, and you're back to, like, monetizing human suffering almost."

Whether they saw themselves this way or not, these boys were profiting off a nationwide wave of Xanax addiction that kept growing. While people understandably focused attention on the fivefold rise in opioid overdoses from 1999 to 2015, benzodiazepine overdoses quietly went up nearly ten times during that same period. (These epidemics often worked together; according to a CDC study that tracked fatalities from 2010 to 2014, more than 30 percent of opioid overdose deaths involved a benzo sidecar.) It was possible to spot this hidden trend in a few different statistics—exponential growth in prescriptions, seizures, hospitalizations, and deaths—and it was easy to hear in the music at fraternity parties. By the time Mikey moved to Atlanta, everyone from SoundCloud rappers to Young Thug sprinkled the feeling of barring out into their songs, rapping over weightless synthesizers about eating

Xanax. The "vibes" kept getting hazier, and on Travis Scott's "Sicko Mode," the most inescapable rap song of the late 2010s, Drake described a private jet flight as "I took half a Xan, thirteen hours 'til I land, had me out like a light, like a light, like a light."

During that same period, I saw a half dozen boys I'd grown up with leave college to quit Xanax. Some of them started talking about anxiety more openly, and some relapsed when they came back to school. "Dude, if there was a Xanax bar sitting right next to me right now, and I knew it didn't have fentanyl or anything in it, I would be tempted," my high school friend told me. "I have so much general anxiety, and when I took Xanax I didn't give a fuck about the things I wish I didn't give a fuck about. I would have this bag of bars, and when an instant of depression or whatever would hit, I'd just take another bar."

During our early batch of phone calls, I asked Mikey what he did after his friend Flip and his grandfather Frank died within a few months of each other. I knew he'd spent more time in Atlanta than in Charleston, going out in Peachtree and working from the Cyan, and I'd imagined he'd felt more rushes of anxiety or sadness than usual. In response, Mikey told me that he'd handled the losses by trying to attach himself to as little as possible. "I was like, 'Damn, the only thing I'm taking with me the rest of my life is my breath,'" he said. "Everything is subject to change." When I told him that he sounded very Buddhist, he said, "It just turned me cold. I didn't really have value for human life after that. I didn't give a fuck about anything. It was the most money I've ever made in my entire life."

Mikey of course wouldn't say where that money came from, but according to one pretrial document it included a two-kilogram cocaine shipment to the College of Charleston. A few weeks after spring break, Mikey met a KA driver at either a Publix grocery store or an Atlanta golf course and handed him 70.54 ounces of cocaine, which the driver took back to campus. By the document's math, 35.22 of those ounces went to Zackery Kligman, who never met Mikey or learned his name. During the exchange, Mikey remained in Atlanta and Rob stayed in Charleston, using fraternity drivers to run their multistate drug network without personally exposing themselves to customers or the highway patrol.

Mikey Schmidt: We just move in the shadows and count crazy
Rob Liljeberg: Exactly
Mikey Schmidt: Always put someone in between us
Rob Liljeberg: Agreed
Mikey Schmidt: To bad they are fucking retards
Rob Liljeberg: Everyone is

Later that week, Zack Kligman called Rob to order more cocaine. While an episode of *Impractical Jokers* played on the TV in the background, Kligman started the conversation with a long "Yooo." On the other line, Rob kept his "yo" brief. While they talked, Rob said one word for Zack's every five. I don't know if Rob would have agreed with the 97 Smith Street

Xanax dealer who called Zack Kligman a try-hard, but while Zack called his customers "players" and Xanax pills "sticks" and weed "tree" and cocaine "ye," Rob usually responded with something like "all right." Regardless, by the end of their call Rob agreed to sell Zack a pound of cocaine, and he said his unnamed guy in Atlanta could get it to them by the end of the school week.

On Thursday, Rob and Mikey had to push their deadline. One issue with using pledge drivers is that they have to go to school, and they were too busy studying for finals to make the ten-hour round trip. While Rob talked to the pledges and Kligman asked when he could expect the product to "touch down," Mikey told Rob he was struggling to find a good price for a pound and a half of cocaine. He wrote, "Everyone tryna charge me 14 homie pulled up in a white Benz with white rims and I was just like no to 14 and he was like get out." With one of his usual sources falling through, Mikey had to look elsewhere. Uncle must've been unavailable, because Mikey told Rob that he now needed to "meet the Mexicans in the hood at 6am" himself. Before he woke up for the meeting, Mikey warned Rob that the cartel prices would either force the KAs to cut the cocaine with Inositol or take smaller profit margins. Looking at those options, Mikey worried that the whole operation wasn't "convenient anymore—or easy or safe." Rob responded, "I am fine taking less or just not doing it at all," but Mikey eventually decided to get up early and meet the source anyway. Before bed he wrote, "Whoever you send to pick this up please tell them not to fuck up."

Near the end of school on Monday, Rob sent a pledge driver to Atlanta. Waiting on specific pickup directions from Mikey, the Kappa Alpha drove north on I-26, cut west through Orangeburg, South Carolina, and headed down through Augusta toward Fulton County. When he arrived five hours later and tried to call, Mikey's phone went straight to voicemail. Every fifteen minutes for the next two hours, Rob texted Mikey things like "Dudeeeeeee," "Dude," "This is shitty as fuck dude," and "I'm kinda worried about you dude you good," but Mikey's phone stayed off. The pledge drove back overnight for Tuesday classes, and two days later Mikey tried to explain to Rob what'd happened. He said he'd been scrolling Instagram on his balcony when he'd dropped his iPhone and watched it fall twenty stories. Because he didn't have Rob's number on his other burner, Mikey said he had no way of contacting Rob or the pledge. Mikey apologized to Rob, and instead of screaming, Rob told his friend that he "One hundred percent got his situation" and understood that tensions were running high. Ultimately, he said he just wanted to get the deal done soon so they could "cash out." Mikey responded that he needed more cash too, and Rob asked him when he'd be free next.

On Thursday, April 21, Rob sent another pledge driver to Atlanta. One of their usual choices backed out at the last minute, but a young KA named Jonathan Reams offered to make the trip instead. Jonathan was a country boy from Easley, South Carolina, and his Instagram bio quoted a Zac Brown and Jimmy Buffett lyric: "Mind on a permanent vacation, the ocean is my only medication." Jonathan came from working people and didn't own a car, and he needed the $200 Rob usually paid for trips to meet Mikey. As had been the case the last time Jonathan drove to Atlanta, no one told him exactly what he was picking up, and after he took the keys to Rob's mom's 2002 Toyota Tacoma, he agreed not to look in the bags when he arrived. Excited by the pledge's team spirit, Rob called Jonathan "Goatathan," and Mikey texted back, "This kid gets pulled at night and I'll kill someone. Like I don't have a good feeling about this."

While Jonathan arrived in Atlanta and waited outside a Publix grocery store between a Walgreens and a Jersey Mike's, Rob told Mikey to hurry. "Dude," Rob said, "he's got an exam." One hour later, Mikey's runner showed up carrying a few grocery bags. One bag held a 40 percent reduced-fat bag of Cape Cod kettle chips, which he'd emptied out and resealed around a quarter pound of weed. In other plastic bags he'd stuffed 3,984 "Green Hulk" pills, which mixed alprazolam powder and synthetic marijuana, and a purple box of Ronzoni Smart Taste Pasta concealing 702.7 grams of cocaine. Mikey had bagged up a pound of coke for Zack, plus another half pound for Rob's other customers, and he'd warned Rob that people might not like the cocaine because it wasn't as "methy" as the impure stuff C of C kids were used to. In response, Rob texted "these idiots will love it."

Rob Liljeberg: Thanks dude sorry about all this. We should take a trip this summer that's relaxing and drink Coronas

Mikey Schmidt: Yeah dawg we are Imma make a few finesses so we can take some vacations after may
Rob Liljeberg: Worddd sounds good dude
Rob Liljeberg: Thanks again and sorry about the confusion
Mikey Schmidt: My bad again nigga love you
Rob Liljeberg: You're good dude it's all of us love you too

The three main characters in the next morning's events refused to share their memories of April 22 with me. Whenever I asked him about it, Mikey changed the subject, and whenever I reached out to Rob he didn't respond. Jonathan Reams did write me back on Facebook Messenger, but only to say that he'd speak to me only if I paid him $150. If Rob and Mikey texted each other that Friday, I never saw the screenshots, and the same goes for any messages to or from Jonathan. Without knowing what Mikey, Rob, or Jonathan had to say, I consulted the memories of the Charleston policemen who were parked outside 7 Montagu that morning, plus a few wire recordings, a dozen assorted files, and an interview with a younger KA who'd just moved into Rob's house.

According to one of those sources, Rob woke up at 7 Montagu around seven that morning. Using his scales and his heat sealer, he weighed out sixteen ounces of cocaine and sealed it inside a large bag of popcorn. He stuffed the popcorn into a drawstring backpack, and he hid the remaining half pound of cocaine, plus the weed and pills, elsewhere in the house. He hadn't planned on living at 7 Montagu that semester, but after some apparent turbulence with his Chi O girlfriend, he'd needed a place to stay, and luckily the house had an empty room upstairs. Around eleven fifteen a.m., while some of his Kappa Alpha housemates were still asleep, Rob texted Zack and asked when he'd be ready to meet.

At 11:33 Kligman pulled up to 7 Montagu, and Rob called and told him to park in the driveway across the street. Rob stepped out among the centuries-old mansions in a Dri-Fit shirt and midcalf socks, and he tucked the drawstring bag into his chest like a football. When he dapped up Zack and ducked into his Cadillac, Zack said, "Yooo dude, I appreciate you man." Rob sat down and asked, "You brought all the cheddar right?" Zack said he'd come back in ten minutes with the money, and they talked through the $19,350 Zack owed Rob for cocaine, accounting for the $6,250 Rob owed Zack for Xanax. Gripping the drawstring with his fist, Rob pulled out the popcorn bag and set it between his legs. Bobbing his head and shoulders, Zack asked Rob about his Atlanta source's delays, saying, "That guy, I was worried you were getting fucked over for a second." Rob responded, "Naw, he's just slow as shit." Zack dapped him up a second time, and when Rob stepped out he drove off.

Once he was back inside 7 Montagu, Rob called Mikey to say that he was waiting for Zack's money. After he hung up, he worked to flush the rest of his drugs out of the house. While he gathered the coke, weed, and pills and got ready to hide them in the back of his mom's truck, he told Jonathan Reams to come over for another pledge task. When Jonathan arrived, Rob handed him a large bag of potato chips with directions for a "drop." He told Jonathan to head toward a secret location near campus, where he'd leave the bag for a Xanax customer to pick up. Leaving the house, Jonathan straightened his ball cap and walked outside, heading up Saint Philip and toward Calhoun. Because the chip bag was too big to fit in his khaki pockets, he carried it by hand. When he sat on a bench near the campus Chick-fil-A, a large man in a golf shirt walked up and identified himself as a police officer. When the detective took out handcuffs, Goatathan began to sob. The man put him in an unmarked car, and Jonathan heaved and repeated, "I didn't have anything to do with it. I didn't have anything to do with it!"

Around the same time, Rob carried the rest of his drugs to his mom's old Toyota pickup. Entering a side street three houses down, he placed a canvas tote and a few grocery bags in the Tacoma's back passenger seat. He stepped back on Montagu and saw two men wearing POLICE tactical vests walking toward him, and he dropped his keys onto the street before they told him to put his hands in the air. While one officer put him in handcuffs and the other picked up the keys, they read his Miranda rights and asked, "Are there any narcotics in your residence?" Rob told them he'd left five to seven ounces of cocaine in his truck, and he described where he'd parked it. While a tow truck arrived to haul the pickup into evidence, the two detectives led Rob into their unmarked SUV and drove him to a municipal building on the Ashley River.

+ + +

At 12:30 p.m., undercover officers from the Charleston Police Department Special Investigations Unit (SIU) converged on 7 Montagu, some in unmarked Tahoes, others on leisure bicycles, and some on foot in golf shirts or pink shorts. These officers blended in with the neighborhood, but the six-man SWAT team that accompanied them did not. Leaving the third-floor bathroom in his boxers, a 7 Montagu sophomore heard their tactical boots coming up the stairs. When he stepped into the hall he saw a few large pistols in his face and heard, "Get the fuck on the ground!" Soon the police herded the boys onto the sofas downstairs, each pair of KAs handcuffed with a policeman between them. While the boys sat there, a dozen officers searched the house, opening safes, stripping the kitchen, and sorting through their clothes.

Sitting on the couch, one KA turned to a policeman and asked, "When can I get out of these cuffs? I want to play golf today." The officer ignored him, and his partners continued to tear up the bedrooms. Eventually the policemen brought each KA into the dining room for one-on-one interviews, which didn't reveal much. After the search team confiscated only a heat sealer and scales, plus a couple pills from one KA's blazer pocket, they handed 7 Montagu's keys back to its twenty-one-year-old owner. Taking another look at a house that cost more than a few of theirs combined, the officers left the boys to enjoy their summer break.

A few hours later, two KAs sat on the downstairs couch

and discussed what had just happened to them. The chapter GroupMe was blowing up with rumors, and even though they hadn't been arrested themselves, the boys wondered how much they should tell their parents. While they talked, Rob Liljeberg opened the front door wearing the same Dri-Fit shirt and mid-calf socks. After he made eye contact with them, he turned and jogged upstairs. The younger boys followed him and asked what had happened, and when Rob reached his room, he turned back and said that the police had taken his passport and told him not to leave town, but otherwise he was all good. Before Rob closed his door, he said, "Yeah, no, I'm fine."

CHAPTER 13

I'M YOUR PLEDGE

For the month of April, Mikey's only link to the world outside Atlanta came through his phone. After he'd driven home from spring break when Frank died on March 13, he didn't return to Charleston until May. Keeping pledge drivers between his operation and Rob's, he worked while his mom planned his grandfather's funeral. He'd gotten to the point where he could offload $10,000 in inventory with two weekly phone calls, leaving him time for sessions with 808 Mafia and nightclubs with Biscuit. When he wasn't working, he liked to go on his balcony at the Cyan and check Snapchat and Instagram. He'd been taking more Xanax himself since Frank died, and after he'd eat a QB and smoke a blunt, he'd lean above Del Frisco's and watch his friends' stories. In South

Carolina, SAEs posted drone videos of parties at their lake houses, and in Georgia Mikey's coworkers posted from their G-wagons. Two days after Frank's service at Saint Luke's Presbyterian in Dunwoody, Mikey got on his phone and saw that his ex-girlfriend Alexis was *Total Frat Move*'s "Babe of the Day." Her friends had nominated her as a joke, and now her swimsuit and disc golf photos were on the site's front page. Alexis told me that she'd first thought it was pretty cool to be featured, but then her sorority sisters started blaming her for affecting their reputation. Below the photos, the *Total Frat* readers had posted a classic *TFM* comment thread.

Fratty_Boh 24: She could have kept the Titanic afloat with those chest flotation devices.

UncleJimmy: Even if ISIS filled those fake knockers with C4 I'd still tickle her nipples with my peepee.

Youngmellow: Fuck ISIS and fuck you.

Colonel Reb forever: I attend [her college] as well. She's a good one, so y'all be nice.

Frat_jim: Do you think that's gonna get you laid or something?

Colonel Reb forever: No, it won't get me laid because she doesn't know I'm on here.

Larry_Sellers: Is expressing my desire to repeatedly ram my fuck piston between her chest howitzers considered nice?

Joyceharvey45: Commence your Home Business right now. Hang out with your Family and Earn. Start bringing $60/hr just over a computer. Very easy way to choose your Life Happy and Earning continuously. Begin here..... ——— http://incomenews11.cf

Whatever feelings the thread stirred up in Mikey, he didn't dwell on them. Instead, he handled the pains of his April C of C shipment—the six a.m. cartel wakeup, the shattered phone—and focused on getting paid. After Rob sold their pound of cocaine to Zack Kligman, he called Mikey to talk about their KA money laundering, and he mentioned that Zack had paid only $6,500 of the nearly $20,000 he owed them. Mikey responded, "Dude what the actual fuck." Thanks to his laundering and spending, Mikey was cash poor, and he told Rob he needed money now. When Rob said that Kligman wasn't answering his calls, Mikey asked himself if he should worry about deeper problems. Perhaps Kligman was daring Rob and Mikey to confront him over the $14,000, knowing that they didn't have the "muscle" that Kligman did, or perhaps Zack couldn't pay them because he was under other constraints.

Mikey, who trusted his own catlike sense about these things, started to worry that Zack had been "caught and released" by the police. He wondered if the Charleston PD had arrested Kligman with a small amount of Xanax and sent him back outside to work as an informant. Mikey floated this idea to Rob, who responded, "I'm actually scared dude. Please tell me you're just being paranoid." To confirm one way or another, Mikey asked Rob to drive to Zack's house near President Street and investigate. Mikey told his friend to order ten thousand more Xanax bars, using the deal as an excuse for Rob to "look at him in the eyes and feel his vibes." If Zack's blue irises looked shifty, Rob and Mikey would know they were dealing with a police informant, and they could destroy their phones and clean out their safes. If his eyes had a trustworthy energy, Rob could ask for their money and then pay Mikey back for the pound and a half of cocaine. This plan scared Rob, who didn't want to confront a potential informant who owned a grenade launcher. He messaged Mikey, "It's still risky to stare at the sun," and Mikey wrote back, "Nah your good put some ray bans on."

Each time they texted each other about Zack Kligman that week, Rob expressed more fear and Mikey expressed more anger. Whenever Rob said he wouldn't drive to Kligman's house north of campus—telling Mikey "I'm actually scared dude," or "Get us protection dude I can't handle this stress," or "Dude I'm so scared"—Mikey pushed his friend harder. Mikey wrote, "Everyday I don't have money I get more mad I wake up pissed if I sleep I don't sleep easy I wake up ready to rip someone's head off." Rob offered to pay Mikey out of his savings account, even if it meant his mom and dad asking questions, but Mikey told him he didn't have to do that. Still afraid to face Zack, Rob ultimately offered to sell Mikey's cocaine around C of C for free. Over a long series of texts, he tried to convince his friend to let him work off his debt:

Rob Liljeberg: Call me later. I will raise mad $ if you gimme work when you're comfortable with it to make your money back
Rob Liljeberg: I know I owe you and I won't nig out on it
Rob Liljeberg: I'm your pledge until this is over.
Rob Liljeberg: Also there's a black guy selling quarters for 450 out of midtown right now and I really wanna put him outta business

Rob Liljeberg: The game is struggling without you mi amigo
Rob Liljeberg: Send me a shitty key and watch me work my magic
Rob Liljeberg: I will earn your money hard. You can drop off and leave and go drink coronas on the beach while I hustle my balls off for you

With senior beach week and Charleston Affair alumni weekend coming up, Rob told Mikey that he could easily sell a kilogram of mediocre cocaine. This approach wouldn't reveal whether Zack Kligman was a police informant or not, but it at least would get Mikey paid in full, and eventually Mikey agreed to meet a KA driver in Atlanta. Rob texted him, "Thanks for working with me man. I feel like an idiot and I really wanna make it up to you . . . Go have a corona you deserve it." A few minutes later, Mikey sent a photo of a Corona longneck sweating on a Goose Island coaster, and he wrote, "One step ahead as always."

For some dealers at the College of Charleston, news of the bust at 7 Montagu had felt like an extinction-level event. Although the police hadn't found much inside Rob's house, the idea that anyone in a Chevy Tahoe or pink shorts might be an undercover detective turned the C of C campus into a minefield. Instead of going to class, some dealers gave into paranoia. According to several sources, two or three C of C dealers left town in the middle of finals and went to Florida, and two others started researching a postgrad move to Bali. Most of these boys were afraid of the Charleston PD's new willingness to raid million-dollar homes one block from campus, but others worried about Rob Liljeberg himself. After the bust, Rob's mom had driven up to help him move out of 7 Montagu and into a house on Cannon Street, and some kids wondered if he'd escaped jail time only because he'd snitched on other dealers. Even though the Charleston PD had never officially arrested Rob, these police rumors made it hard for him to socialize. One night he walked into a party where lacrosse players were doing cocaine on a table, and when they looked up and saw Rob they slammed a book on the powder. Before the white dust resettled on the table, the boys high-fived each other and got up to leave.

Of course, Mikey wasn't there to see any of that. His only sense of what was happening at the College of Charleston came from his phone. Rob himself hinted at an anxiety among fraternity guys, telling Mikey that "everyone [is] super nervous. But everyone's doing loads of shitty blow and paying $70 a g," but he didn't tell Mikey about the police raid or the chatter that followed it. Eventually guys started texting Mikey different "I heard Rob got busted" stories, and one day while Mikey drove home from getting his Porsche fixed a Charleston girlfriend called to tell him the same thing. After that, Mikey warned Rob about the smears.

Mikey Schmidt: People keep texting me sayin you're a snitch
Mikey Schmidt: Lol
Rob Liljeberg: No they don't
Mikey Schmidt: An I'm just like nah there no chance

Rob Liljeberg: You'd know dude especially with those connections you have

Mikey Schmidt: Thanks for tellin bro so that I could clear everything up

Rob Liljeberg: People tried to tell me I got arrested with a kilo

Rob Liljeberg: I was like dude seriously?

Rob Liljeberg: You think I'd be drinking corona at midtown if they found a fucking kilo on me

Mikey Schmidt: Hahahah nah

Mikey kept defending Rob. He didn't want to let paranoid rumors change the way he saw his best friend. Eventually, though, he heard stories that edged closer to what people had seen on April 22. One Atlanta friend—immediately following the text, "I'm tryna fuck I slapped her ass so hard when she was walking away"—told Mikey that he'd heard that Rob had his passport confiscated by the police. Mikey sent Rob a screenshot of the message, and Rob responded, "That shits not anywhere close to true." After that, Mikey got a longer text from a KA brother nicknamed "Ders" who'd been at 7 Montagu during the police seizure. Ders said that officers had torn up the house while the KAs sat on the couch in handcuffs, and although they'd expected never to see Rob again, "3 hours later he's back and we are all just like wtf then he tells us they took his passport." In the days since the raid, Ders swore he'd seen undercover officers watching Montagu Street, and he was so scared that he'd moved home with his mom and dad. After calling Ders "a little pussy," Rob finally admitted that the police had taken him downtown while they searched 7 Montagu and released him when they didn't find anything. "I'd be in jail regardless of what I said if they actually caught me with what you sent me," Rob wrote. "I get you're concerned, like very concerned. But all I can say is that time will tell [. . .] and I'm working to raise money for you."

Mikey agreed that the police wouldn't send a boy who'd been caught with a pound and a half of cocaine back into the College of Charleston nightlife. Still, while he stewed in his condo he imagined other worst-case scenarios. Even if the police hadn't found anything at 7 Montagu, the fact that they'd known to raid the house meant they were getting closer to the Kappa Alpha network. At this point, maybe undercover operatives really were parked outside Rob's old bedroom; maybe they were parked outside the Atlanta Del Frisco's downstairs. Mikey wondered who else the Charleston sting had targeted, and he went on SouthCarolina.arrests.org and typed in "Zackery Kligman." After a baby-faced 2011 mug shot, Mikey saw a photo of Zack with a manicured beard and a 2016 charge for TRAF COCAINE. The time of arrest was listed as 2:06 a.m. on April 2, 2016, twenty days before Rob's and Mikey's most recent deal with him. While Zack's eyes looked coolly at the screen, Mikey realized a few things about his own situation. Although it was unlikely that Kligman was a snitch—for obvious reasons, when the police "catch and release" someone for confidential informant work, they don't publicize the arrest or release a mug shot—Zack's cocaine trafficking charge in April meant that Mikey probably wasn't getting any money from Zack. If he was smart, Kligman was laying low now, and even if he wasn't smart he was almost certainly using the profits of their April 22 deal to pay the legal fees for his April 2 case. Looking at Zack's mug shot, Mikey sent the link to Rob.

Rob Liljeberg: Jesus dude. He got arrested on the second?
Rob Liljeberg: I can't believe we didn't stop to think
Mikey Schmidt: I did!!!!
Mikey Schmidt: We would have been golden if we never served him up
Rob Liljeberg: I'm sorry man
Mikey Schmidt: Your good
Mikey Schmidt: When you love the money shit like that happens
Mikey Schmidt: I love the money
Rob Liljeberg: Haha yes we both love the money

If Mikey played it semicool over text, his anxiety spiraled when he was alone. Now that they'd arrested Zack Kligman, the Charleston PD almost certainly wanted to look further upstream and find Zack's "source of supply." Mikey could find some comfort in the fact that Zack didn't know Mikey, but ultimately Mikey was one of Zack's cocaine sources, and the Charleston police had arrested Zackery Kligman for trafficking cocaine. Mikey canceled his next deal with Rob, and even though he lived a state away from the Charleston Police Department, he struggled with paranoia whenever he left his apartment. Driving home after serving a party at Ole Miss, he looked out both windows and saw unmarked Dodge Chargers in either lane. If other people thought the drivers were just Mississippians celebrating the American muscle car tradition, Mikey wondered if they were men paid to follow him. While he listened to Lil Uzi Vert's "Money Longer"—nodding along to "smoking that gas, gone off that Xanny, she on the powder . . . money got longer, speaker got louder, car got faster"—Mikey saw a third Charger pull up. He tried to focus while the three cars hovered around him, and his fear got deeper when they all left the interstate at once.

At home in Atlanta, Mikey hired a special mechanic to install a "combination safe" behind his car radio. He'd often used hidden compartments in his cars, but this safe wouldn't open unless he turned on the left blinker, turned the heat up to 72 degrees, and put the car in neutral. When he took the car for a drive, a police Tahoe came up behind him and turned on its sirens. While Mikey pulled off the road his anxiety went into full bloom, and he tried to control his breath as his father had taught him when he was three. When the breathing exercise didn't work, Mikey saw a white pill on his dashboard and ate it. The Xanax went down his throat while the Tahoe opened its doors, and when the officer came to ask questions about his driving, Mikey was able to make eye contact and offer a feeling of safety. Even when a canine sniffed the car, Mikey felt relaxed. On his way back home without any charges, he felt grateful to his benzo supplier.

Mikey Schmidt: I had a Zan on the dash so I ate it and I was the least stressed of all during the situation calm cool collected and so incredibly respectful

Mikey Schmidt: Thanks Zac
Rob Liljeberg: Haha I grunt laughed at that
Rob Liljeberg: "Thanks Zac"
Rob Liljeberg: Quote of the year

In early May, Rob invited Mikey to his College of Charleston graduation. Rob's parents had rented a condo on Folly Beach with plans to boil fifteen pounds of shrimp, and they had two extra tickets to the commencement ceremony for Mikey and his mom. The weekend would give Mikey a chance to see Rob before his postgrad trip to Asia, and it'd give him time to go out in Charleston before everyone left for summer break. Although his mom wasn't going to make it, Mikey told Rob he'd be there. Mikey also planned to use the trip to pick up his PlayStation 4 and meet a top local defense attorney. "I got six figure legal money comin in I'm not a fuckin idiot," Mikey texted Rob. "Calculated risks aren't worth it anymore we are all over the radar our names and legacy won't die cause no one in that city will do it like us."

Two days before Rob's commencement, Mikey went to Charleston's French Quarter to visit the law offices of Tim Kulp. Earlier in the week, Kulp had taken a phone call from the most famous DUI attorney in Atlanta, who'd said, "Got this guy I'm sending you. Young fellow. He's afraid he's going to be arrested in a significant cocaine trafficking case." When Mikey walked in from the third-floor porch, Kulp was surprised that his potential client looked like Justin Bieber. Mikey grabbed at his teeth with his pointer finger and thumb like he was feeling for braces, but he also told Kulp that he would never cooperate with the police. Sitting over a Persian rug and under a framed Frank Sinatra mug shot, they talked through Mikey's police fears for the next three hours. Kulp gave him a few numbers to call if he did get arrested, and he repeated different versions of the advice "Don't fucking talk to anybody except for your family and me." Kulp didn't charge for the consultation, but he told him there'd be a significant fee if they ended up working together, and he didn't take cash. Mikey responded, "That's not a problem."

When Mikey left Kulp's office and walked through downtown, he felt sure he was being followed. In addition to the many uniformed policemen he saw greeting families in town for graduation, Mikey thought he spotted two casually dressed white men in their thirties tracking him. Heading east, he tried to lose the men in parking garages, slipping into the decks on his way to the river. These shortcuts led him to the safety of The Vendue hotel, which had his favorite rooftop bar in downtown Charleston. He'd come to see Rob for the first time since Frank's death, although it'd taken some convincing to get Mikey there. Before Mikey had driven to South Carolina, his anxiety had spun out again, and he'd called Rob to say, "Dude, I love you like a brother. I'll do anything you need, but don't set me up. Put any person in a place they need to be, but you don't set up family." Rob had been patient with his friend's fears, and he'd texted him, "I owe you money, not heat." When Mikey had calmed down, he'd agreed to meet at The Vendue to drink and talk through the ways Rob could pay him back.

Now Mikey took the elevator up to meet his friend. When he arrived, Rob dapped him up and said he needed to go downstairs and say hello to his grandfather real quick.

While Mikey waited for Rob, he got a table next to a loudspeaker disguised as a rock feature. He ordered his all-time favorite mustard truffle fries and looked over the river. An early summer wind came in from the barrier islands, and when Rob came back up they ordered drinks and talked through the disaster of their April cocaine deal. Sharing the fries, they agreed that "buddy" [Kligman] was never going to pay them back, and Rob shared his plans to pay Mikey back instead. Mikey thanked Rob for not selling him out when the cops had raided 7 Montagu, and he promised to help Rob work out a strategy for future coke and Xanax deals. They finished drinking and took the elevator back down into graduation weekend.

The College of Charleston is said to host the prettiest commencement ceremony in the South. Under the live oaks of *Travel + Leisure*'s Most Beautiful College Campus in America, nestled in the middle of *Travel + Leisure*'s Best City in the World, students walk the quad where Rachel McAdams eyed James Marsden in *The Notebook*. On the morning of May 7, 2016, Rob and his male classmates pinned roses onto their white dinner jackets, and the women of C of C carried bouquets over their white gowns. While the crowd sat under fingers of Spanish moss, President Glenn McConnell approached the podium. McConnell had made it through the Confederate memorabilia protests and won the college president job. Now, after a long year that'd included a $125 million capital campaign and the off-campus death of Patrick Moffly, he leaned into the microphone. "Looking out across a sea of smiling faces, I am indeed inspired today. . . . All along, we knew you were different. You were smart, you were curious, and adventurous in ways that others weren't." He encouraged the class to "know thyself," and after a fundraising plug and other rituals, the college gave out its 2016 bachelor's diplomas. When Rob walked onto the stage he gave out a few extroverted handshakes, and when the voice on the PA said "Robert Louis Liljeberg III" he let out a very slight smile.

Later that evening Rob invited Mikey out to Folly Beach for steaks and Coronas, but Mikey didn't want to face the traffic on Highway 171. Instead, Mikey slept at his Charleston girlfriend's apartment with plans to wake up Sunday and drive to Atlanta for Mother's Day. When he got out of bed the next morning, though, he realized that his girlfriend hadn't moved his laundry from the washer to the dryer. Mikey really liked to have a fresh wardrobe, and he made her move his wet clothes while he rolled a blunt and turned on some music. He smoked in his boxers while the load spun around. Once his laundry was ready, he piled a few thousand dollars' worth of golf shirts and khakis into his BMW trunk, next to his Gucci loafers and PlayStation 4. When Mikey got in the driver's seat, his phone had a text from Rob: "Tell your momma happy Mother's Day. I hope y'all have fun today."

Mikey turned on 2 Chainz's "Feds Watching" and dropped the top on his BMW. When he pulled onto Smith Street he saw blue Charleston PD lights spinning behind him. Without a Xanax bar on his dash to swallow, Mikey could only pull over and watch as an officer approached his car. After the policeman read Mikey's ID, he leaned into his radio and said, "Take him." Tahoes pulled up and men in windbreakers stepped out, and Mikey encouraged them to search his convertible. The men combed through the warm clothes and PlayStation games while a tow truck arrived. After the truck dragged Mikey's 335i away, Mikey got in a police car and met the same two casually dressed men he'd seen following him two days before.

At the police station, Mikey learned that one of those men was Detective Patrick Gill of Charleston's Special Investigations Unit. Gill was known locally as a young swashbuckler—one defense lawyer called him "an Irish cutie and a cowboy" who liked to give his informants Hollywood-friendly code names—but when Mikey looked at Gill, Mikey just started laughing. He giggled more when they arrived at police headquarters, probably because Mikey was still high, and when Detective Gill started their interrogation Mikey kept cracking up. Looking at the detective, Mikey saw a Citadel military school try-hard, the kind of guy whose cap KAs liked to steal on King Street. At the same time, Mikey told me he assumed Gill saw him as a "little frat boy who lives like a fucking rock star and hangs out with every girl he wishes he could talk to." When Detective Gill told him he knew all about Mikey's trust fund from his grandfather, Mikey responded, "Oh, all right buddy." He wasn't intimidated by Gill's intimation of knowledge, in part because

Mikey knew that Gill's team wasn't going to find any drugs or money in his apartments or his BMW.

On the other side of the table, Gill read from a document that listed some of the things he'd learned about Mikey. The file drew from nearly a dozen confidential informants, with code names like "Fireball," "Buddha," "Mr. Sorry," "Clint Eastwood," and "Hunter Thompson." Thanks to "Hunter Thompson" in particular, Gill knew about Mikey's weed sourcing, Xanax dealing, money laundering, and cocaine trafficking. Mikey felt soberer now, and when Gill told him some facts from the document, Mikey said he wouldn't even state his name without a lawyer present. While they waited for Tim Kulp, an irritated Mikey called the fit, long-haired Gill a "mermaid." Later, Kulp arrived sweaty from yard work at his house on Johns Island. He advised Mikey that the police would negotiate a friendly bond if Mikey agreed to cooperate with the police, but when Mikey tried to offer fake names and stories about low-level dealers, Gill cut him off.

At least as Mikey remembers it, Detective Gill slid an affidavit across the table. Looking down, Mikey saw the names "Hunter Thompson" and "Michael Schmidt" paired a dozen times. Over the past two weeks, the Thompson informant had given the Charleston police an on-the-record interview about Mikey, and he'd also provided two dozen recorded phone calls, a wire recording over truffle fries on The Vendue roof, and all the text messages between Mikey and Rob I've used in this book.

CHAPTER 14

STORAGE LOCKER

Mikey spent the night in the open ward of the Charleston county jail waiting for his bond hearing. He'd arrived at the Sheriff Al Cannon Detention Center with a manicured stubble and a few hundred dollars in canteen money, and he was the only white person in his cell. Sitting down, he tried not to make eye contact with the men speaking Gullah creole across the room. He didn't use the toilet once, and the next morning he felt happier than he'd ever been to see his mother. After his hearing, he signed a $75,000 bond for trafficking cocaine. Under the terms of the agreement, as long as Mikey remained in the state of South Carolina and didn't get arrested for as much as public intoxication on King Street, he was free to go.

On the highway with his mother, Mikey checked the mirror for undercover cars. He'd once told me that he'd grown up quiet because his mom had so much to say, but now they both were silent. When they stopped for a salmon salad at a restaurant, he thought he saw undercover agents eating next to him in duck boots. His anxiety kept corkscrewing when he and his mom reached his family's vacation condo at the Kiawah Island Golf Resort. Instead of talking to his mother, Mikey turned over the last two months in his mind. He thought back to early March, when he'd stood on the grass in flip-flops and watched police cruisers driving past him on Smith Street. He of course hadn't known it at the time, but he'd witnessed a link in the chain of events that led to his own arrest. While he sat on Kiawah Island, he realized that Rob probably wouldn't have betrayed him if Patrick Moffly hadn't been found murdered and surrounded by GG249 pills on the first Friday of spring break.

At 3:49 p.m. on Friday, March 4, when police dispatch reported a "shots fired" call a block from the College of Charleston library, the nearest patrol car turned on its sirens and took a U-turn on Calhoun. Officer Jonathan Fowlkes arrived minutes later at 97 Smith Street and saw two upperclassmen waving him inside. He left his car and stepped over ten-or-so white pills running like bread crumbs from the driveway to the porch. After he'd confirmed with the boys that the gunmen had already fled, he walked in and saw Patrick Moffly lying six feet from the entrance. He was at the bottom of the stairs, with his sneakers facing up at the door. His left arm was in a cast, and his good arm held Chipotle napkins to his chest. Spread out in pools around his body were hundreds more white pills.

After calling for backup, Officer Fowlkes turned on his body camera and knelt in the Xanax pile next to Patrick. He saw blood pooling in the Chipotle napkins, and when Fowlkes pressed his hands down Patrick moaned. Fowlkes, who was only a year older than Patrick, asked, "Do you know who did this to you?" and Patrick closed his eyes. The officer pushed the disintegrating napkins further into Patrick's chest. "Stay awake for me. Hey, hey, hey, stay awake for me." Speaking over his own gurgling, Patrick responded, "Jordan Piacente and Dollar Tee robbed me." The officer asked if Jordan had shot him, and Patrick shook his head. When Patrick started to close his eyes again, the officer said, "Hey, sir, look at me." While blood ran out of the hole in Patrick's chest, he didn't answer Fowlkes's other questions about the shooters. But after the officer told Patrick to keep his feet up and that the EMS would take care of him, Patrick said, "They were in a red car."

While the EMS team carried Patrick into an ambulance, one paramedic recognized him from her son's middle school class. After they left for the Medical University of South Carolina, more police cruisers arrived at 97 Smith Street. Officers formed a perimeter to the end of the block, stretching yellow tape to cut off a growing crowd of rubberneckers. From there, detectives began to search Patrick's house. One officer indexed the 397.92 white GG249 tablets from the street to the floor where Patrick had been shot, and another picked up a spent .45-caliber Hornady shell next to a downstairs cubby. Others went up to Patrick's room, where they found scales, USPS boxes, codeine bottles, Inositol powder, baggies of "plant-like material," and a mirror smeared with white powder under a "Don't Tread on Me" Gadsden flag. While some officers bagged up these items, others went outside to interview witnesses before news trucks arrived, and a few detectives began to interrogate Patrick's housemates.

Answering questions in the driveway, the 97 Smith boys had a few things they wanted to hide from the Charleston Police Department. First, there was the fact that one of them had sold Patrick ten thousand GG249 Xanax bars that morning. When the housemate got out of bed and found Patrick watching *The Wire* on the couch, Patrick told him that one of his customers wanted ten thousand pills in a few hours. Because Zack Kligman had cut Patrick off after the USC tailgate cocaine trafficking arrest, Patrick needed another source for benzos, and the housemate told Patrick that he could get ten thousand sticks for one dollar each. After that, the housemate just texted Zack, who bagged up ten ziplock bags at the Treehouse and dropped them off in a USPS box for seventy-five cents a pill. Enjoying a tidy profit for a quick flip, the housemate gave the box to Patrick, who put the ziplock bags under his Gadsden flag and made his "Maybe im the plug?" Snapchat.

Talking to the detectives, these housemates didn't mention that morning's GG249 sale, and they left out their broader role in the wholesale/retail alprazolam economy. Instead, they focused on what they'd witnessed before the shooting. According to their testimony, a few of them were playing *Call of Duty* in a downstairs bedroom at 3:45 p.m. when they heard voices above them. On the second floor, another housemate pulled up the curtain on his door window and saw a young-looking Black man step into the upstairs bathroom. The housemate told the Charleston PD that he "didn't agree" with Patrick's Black friends, who included Josh Bowman and other guys from the Silver Dollar bar, because they came over and "played their rap music very loud." With that in mind, the housemate closed his window curtain and stayed in his room. Less than five minutes later, Patrick's housemates heard four pairs of shoes tumbling down the staircase. After the sound of either running or fighting, Patrick said clearly, "Are you really gonna shoot me?" Over the reverb-heavy explosions of *Call of Duty*, the boys heard a numb pop.

Patrick called out, "Help, I've been shot!"—and more than anything else from that day, the housemates didn't want the detectives or anyone else to know how they'd reacted then. When they reached the bottom of the stairs, they saw Patrick grabbing his chest on the floor. Around him were hundreds of loose GG249 bars and a punctured ziplock bag, and next to him were two other full bags of pills. While Patrick bled out next to them, one housemate grabbed the two bags and ran to their neighbor's backyard, where he hid the pills under beer cans in the trash. A second housemate walked up and kneeled down next to Patrick, but only to clean up some Xanax and swallow a pill. After that, as Patrick slipped in and out of consciousness and a third housemate flushed some drugs down the toilet, the second boy dialed 911. Figuring it would take too long to scoop up the Xanax around Patrick, he walked to the yard to bury his own pills.

With his friends busy destroying evidence, the only boy left to help Patrick was a C of C student who didn't really know him. He'd come to 97 Smith to play Xbox and buy some Xanax for his spring break trip home to Greenwich, and while Patrick's housemates flushed and buried their pills he went to the kitchen to find something to stop Patrick's bleeding. He hoped for a dish towel or at least a paper towel but only found Chipotle napkins. He pushed them into the hole in Patrick's chest, and although the recycled brown paper was too thin to absorb much blood, he tried to apply pressure with his hands. The .45 round had passed through Patrick's right lung and liver before lodging in the soft tissue of his back, and while the boy pressed down he could smell Patrick's skin burning. Patrick said "Tell my family I'm sorry," and the boy kept pushing the napkins until Officer Fowlkes arrived and sent him to the driveway to be questioned with Patrick's housemates.

While the 97 Smith residents answered questions outside, an investigative team searched the house. One housemate watched the police fail to check the neighbors' trash can, and another remained calm thanks to the Xanax he'd eaten. Without the help of pills, though, the C of C student from Greenwich who'd pushed the napkins into Patrick's chest was starting to feel like he needed a cigarette, and when he reached into his pocket and pulled one out, a GG249 bar fell out with it. A policeman saw the Xanax hit the ground, and when he asked the boy where he'd gotten it, the boy pointed to one of the housemates. Later, another detective came out holding a paper lease agreement to a carriage house at 43 Gadsden Street. Realizing that Patrick's housemates knew more than they'd admitted, the officers took them to department headquarters. Other investigators drove to the Medical University of South Carolina emergency room, where Patrick was in surgery, and dozens of police cruisers searched the Charleston area for a red car.

After trauma surgeons declared Patrick dead at 7:15 p.m., his picture ran all over the next morning's papers and the next evening's local news. Most stories led with a photo of him in a pink button-down and a striped bow tie, and others used a shirtless selfie taken in a marble kitchen. Some outlets called him "popular among his social circles at C of C" or "a well-known area surfer and skateboarder," and nearly all of them mentioned his mother's political career. The stature of Patrick's family in the Low Country, combined with the proximity of his death to the C of C quad, made his murder one of Charleston's highest-pressure cases since the Mother Emanuel shooting. Facing the press outside his office, Chief Mullen knew he needed to do two things to respond credibly to the homicide. Of course, Mullen's people needed to find the men who'd killed Patrick, but they also needed to unravel the drug ring that had given him his GG249 Xanax pills.

The Violent Crimes Unit started by investigating Patrick's dying claim that "Jordan Piacente and Dollar Tee robbed me." Jordan Piacente had an alibi—she'd flown up to New York that morning for a wedding—so detectives began looking for "Dollar Tee." Less than an hour after the murder, they found a teacher at an all-girls prep school down the street from 97 Smith who said that she'd seen three Black men running out of Patrick's house looking like they'd "robbed a bank" in a movie. The witness taught art classes and prided herself on her sense of detail, and she remembered that one of the men carried an open carton of Marlboro cigarettes, another ran so fast he nearly overshot the car, and a third had high cheekbones and a "more attractive than average" face. They all got into a "sporty little red Jetta," and one of them shouted, "Go! Go! Go!" While the Volkswagen drove away, the witness made sure to note its green and white dealer license plate, which had the word "Time" on it. After the car turned off Smith Street, she looked up at Patrick's house and saw a white male in a blue polo looking down from the second-floor window, but he never came outside.

After some internet research, detectives concluded that the license plate came from DriveTime Used Cars on the other side of the Ashley River. That evening an officer visited the dealership, and he searched the DriveTime books for red Volkswagens bought recently enough to use temporary dealer plates. He found one car that fit the description, a red 2014 Jetta that a twenty-one-year-old named Charles Mungin III had purchased three weeks before. Police dispatch put out a "BOLO" (Be On Lookout) for the Jetta, describing Mungin as a five-foot-eleven "Black male with dreadlocks" weighing approximately 160 pounds.

At eleven p.m., a Charleston PD sergeant and another patrolman saw a red Jetta with a temporary plate on Tripe and Main Street, west of the Ashley River. After the car parked in a quiet, overgrown corner of the Ashleyville subdivision, the patrolmen watched a man with dreadlocks leave the driver's seat and walk toward the trunk. The officers approached him, and when they looked into the car window they saw "marijuana located within plain-view." They arrested Mungin for marijuana possession and had his car towed downtown for crime scene investigation. Officers searched the VW, but besides FAFSA student loan paperwork and some generic Wellbutrin, the interior was mostly clean. Then investigators removed the driver's seat and pulled up the floor mats, and they found seven white GG249 Xanax pills wedged into the railing. Two weeks later, after GPS records showed Mungin's Jetta outside 97 Smith Street at 3:45 p.m. on March 4, and after Patrick's phone contacts showed Mungin saved as "Tee," the Charleston PD had an arrest to broadcast on the local news.

From one point of view, the Violent Crimes Unit had made quick work of their murder investigation. With Charles Mungin in custody, the homicide detectives could spend the following months piecing together surveillance evidence and finding a motive before his case went to trial. Although they continued to look for the other men in the red Jetta, they didn't arrest Jordan Piacente, and they felt confident enough to let Patrick's housemates leave for spring break in Puerto Rico.

Still, the Moffly case wasn't a self-contained murder investigation. If it had been, it wouldn't have led the police to Mikey Schmidt. But after officers found GG249 tablets around Patrick's body and in Mungin's car, they decided to follow the trail of Xanax pills to its source. This narcotics investigation had a head start, because Patrick Gill had been exploring the college drug market for five months already. In late 2015, Detective Gill had started working a drug tip about a Citadel cadet named Jake Poeschek. Jake was the son of Rudy "Pot Pie" Poeschek, one of the great fistfighters in NHL history. Jake had enrolled in the Citadel in 2012, and in the fall of 2015 he sold a banned substance to one of Gill's informants. In November the Special Investigations Unit raided Poeschek's girlfriend's apartment and discovered false-bottom Arizona ice tea cans; a snorting straw; and enough cocaine, marijuana, and Xanax for a few "possession with intent to distribute" charges. From there, Detective Gill turned the screws on Jake Poeschek—charging his girlfriend for possession and Jake for dealing within half a mile of a public park—until Jake opened up about the boy who'd supplied him. After that, Gill gave Poeschek the confidential informant nickname "Buddha" and started investigating Zackery Kligman.

When detectives learned that one of Patrick's housemates had signed a lease to a rental at 43 Gadsden Street, Detective Gill already knew the address well. It was Zack's Treehouse. Thanks to Buddha and other college informants, Gill had been monitoring Zack since Christmas break, when the Charleston PD had installed a camera on the telephone lines above Gadsden Street. One source had also mentioned that Zack had some unnamed "ego issues" with a local skater named Patrick Moffly, but Gill had lacked the resources to chase the lead. Up until March 4, Gill's low-budget investigation had led only to Jake Poeschek's possession charges, and the Treehouse surveillance camera hadn't revealed anything yet. After Patrick died, though, the department made college narcotics a new priority. As Sergeant Todd Hurteau, who co-led the operation with Gill, told me, "There was no real concrete case at first. They did have some surveillance that was put up, but really what spearheaded this whole thing was the Moffly murder. . . . We were asked to find who was distributing this stuff throughout the city, because there was now a homicide."

The evening Patrick died, the Special Investigations Unit filed a Treehouse search warrant. Pulling up across the street from the Gaillard-Bennett House, they hoped for a major seizure. Gill's informants had told him they'd seen five to ten pounds of weed, up to one kilogram of coke, and as many as "one million pills" at Zack's stash house. Patrick's death hadn't been broadcast on the local news yet, and Gill had reason to believe that Kligman might not have known to move those supplies. But when they walked inside they found only drug residue and an Extra Space Storage lock. Defeated, Gill's team returned to the office and watched the day's footage from their hidden camera. At 4:10 that afternoon, only twenty minutes after Patrick's housemates had called 911, Zack Kligman had walked up to the Treehouse carrying pizza boxes. At 4:30 a car had backed into the driveway, and Zack had gotten in with his boxes and left.

✦ ✦ ✦

Once they were back from Puerto Rico, Patrick's housemates shared more of what they knew about GG249 pills. None of the housemates told Gill about their years of dealing Xanax or the two bags hidden in their neighbor's trash can, but one did admit to selling Patrick the ten thousand bars he'd been killed with. Another explained how Zack knew to clean out the Treehouse twenty minutes after Patrick was shot. One of the 97 Smith boys, a C of C senior whom Detective Gill nicknamed "Fireball," admitted that he'd told Kligman about the murder before the police had even arrived at 97 Smith Street. When Fireball had seen Patrick bleeding on the floor, he'd texted Zack the phrase "move your clothes." This admission, combined with the signed Treehouse lease in Fireball's room, gave Gill enough leverage to convince Fireball to increase his cooperation.

On March 30, Detective Gill put a recording device in Fireball's front pocket and sent him to the Treehouse to meet Zack. Because they were moving out at the end of the month, Fireball had offered to help Zack clean the house. On the drive, he listened to "Famous" off Kanye West's *The Life of Pablo*, and when he walked into the house, Zack gave him a cheerful "Dude, how you been man?" Fireball responded that it had been one of the most depressing months of his life, and Zack agreed that March had moved by slowly. While they swept the trash and talked through the logistics of boxing everything up, Zack gave Fireball his theory as to who killed Spilly, adding,

"Patrick was really hanging out with a bunch of thugs." Zack pointed out some cocaine powder and an old green Xanax tablet still on the floor and thanked Fireball for giving him a heads-up after the killing. "I had a brick of blow, a hundred thousand dollars, and like twenty to forty pounds of weed, plus a bunch of money here. So yeah, [another 97 Smith housemate] texting me saved lives." Fireball chuckled and said, "Good shit," and they dapped each other up. After that, Zack went "Fucking right!" and Fireball responded, "We gotta move on, baby." Once they'd discussed a future Xanax deal and finished moving boxes, Fireball said, "Later bro," and Zack told him "Peace."

Fireball listened to the rest of Kanye's "Famous" on the drive back to Gill, and then he played 2 Chainz's "Rolls Royce Weather Every Day." He handed the recording device to the SIU operatives, but the audio mostly just confirmed what Gill's team already knew. What had begun as a one-man campus investigation had grown into a thirty-person task force, with liaisons representing the South Carolina Law Enforcement Division and the Drug Enforcement Administration. These men had tracked Zack Kligman for all of March. Consulting FBI surveillance and the US Postal Service inspectors, Gill's team had a sense of Zack's mail order supply chain, and their in-person surveillance had revealed Zack's Cadillac's routes from north of campus to around the Low Country. The Special Investigations Unit had gone through Zack's phone records and arrest reports, and they'd developed a new informant code-named "Jena Clark," who'd heard from Zack's girlfriend that Kligman had moved his Treehouse narcotics to a rental storage unit across the Ashley River. Because Gill's people had found an Extra Space lock during their Treehouse search warrant, they visited the dozen Extra Space facilities around greater Charleston.

Five days after the murder, one of Gill's operatives drove to the Ashleyville Extra Space off Highway 61. The facility backs into the overgrown corner of Tripe and Main Street, and the officer had an employee pull the security footage from the day of Patrick's murder. At 5:02 p.m. on March 4, about thirty minutes after Zack left the Treehouse with the pizza boxes, the camera showed him walking into Extra Space with a large plastic container. Zack took the elevator to a unit on the second floor, and when Gill's team subpoenaed Extra Space they learned that the unit had been leased by a boy named Daniel Katko. Jena Clark told Gill that Katko worked with Kligman. (Years later, an SAE dealer described Katko to me as "huge-gauge holes, super-baggy pants, big-ass Osiris skateboard shoes, a paintball jersey, and Gucci sunglasses. Just like, 'What? Can you please get in my house and leave really quick so nobody sees me?'") Tracking Katko's key card, Gill's team saw him use the storage locker every day from March 4 through March 18. In addition, the Extra Space cameras showed Kligman, Katko, and other boys carrying large boxes to and from the second floor at different points all month. When March ended, Gill's team sent an undercover operative to loiter in the parking lot and monitor the storage unit.

The first morning that Gill's man went to Ashleyville for "stationary and physical surveillance," a good chunk of the

Special Investigations Unit had to work the Cooper River Bridge Run kids' run. The annual charity event marked the beginning of April 2016, and SIU officers served as undercover guards for the Toddler Waddler and the 400-meter dash. Near the bounce castle, they heard from their Ashleyville operative that Daniel Katko had just used the second-floor Extra Space unit and driven away. Later, they learned that Zack Kligman had arrived outside Extra Space holding a large box. The officer watched Zack take the elevator past the second floor and up to the fourth, where he walked into a unit the Charleston PD didn't know he'd rented. After Zack left unit 4249 with two USPS boxes, the SIU sent an agent to follow him. He tailed Zack's Cadillac to a nearby post office, where he seized a box containing $25,000 in cash after Kligman dropped it off. Armed with this new information, Gill's team filed a search warrant for the second-floor unit and the previously unknown fourth-floor rental. When the kids' run ended, Gill's operatives drove west across town toward the Ashley River.

Gill's unit approached Extra Space at sunset. With the help of the Charleston County Metro Major Case Unit, which had jurisdiction in Ashleyville, they carried their warrant inside and up to the second floor. They walked down the concrete hallway and cut the lock to unit 2049, and when they pulled up the door they itemized the mess. Among other things, the officers' report lists USB sticks and laptops, notebooks and ledgers, pressure cookers with green residue and spoons with white residue, a hollowed-out book, and two firearms. One of the guns was a black Springfield Armory XD-EM Elite compact pistol, with two loaded magazines and a laser sight, and the other was a black Mossberg International assault rifle. The Mossberg was a semiautomatic tactical weapon with the ballistic form factor of an AR-15. Zack had bought a Tac-D .22-millimeter grenade launcher to attach to its barrel as an accessory. Short of a few precursor chemicals and 101 grams of alprazolam powder, though, the space didn't reveal any drugs.

After that, the search team went upstairs and cut the lock to unit 4249, which was cleaner than the second-floor unit. Past the metal door, the officers found a brown box, a large plastic container, and three Priority Mail envelopes. They opened the container and saw thousands of ziplock bags. One of the bags held 27 grams of cocaine, and a few thousand others held a few hundred GG249 bars each. After sorting through the ziplocks, they listed their seizure as 6,947.62 grams of alprazolam, which, by a math of 2 milligrams per pill, comes out to about 3.5 million Xanax bars.

At 9:56 that night, twenty-eight days after Patrick's murder, Gill's team arrested Zack Kligman on US Route 17 and drove him to his house north of campus. Using a K-9 team for a "narcotics sniff," they found 25 grams of MDMA and 169.49 grams of Xanax powder in a backpack next to the TV, in addition to a black 9 mm handgun in the nightstand by the couch. Around midnight, they took Zack to Charleston police headquarters to book him for a historic one-boy seizure: two pistols, a laser sight, a black Cadillac CTS, 27 grams of cocaine, 25 grams of molly, a military-style assault rifle, an attachable grenade launcher, 169 grams of alprazolam powder, and 6,947.62 grams of alprazolam pills. The pills alone were worth seven figures wholesale, and retail they could yield eight.

Sitting across from Gill, Zack faced far worse charges than those resulting from his 2011 Mount Pleasant arrest, which had made him weep "I am so fucked" on the side of the highway, or the 2012 Georgia arrest for trafficking MDMA and possessing LSD, marijuana, and ketamine with intent to distribute. Still, he hadn't gone to prison for either of those charges, or for his 2013 flunitrazepam arrest in Myrtle Beach. Facing detectives in the interrogation room, Zack apologized and made the Charleston PD an offer. Kligman said there was a man above him in his pill press operation, and he promised to lead the Special Investigations Unit to him. After Zack gave a proffer about Eric Hughes's pill press operation, Gill gave him the codename "Mr. Sorry" and sent him out to work as an informant.

The Special Investigations Unit went to bed around four a.m. that night, and they woke up at five a.m. to work the Cooper River Bridge Run adult run. Over the next few days, though, they realized they'd made a clerical error. By the time they'd agreed to catch and release Zack Kligman, they'd already booked him and published his mug shot online. Zack was listed with an April 2 "TRAF COCAINE" charge on websites like SouthCarolina.arrests.org, which people like Eric Hughes checked nearly every day. Eric had been paranoid enough after Patrick Moffly's death to move his operation from South Carolina to Georgia, and when he read about Zack's arrest he cut Kligman off completely. Eric wasn't answering Zack's calls, which meant the Charleston PD or the DEA couldn't set up a "controlled buy" between Eric and Zack or discover the location of Eric's Georgia beach house. Facing potential charges for cocaine, MDMA, Xanax, and possession of a weapon during a violent crime, Zack needed to inform on boys who didn't know to check online mug shot databases.

During one of Zack's first recorded calls with Rob Liljeberg, Gill's people turned on *Impractical Jokers* to make Zack sound like he was casually watching TV. In the episode "Strip High Five," two of the Jokers have to ask random pedestrians for high fives, and for every stranger who doesn't give them one, the Jokers have to remove an item of clothing. While the men stripped down and their friends yelled "Take it off!" Zack dialed Rob's number. Zack had admitted to Gill that he'd sold ten thousand Xanax bars a week to Rob and received coke from Rob's source in Atlanta, and now Gill wanted Zack to set up a cocaine handoff. When Rob answered, Zack told him "yooo" and said he had a player in Columbia who needed coke by Tuesday. If some boys thought Zack talked like a "try-hard," his voice didn't quiver when he discussed the pound of "ye" he wanted to buy. Before they hung up, Rob agreed to have the delivery by the end of the week.

Of course, thanks to the pledge drivers' schedules and Mikey dropping his phone twenty stories, Gill had to wait three weeks for Zack's delivery from Rob. Finally, on the morning of April 22, the Special Investigations Unit met Zack at a lot near the

Citadel and rigged his Cadillac with a camera and a micro-phone. The lens faced down from the roof, and when Zack drove toward 7 Montagu the camera showed his head bob-bing while the shadows of trees rolled over his lap. When he arrived, he called Rob and said "I'm pullin' up right now," and when he parked, the hidden camera and mic captured every moment of the handoff. Gill's people could hear Zack telling Rob that he'd been afraid that Rob was "getting fucked over" by his source in Atlanta, and they could see Rob emptying his drawstring bag onto the floor. After Kligman told him "Dude I appreciate you" and drove away, he spoke into the microphone, "I got it. It's inside this popcorn bag in my car."

Within the hour, Gill's team seized Rob Liljeberg and led him to their unmarked car. Once they reached police head-quarters on the western edge of downtown, Gill left Rob alone in an interrogation room to stew. Rob sat there in his Dri-Fit shirt and midcalf socks, resting his elbows on his knees and his forehead in his hands. At one point he balled his fists and stretched them above his head and went "oooooowwh." At an-other point an officer came inside to say, "I ain't gonna preach to you. I'm not your dad. I've got friends who are still in jail for doing shit like this when they were your age. You know what I mean? I've got friends who are dead. You've just gotta get smart from here on out." Later, Gill returned and sat down. He was still dressed in his undercover clothes—blue jeans, white polo, long hair tucked behind his ears like the golfer Tommy Fleetwood—and he set a pen and notepad on the table. Rob had been offered an attorney and declined, and now he folded his hands like he was praying. Because of mandatory minimum sentencing laws in South Carolina, Rob was facing twenty-five years in prison without parole, and it was up to him to negotiate with Gill, who wanted to know where he'd gotten his cocaine.

One night last summer I told some of my oldest friends about the dilemma Rob faced when Patrick Gill asked him to inform on Mikey Schmidt. We were on a rooftop bar overlooking a river, and when one of them asked what I was working on, I told him how the College of Charleston Kappa Alpha president had worn a wire on his best friend to limit his own prison time. Two of the boys on the roof had been Kappa Alphas themselves, and the third took the rules of male bonding just as seriously, and I expected them all to say something like, "Damn dude, that's fucked." Instead, one former KA said, "Max, I love you, but I'd never go to jail for you." I thought about that for a while and realized that I'd inform on him too. We talked it through, and everyone at the table agreed that if we ever got arrested for, say, insider trading, we'd flip on anyone but our immediate family if it kept us out of prison. Someone suggested that anyone who wants to die on the cross for more than their relatives has a messiah complex, and another said, "You can't spell 'frat' without 'rat.'" So as narratively satisfying as it would be to paint Rob Liljeberg as a special kind of traitor, I should admit that I would've flipped on my bros too.

Anyway, that's what Rob did. Sitting down for a full interview under the code name "Hunter Thompson," Rob made a proffer in the hope that Gill would help dismiss his charges. Hunter told the Charleston PD that he got his cocaine from Mikey Schmidt, who got his cocaine from his "uncle" in a gated community in Atlanta. Rob also gave up Mikey's clients at C of C, a group that included KAs, GDIs, and boys in other fraternities. He listed the names and addresses of a half dozen other Kappa Alpha dealers and reported that Mikey's operation stretched to UGA, USC, Clemson, and Ole Miss. After Rob led Gill to a few KA dealers' Facebook profiles, he gave the detective a year of text messages with Mikey, which Mikey had mostly deleted but Rob had not. Those texts had plenty of incriminating material already, but he continued to text Mikey for the next week, calling his friend his "massa" and coaxing out more statements of guilt while acting guilty himself over the money Kligman hadn't paid. Starting that night, Rob also set up recorded phone calls with Mikey, talking about cocaine they'd sold and money they'd laundered through their fraternity. And when Rob finally talked Mikey into driving to Charleston from Atlanta, he wore a wire to the rooftop bar at The Vendue hotel. After that, Gill allowed him to walk during College of Charleston commencement and accept his diploma by hand.

In the days after graduation, the police booked Mikey and two other C of C dealers. Gill saw Mikey as the most important name on his corkboard, but his team also used Kligman's information to book two SAEs. First they arrested SAE socialite Russell Sliker for two counts of Xanax distribution, and then they came for SAE bodybuilder Ben Nauss. Five days after

Mikey's arrest, Ben came home from the gym and took off his shirt in his living room. Sitting by the TV with his meal-prepped spaghetti, he heard a knock on his door. Through his blinds he saw a cluster of SWAT officers holding assault rifles. While the battering ram started, Ben ran up the stairs and toward his room, where he had a vault that contained four pounds of marijuana, 90 milliliters of anabolic steroids, and a few hundred of his alprazolam pills. While the officers smashed into his living room and approached the stairs, Ben grabbed a plastic sandwich bag of pills and took it up to the roof. Stepping into the 90 degree heat, he wound up and threw the Xanax bag into the sunshine, and only as the projectile left his hand did he realize he'd never sealed it. The plastic bag exploded in the air like a skeet, and before he went downstairs to get tackled and cuffed, he watched the GG249 pills rain back down onto the street.

CHAPTER 15

SOME CONSEQUENCES

Because his mom had to be at work in Georgia and the judge wouldn't let him leave South Carolina, Mikey spent most of the summer alone at the Kiawah Island Golf Resort. He woke up every morning at his family's beach condo, where he smoked weed and Marlboro Ultra Lights and looked at the coastal foliage. He was a five-iron shot from the Turtle Point Golf Course and a cart ride from the island's four other courses, and he played eighteen holes more or less every day. Mikey could drive it 260 yards off the tee, and when he didn't break his clubs on his knee he had a nice short game. When he finished playing Turtle Point, which was designed by Jack Nicklaus, he walked to the Sanctuary Lobby Bar, where he talked to older women. Some nights he passed out in the sand, and one morning he woke up to a screaming call from his stepfather about a $5,000 bar tab. Another evening Mikey walked drunk into an ice cream shop wearing aviators and no shirt, and while he ate two scoops of cake batter he looked at the TV and saw himself on the news. A reporter was broadcasting live from Charleston police headquarters, where the department had just announced one of the largest narcotics busts in city history. The first name on its press release was "Michael Schmidt, 21, of Shadow Glen Court, Atlanta, GA."

At Chief Mullen's June 8 press conference, his officers arranged their seizures on long tables. They stacked plastic bags of coke and weed, laid out a buffet of Xanax and "Green Hulk" pills, zip-tied seven firearms into cardboard boxes, and enlarged a picture of $214,161 in bills for the TV above the podium. They charged the KAs—Mikey Schmidt, Rob Liljeberg, and Jonathan Reams—with cocaine trafficking, marijuana possession with intent to distribute, and possession of synthetic marijuana pills, and they booked SAE Russell Sliker for Xanax distribution and SAE Ben Nauss for possession of marijuana with intent to distribute and possession of Xanax. Kligman's associate Daniel Katko faced six different charges for distributing or trafficking four different drugs, and the Citadel cadet Jake Poeschek and his girlfriend faced four counts including Xanax possession and "Possession of Cocaine with the intent to Distribute within Close Proximity to Park/Playground." Zack Kligman, on the other hand, was charged for possessing 27 grams of cocaine but not for his assault weapons, marijuana, MDMA, and benzodiazepines. While the Charleston Police Department spread the other boys' drugs on the tables, they never mentioned the 6,947.62 grams of alprazolam they'd seized.

After the C of C arrests, Zack wasn't charged for the millions of Xanax pills in his Extra Space locker. When I filed a Freedom of Information Act request for documents, the department's packet didn't include any mention of the seizure. After I obtained the original affidavit describing the 6,947.62 grams of Xanax, though, Sergeant Todd Hurteau and Captain Andre Jenkins confirmed the magnitude of what they'd found in Zack's locker. The officers said the pills had been bagged up by the hundreds in small ziplock bags, and when I asked why local and federal authorities had decided not to press charges against Zack, Sergeant Hurteau told me, "That's something I don't necessarily want to comment on." When I pressed, Captain Jenkins said, "That comes from a lot of different things. The amount of cooperation he gave, what he was found with, a lot of other things involved."

Regardless, Chief Mullen didn't need to announce that his officers had confiscated fourteen million dosage units of benzodiazepines for their press conference to succeed. On the City of Charleston Police Department's Facebook page, one social media user commented: "Wow! 43,000 pills? I work in a narcotic vault, and I'm pretty sure I don't stock that many pills! Good job!" The boys' drugs and mug shots still ran on the local news after the NBA Finals, including on the TV in the restaurant where Ben Nauss had been bartending. Two weeks later, the Charleston *Post and Courier* published an investigative deep dive titled "Cocaine, Pills . . . and Textbooks" about a "network of present and former College of Charleston students and other 20-somethings accused of funneling hundreds of thousands of dollars of cocaine, pills and other narcotics into downtown's white-hot party scene." The New York *Daily News* picked up the story, as did the progressive news aggregator *The Raw Story*, which ran the headline "Criming while White: Frat Bros Ran Massive Campus Drug Dealing Operation—Right in Plain Sight."

The same week as Mullen's press conference, the New York *Daily News* ran another item about the extended college narcotics network. In May 2016, Bradley Felder, the Clemson baseball star who'd allegedly sold molly and Xanax to C of C Sigma Nus and impressed Mikey with his rose gold Yacht-Master at a strip club, had pled guilty to federal drug charges. After he'd left Clemson and failed a tryout with the Atlanta Braves, Felder had joined the Hendrick Motorsports NASCAR pit crew, where he'd used his arm strength and foot speed to carry seventy-five-pound tires faster than a normal mechanic could. During a work trip to California, he'd met a man named Curly who offered to sell him marijuana in bulk. After local Missouri police found sixty pounds of weed in Brad's truck, and after South Carolina law enforcement seized another thirty pounds he'd shipped from San Francisco, and after these cases petered out in local courts, the DEA opened a case on him. When agents intercepted nine packages from China holding nearly twenty kilograms of MDMA crystal, they decided to raid his parents' dairy farm in Bowman, South Carolina. Out in the pasture, in a freshly stirred plot of dirt, they dug up a waterproof bag holding $1,768,031 in cash. Brad admitted to trafficking thousands of pounds of marijuana and over forty kilograms of MDMA over the previous four years. The *Daily News* wrote, "The field of dreams for one former college baseball player-turned-drug dealer has gone up in smoke."

An hour north of the Bowman dairy farm, another sting began when a University of South Carolina student complained that the weed smell in her apartment hall gave her a headache. After two Columbia PD officers sniffed around the cracks of a storage unit, they called in a warrant and discovered one hundred grams of hash oil, an AR-15 rifle, Aczone topical acne medication, stacks of USPS Priority Mail boxes, two Tec-9 submachine guns, and 29,139 GG249 Xanax pills. The pills and guns belonged to Matt Garnett, a USC fraternity kid whose father was the president of the National Bank of South Carolina. When they arrested Matt his nose was scabbed from a bar fight, and when they booked him they learned he'd worked with Patrick Moffly, Zackery Kligman, and Eric Hughes. The arrest was another step toward charging Hughes, whom the DEA had tracked to a beach house in Tybee Island, Georgia. Agents watched Hughes's pill press operation from a distance until the following summer, when Eric drove a thirty-two-inch toolbox full of pressed Xanax bars down a Georgia highway and smashed into a tow truck hitched to a boat. While Eric's car flipped several times, a few hundred thousand white pills spilled onto the road. Federal investigators arrested him a few days after he left the hospital, and when they raided his beach house they found his employees trying and failing to clean up the alprazolam dust.

After summer break 2016, two representatives from Kappa Alpha nationals traveled to Charleston to host a mandatory meeting. Facing a room of forty or so C of C KAs, the men from Mulberry Hill told the boys that they were launching a membership review. To apply to stay in the fraternity, each brother had to sit for a one-on-one interview, turn in his College of Charleston transcript, and submit a hair follicle for a drug test. The process took about a week, and according to one of the surviving KAs, about 90 percent of the boys failed some part of the review. When I asked him what the follicle exam tested for, he said, "If they were looking for weed, I wouldn't have made it." (An attorney for the KA national organization stated that the drug screen "tested for a wide range of legal and illegal drugs" and that "[d]etails of that drug screen, both individually and collectively, have been discarded consistent with [KA's] document retention policy and privacy concerns.")

After that, the Interfraternity Council and Mulberry Hill invited the remaining brothers to campus and asked them to keep the chapter alive, but the boys didn't want to belong to a ten-person fraternity, and they voted to shut C of C KA down. When the college publicized its decision, *Total Frat Move*'s Bogey Wells published a eulogy: "Writing about the closure of a chapter is right at the top of my list of the shittiest aspects of this job. . . . While I cannot make any judgment on the merits of the removal of the College of Charleston Kappa Alpha chapter, any chapter that has survived 112 years is truly a historic treasure to lose."

Kappa Alpha wasn't the first College of Charleston fraternity to close that semester. The Alpha Epsilon Pis lost their charter at the end of August, three days after they hosted a 130-person Bid Day darty with strippers and a waterslide. At the day party, according to police records, an AEPi brother pulled a drunk seventeen-year-old freshman by the arm to a bedroom, where he locked the door, made her keep drinking and try cocaine for the first time, took her clothes off, and ordered her to perform "sex acts" while another AEPi took photos. (The AEPi photographer sent a picture to a friend, who texted back, "Ewwww. Who is she." The photographer responded, "Lol random drunk chick that was in my room for some reason.") AEPi nationals closed the chapter three days later, and President McConnell announced a fraternity and sorority alcohol ban the next week, right after the *Princeton Review* named C of C one of the twenty top party schools in America. The shutdowns continued into October, when the college suspended the Sigma Nus for "allegations involving alcohol, drugs and hazing," and in April, when they suspended the Betas for hazing with "personal servitude and calisthenics." The college lost a fifth chapter before the end of the year, after a Pi Kappa Phi punched a new member for flirting with his ex-girlfriend. Following the punch, another Pi Kapp called out the puncher on their "Shotcallerz OG" Facebook group, writing: "We will get 80 bros behind us to bury you fucking queer. . . . you are the biggest pussy to step foot on planet earth." After the puncher went to bed that night, according to a later-filed lawsuit, four of his fellow Pi Kapps broke into his house, ripped his door off the hinges, turned over his washing and drying machines, broke his ribs, and allegedly beat him until he lost consciousness.

I remember wondering around then if fraternities would survive in America. It had been a rough four years for Greek life PR, from the "n——chant" at OU SAE to the hazing-related deaths of Peter Tran at San Francisco State Lambda Phi Epsilon, Michael Deng at Baruch Pi Delta Psi, Armando Villa at Cal State Pi Kapp, Tucker Hipps at Clemson Sig Ep, Nolan Burch at West Virginia Kappa Sig, Trevor Duffy at Albany ZBT, Ryan Abele at UN Reno Sigma Nu, Tim Piazza at Penn State Beta, Maxwell Gruver at LSU Phi Delt, and Andrew Coffey at Florida State Pi Kapp. Plaintiff's attorneys were suing fraternities for sexual assaults and personal injuries at record rates, and outlets like MSNBC and *The Atlantic* were calling to abolish or radically transform the whole system. One *Bloomberg* investigation discovered over one hundred fraternities that were "shut down, suspended, or otherwise punished" during 2015's spring semester alone, and on Wednesday, March 18, 2015, *USA Today* ran these three headlines: "U. of South Carolina Fraternity Suspended after Student Death," "Wisconsin Frat Booted for Hazing New Members with Food Deprivation, Forced Drinking," and "Party's Over for Frat after Ski-Resort Rampage."

By the C of C bust in the spring of 2016, it was getting harder to ignore the ways other people looked at bros. The word itself was now a vague insult, like "finance bro" or "Bernie bro." When other university students talked about fraternities, they were less likely to even say "bro" and more likely to use such phrases as "institutional racism," "rape culture," "toxic masculinity," or "fuck the patriarchy." For a group of guys used to being the heroes of stories, this was a cold plunge. If bros saw themselves as kings or jesters, other people now saw them as villains. No one wanted to hear about philanthropy drives when fraternities went viral for Confederate uniforms or sexual assaults, and no one saw fraternity life as a National Lampoon comedy when they read about narcotrafficking and dead freshmen. (In the fall of 2016, Nick Jonas starred in a sort of anti–*Animal House* fraternity drama called *Goat*, in which fraternity brothers traumatized their pledges and pelted a boy to death with rotten fruit. The movie's slogan was "Cruelty. Brutality. Fraternity.") In the rapidly heating political climate, it was hard to imagine mostly white, mostly rich, all-male pleasure mansions surviving more bad press. The November election was approaching and Confederate statues were coming down, and it seemed like America wanted bros to taste the consequence of a life without consequences.

Thanks to British colonial style, South Carolina calls its criminal court the "Court of General Sessions" and its attorneys general "solicitors." After Patrick Moffly's homicide and Mikey Schmidt's arrest, the Charleston solicitor assigned one managing assistant solicitor to prosecute the entire C of C drug network. The same lawyer, Stephanie Linder, would try the nine suspects named in Chief Mullen's press conference and the two men charged in the Moffly homicide. Linder, who often prosecuted gangs and sometimes handled federal cases as a special assistant US attorney, would spend much of the next four years working on the C of C trials. From her office downtown, she coordinated with local and federal agents and managed the web of informants who brought the cases together. Whenever she met the drug network's defense lawyers, she told them that she believed many of their clients had never been checked by anyone in their lives, and she had no interest in handing out suspended sentences.

Even compared with the other boys, Mikey knew he'd struggle against Linder. Although the police hadn't found any narcotics when they'd searched his apartments and cars, Mikey had admitted to selling cocaine and Xanax over his texts and calls with Rob and his wire recording on The Vendue hotel roof. In addition, Rob and Jonathan Reams had agreed to testify against Mikey if his case went to trial. With his friends volunteering to speak against him, Mikey found himself in the most dangerous place on the college drug informant food pyramid. While Zackery Kligman could admit that he got his cocaine from Rob without fear of violence, and Rob and Reams could admit that they got their cocaine from Mikey without fear of violence, Mikey couldn't tell Linder the name of his cartel-linked Atlanta cocaine sources and reasonably hope to survive. Unlike fraternity drug dealers, Mikey's Atlanta contacts might actually kill an informant, so he had to turn to Tim Kulp for other legal strategies.

Instead of cooperating with Stephanie Linder, Kulp hoped to analyze and attack the rest of her docket. His plan was to find bits of evidence that jeopardized Linder's other cases until she felt inclined to offer Mikey a plea deal. He described this plan as "hitting the cases in the stomach everywhere I can. 'Body blow, body blow, body blow,' until finally I hit something that's really sensitive." Sitting with Mikey under Kulp's mounted eight-point buck, which had lost the 2009 regional biggest buck contest by one pound, Kulp believed the way to pressure the assistant managing solicitor was to focus on Zackery Kligman.

After reading through hundreds of discovery files, Kulp realized that most of Linder's cases owed their life to "Mr. Sorry." Thanks to Kligman's proffer interviews and controlled buys, Linder had the evidence she needed for trials against Rob Liljeberg, Jonathan Reams, Russell Sliker, Ben Nauss, and Mikey Schmidt. But if the police were supposed to use informants to build cases up the ladder toward the people in charge, here they let a trafficker near the top inform on five dealers below him. Looking at the hundreds of thousands of dollars of narcotics that the other boys had been charged with, and comparing it with the millions of dollars of narcotics that Kligman had never been charged with or publicly linked to, Kulp found something to attack. He filed motions asking the solicitor's office for evidence about Zack's prior arrests, and he shared Kligman's 6,947.62 grams of Xanax with journalists like me. But the heart of Kulp's campaign drew on the investigative skills he'd honed briefly working for the FBI in Miami during the late 1970s. Mikey told Kulp that he'd heard a theory that Zackery Kligman had been involved in Patrick Moffly's homicide, and Kulp saw a few reasons to ask if it was true.

To Kulp's eye, Kligman had a reason for wanting Patrick Moffly dead. According to the Moffly family themselves, Patrick had been arrested trafficking Zack Kligman's cocaine at a Gamecocks football tailgate. The Columbia solicitor's office had almost certainly promised to ease Patrick's fifteen-to-thirty-year sentence if he told them where he'd gotten his drugs, which meant informing on the Kligman network. During these meetings, Patrick had used his parents' lawyer and denied Zack's alleged request to control his legal defense, a decision that left Patrick so afraid that he'd hidden on his parents' farm for a month. He'd returned to campus on March 3 and he'd been murdered the next day, one month before he was supposed to go to trial. Of course, Zack didn't fit the description of any of the three men who sprinted toward the red Jetta after the shooting, but Kulp believed that Kligman had the means and the motivation to set up a hit. Not only did Zack sit near the top of a multimillion-dollar narcotics operation, but according to David and Elizabeth Moffly, Patrick had said he was afraid of what Zack might do to him.

To undermine a key informant against them, Kulp and Mikey set up their own gumshoe Kligman investigation. Mikey listened for any information about Zack that his friends heard on King Street, and he also used Google to research Albert Kligman, a Pennsylvania dermatologist who'd tested prisoners with Agent Orange during the 1950s and '60s and who probably wasn't related to the Myrtle Beach Kligmans. In the meantime, Kulp traveled around town with a 191-page black Shinola hard linen journal. In the center of one page he wrote KLIGMAN in black ink, circled the name in orange, and drew more than twenty different arrows toward the names of different associates and girlfriends. In his spare time, he poured through the Kligman family's property holdings and went on his own surveillance missions, staking out Zack's house north of campus from a friend's place across the street. When he saw Kligman walk outside with what Kulp remembers as a labradoodle, he called Mikey. "He's a dog guy?" Mikey didn't know Zack personally, but he said he'd heard that Kligman kept a pet with him to throw off K-9 units that tried to sniff his Cadillac.

Without the power to compel any witnesses, Tim and Mikey could learn only so much. Kulp asked the Charleston Violent Crimes Unit to look deeper into Zackery Kligman, but the police had every reason to focus on convicting Charles Mungin III and finding the other men who'd run into his Jetta. The detectives continued to build their surveillance case against Mungin, who refused to cooperate, and in early 2017 they tracked down one of his passengers. Presented with a lineup, a 97 Smith Street housemate identified a twenty-two-year-old named John "Jonny" Glover as the man he'd seen walking into Patrick's bathroom before the gunshot. After another witness corroborated the ID, the police had a second arrest to broadcast on the local news. Talking to the press, the Charleston PD explained the homicide as a "drug robbery gone wrong." They'd learned that Patrick had texted Charles Mungin on the morning of March 4, saying, "Looks like I'll be here if you need anything. I broke my arm in 4 places so I can't go on the snowboarding trip." Mungin had responded, "U got 10,000 bars?" The detectives believed that Mungin, Glover, and another, as-yet unidentified man had driven to Smith Street planning to rob the dealer with the broken arm, and when Patrick fought back they'd shot him and fled. This version made sense for a few reasons: the torn bag of pills, the commotion going down the stairs, the shared belief among friends and family that Patrick was the kind of person to fight three people with a broken arm. It also explained why the men shot Patrick at the foot of the stairs instead of in his bedroom, and it accounted for the lack of evidence that Kligman and Mungin knew one another. Still, the "robbery gone wrong" narrative didn't satisfy Mikey, Kulp, or the people in Patrick's life who'd repeatedly told the police that they should investigate Zack.

Before the trauma surgeons had even declared Patrick dead, Patrick's friends and family had started asking the Charleston PD to look into Kligman. When I visited the Moffly farm on Paradise Island, David Moffly told me that he'd alerted officers during Patrick's surgery that his son had a cocaine trafficking trial coming up, and that he'd spent the last month at home afraid of Kligman. Sarah Moffly told me she'd arrived at the hospital a few minutes later, and when a detective had asked her if anyone had wanted Patrick dead, she'd said, "the Charleston Kingpin," a nickname for Zack that the officer already knew.

When I talked to Patrick's friend Summer McNairy, she said that she'd told officers twice that she believed Zackery Kligman had set Patrick up, and later a defense lawyer who represented one of Kligman's top associates told me that the client believed Zack had been involved in the shooting too. Over the next few years, David Moffly called the detectives several times to remind them that Patrick had expressed fears that Zack might come after him. According to David, one detective responded, "We're familiar with Kligman, but he's not the guy."

Later, when I found the unredacted Patrick Moffly homicide packet, the Charleston PD didn't mention any of these statements about Zack. The investigative files recapped the detectives' hospital interviews with David and Sarah Moffly and described their conversations with Patrick's friends, but they never mentioned anyone's suspicions about Zackery Kligman. Instead, officers focused on gathering as much information as they could about Charles Mungin III. When I asked Sergeant Todd Hurteau whether he ever considered Kligman a suspect in the Moffly homicide, he told me, "As far as I'm concerned, Zack's not a killer, from what I've learned with him. I can't say that with one hundred percent certainty, but I spent time with him enough."

When I arrived outside the Charleston courthouse in September 2019, I assumed the news trucks had come to follow Charles Mungin's homicide trial, but they were actually there to watch *Southern Charm*'s Thomas Ravenel plead guilty to sexual assault and battery on his nanny. Besides a few lawyers and me, the only visitors to courtroom 4C were Charles's and Patrick's family and friends. The dozen visitors on the left side of the pews could've been mistaken for a Black Baptist congregation with Sunday florals and wood canes, and the dozen on the right looked like white Presbyterians in khaki pants. The separation continued toward the bench, where the only nonwhite person among the lawyers, bailiffs, and judge was Mungin's defense attorney, Jason Mikell.

Mikell was known in the community for his work on DUI cases and smaller criminal charges. Several lawyers had told Charles's mother that it'd cost six figures to defend her son, but Mikell had charged $20,000 for a retainer and allowed her to pay in installments. He'd never tried a murder case before, and his plan centered on getting Charles a good plea deal. From the summer of 2016 to the fall of 2019, Mikell had negotiated with Stephanie Linder, doing what he could to escape the risk of a jury trial. During their conversations, he'd reminded Linder that Charles Mungin was a young man with no record of significance facing a case that relied solely on circumstantial evidence. Linder had started by offering Mungin twenty-five years in exchange for a guilty homicide plea, but after years of persuasion Mikell had gotten her down to ten years for voluntary manslaughter. Because a guilty charge in court would almost certainly mean life in prison, Mikell had left Linder's office feeling ecstatic, but when he'd told his client about the offer, Mungin had declined.

With the trial coming up, Mikell had gathered a half dozen people at the Berkeley County courthouse to ask Charles to take the deal. First, Mikell had enlisted a friendly judge for an off-the-record conversation that compared a ten-year manslaughter plea to an armed robbery and homicide conviction. Then the Moffly family lawyer had warned Mungin that the judge presiding over his case was known for handing out life sentences. After that, Mungin's mother, Evette, had taken Charles out to the hallway. Looking at her son, she'd said, "I know you didn't do it, God knows you didn't do it, but I need you to take the deal." Her oldest son had grown up a happy-go-lucky kid—his little cousin had once asked if he'd come out of the womb smiling—and Evette believed he hadn't lived enough to understand the justice system yet. "They want to put somebody in jail to close this case," she'd said. "You're Black, and if you don't have any money to hire somebody powerful to fight for you, then you can forget it. When they call this the Dirty South, they don't call it the Dirty South for nothing." Charles had told his mom and his grandmother he wasn't going to do any time for something he didn't do. Then he'd gone back inside and told his lawyer, "Mr. Mikell, I want you to know this about me: I'm a strong person."

When Charles Mungin III walked into the courtroom, his hair was tied in braids. He wore a button-down shirt, and his tie stopped above his belly button. His face looked almost tranquil, but his eyes didn't make contact with anyone. He sat next to Mikell, and after the judge warned the jury not to expect the "high drama, intense action, and riveting circumstances" of legal TV, Linder began her case against him. Over the next three days, she called more than thirty-five witnesses for the prosecution. The police had never found a murder weapon or a direct witness to the killing, so Linder retraced Charles Mungin's digital footprints instead. Through his text messages, Linder knew that Mungin had organized a ten-thousand-pill order with Patrick on the morning of March 4. Thanks to cell tower geolocation, she could suggest that Mungin drove around Charleston picking up accomplices while he delayed his meeting with Patrick. Pulling from security footage at the restaurants and prep schools near 97 Smith Street, she could hand out screenshots of a red Volkswagen Jetta approaching Patrick's house minutes before the murder. And citing data from something called a Spireon GPS auto tracking device, which sent Charles's location to the DriveTime dealership every time he started or stopped his car, Linder could map his trip around downtown Charleston. In addition, thanks to the recording devices inside jail phones, Linder was able to give the jury a transcript of a call in which Charles Mungin told his girlfriend, "Hey, make sure you tell granny, my mama, and all of them my name is Charles, because they're looking for a nickname. No Tee or Trey or nothing, just Charles."

As exhibit 9, Linder played Officer Jonathan Fowlkes's body camera footage from 97 Smith Street. The camera's dutch angle mostly shows Officer Fowlkes's legs and Patrick Moffly's feet, but the sound picked up Patrick's gurgling while he tried to speak. In the pew in front of me, Elizabeth Moffly had kept her posture straight all week, but when the screen played the video her back started to curl. While Patrick's legs laid still and the officer kicked him in the foot, Elizabeth said to herself,

"Kick my son one more time . . ." Near the end of the recording, when Officer Fowlkes asked who did this to him, the jury heard Patrick respond, "Jordan Piacente and Dollar Tee robbed me."

When the jurors walked into downtown for lunch, Linder and Mikell talked with the judge about Linder's next witness. To my surprise, the prosecution was going to call Jordan Piacente to testify. When the jurors returned, Piacente walked in alongside her own lawyer. When she stated her name, her voice was a half octave higher than Linder's. Piacente told the jury that she'd been friends with Patrick Moffly, and when Linder asked if she knew someone named "Tee," she said yes. Jordan added that she and Patrick had met "Tee" at the Silver Dollar bar on King Street in the fall of 2015, and she'd contacted Tee for Xanax a few times since then. When Linder asked if she'd heard from Tee the day Patrick died, Jordan admitted that he'd offered her "Zans for two a pop," and she'd responded, "Word, save some for me." Jordan added that she and Patrick sometimes called the Silver Dollar bar "the Dollar," and when Linder asked if she could identify Dollar Tee, she pointed at Charles Mungin.

When Linder finished, Jason Mikell stood up for his cross-examination. Walking toward the stand, he asked Jordan if she'd dated Patrick. After she said, "There were romantic gestures, but it wasn't a romantic relationship," he moved onto a short question about her own Xanax use. Mikell didn't push on her inconsistent alibis from the morning of Patrick's death—first she'd told police that she'd flown to New York for a wedding, and

then she'd told the jurors she'd gone for a cousin's baptism—
and he didn't give the jury many reasons to question her testimony. He didn't ask Jordan why she'd originally told the police
she didn't remember texting Charles Mungin on March 4, and
he didn't mention that her cell phone had fallen into the Atlantic Ocean before the DEA had a chance to look at it. Taking
a nonconfrontational approach, he never reminded the jurors
that "Jordan Piacente" are the first words in "Jordan Piacente
and Dollar Tee robbed me." Instead, he asked Jordan if she and
Patrick ever went to other bars besides the Silver Dollar. After she responded that they also went to Midtown and Public
House, she thanked the judge and left the courtroom with her
lawyer.

Linder rested her case at the end of the third day, and when
it was his turn, Mikell didn't call a witness. The next morning
they both presented their closing arguments. Before Linder recapped her case against Mungin, she told the jury about South
Carolina's "Hand of One, Hand of All" principle. Under this
legal doctrine, which is also the standard in federal court, any
accomplice to a robbery that leads to a murder is also considered guilty of that murder. To the South Carolina justice
system, Mungin didn't need to hold a gun or pull a trigger
to go to jail for the Moffly homicide; he just needed to have
set up the ten-thousand-pill robbery and driven the car. With
that in mind, Linder had only to remind the jurors to read
Mungin's texts and follow his red Jetta. After Linder finished,
Mikell focused on the legal principle of "beyond a reasonable
doubt," holding up a chart showing the gradations of burden

of proof. He asked whether anyone could trust the testimony of Patrick's housemates, and then we left the jury to deliberate.

Less than three hours later, the jury foreman announced the verdict. The bailiff cuffed Mungin's hands before his nose hit the table. Without his arms to shield his face, we all saw him lean on his forehead and weep. I do think the Mofflys got some of the closure they'd hoped for—they'd asked the judge for the maximum sentence, and that's what Charles received—but when the right side of the pews got up to leave, one of Patrick's family members looked back and said, "Now there have been two lives ended."

One month later I drove to Klig's Kites in Myrtle Beach. I understood why Zack Kligman and his lawyers refused to speak with me, but I wanted to see if I could at least talk to his father. I drove past a family-friendly wax museum and a spring-break-friendly tiki bar, but when I walked into the kite shop Zack's dad wasn't there. Before I drove back, I decided to take some notes on the gag gifts. I took pictures of rainbow kites and Confederate flags, and I found the plastic bum shorts he wore in his mooning videos. I filmed some rubber band guns shaped like AR-15s, and then I heard a voice humming along to the guitar solo from a live version of "Dazed and Confused." I looked in the next aisle and saw Zack Kligman sweeping the floor. He hadn't seen me yet, but I lost control of my breathing. I shut my eyes next to a four-foot cutout of Donald Trump giving two thumbs-up, and after I slowed my heart and pulled up Voice Memos on my phone I walked toward him. When I told Kligman that my name was Max, he said, "Yo, Max, how's it going?" and pulled me in for a hug.

Zack's jorts extended below his knees, and while he smiled his weight bounced from his right foot to his left. When I told him I was writing about the College of Charleston drug ring his grin went flat. He told me he didn't want his name or his family's business involved in the story, and when his body started to quiver he said, "Sorry, this shit has me shaking." He was still waiting on his trial against the state of South Carolina, and while his carotid artery pulsated he told me he didn't want to schedule an interview. "I mean the only thing I would say is just that I'm regretful. Very regretful. I'm also sad about what happened to Patrick. He was one of my best friends."

A little while later, Zack left midsentence and walked to the back of the store. Before that, though, he wanted to ask me a question. He said, "Let's go over here for a second" and led me to a quiet aisle. He asked, "Did they get someone for Patrick's murder yet?" When I said that someone had gotten a life sentence for the homicide plus thirty years for the armed robbery, Zack went "Shhoooohh." When I said the man's name was Charles Mungin, his face stayed blank. Then Zack looked around the aisle and asked, "How did they get the information to get him?" I told him they'd convicted Charles with digital surveillance and testimony from the dealers at 97 Smith Street, and Zack said, "Good. I'm glad they got him."

CHAPTER 16

PARTY NEVER ENDS

I n March 2016, while Patrick's family tried to find a place
to host his funeral, they had his body delivered home to
Paradise Island. They debated laying him on his favorite
couch, but instead they left him in his coffin and opened it in
the living room. When visitors walked in on the Mofflys playing Cards against Humanity with Patrick lying next to them,
Elizabeth said "they couldn't get out of here fast enough." With
Patrick resting on the farm, his parents called different venues
around Charleston and asked if they could handle a large party
with an open casket. When restaurants and bars turned them
away for sanitary reasons, Mayor John Tecklenburg offered
them the city-owned Maritime Center, a waterfront venue
south of the aquarium. Five days after their son was killed, the

Mofflys hosted four hundred guests for what they called Patrick's Bohemian Life Ceremony.

David Moffly (father): Effectively, we threw the wedding that Patrick was never going to get.

Elizabeth Moffly (mother): It was a huge-ass party. We spent seventy grand.

David Moffly: We set up a huge tent and did multiple living rooms within the tent. Three open bars, an oyster-shucking station, a big catered spread, and we had Stop Light Observations, a local band that everybody loves, come play. It was a fucking knockout party.

Elizabeth Moffly: "Jeez, Dad, why didn't we have one of these when I was alive?"

William Sawyer (friend): Patrick wouldn't have wanted a serious funeral. He would've wanted people to be drinking, having a good time, celebrating him rather than mourning him.

Skylar King (friend): His funeral might have been the hottest selection of women I've ever seen. The ratio was like two to one.

David Moffly: There was everything from kids in no shoes to the coat-and-tie crowd.

Skylar King: Patrick's wearing a Hawaiian shirt with linen pants and a linen jacket.

Caroline Cordina (friend): Someone did a little cake model of him on a surfboard surfing away.

High School/College Friend: There were police everywhere, but we showered his casket with joints. Hid them in his pockets and his hands.

Victoria Collins (ex-girlfriend): I don't know if his parents know this, but I wrote a letter and put it in his pocket. I told him I forgave him and that I'd always love him.

Johnny Drama (friend): A few of us jumped off the dock, because that's what he would have done.

Austin Moreland (friend): I got pretty drunk and jumped into the harbor in my suit.

David Moffly: After the party we brought Patrick back to the house, and then there was an afterparty. Things got a little fucking crazy out here with all the kids.

Skylar King: It's the last farm party, essentially. About sixty people.

High School/College Friend: I remember going to the bathroom and everyone's eating bars and doing coke. A couple girls offered me an orgy. I'm just like, "You're literally trying to suck my dick by the pool at a funeral afterparty."

David Moffly: A drunk girl tried to climb into the casket with Patrick.

Skylar King: Me and his dad had to rip one of his old exes out of there. She kept trying to touch him.

Austin Moreland: I'm on the back porch, and I look through those big-ass nice windows they have, and I see her pounding on his chest and screaming, "Why did you leave me?"

Skylar King: I'm like, "Yo, he's dead, he's fragile! He's decomposing. You could grab his hand and his arm could completely fall off." It took five guys to drag her outside.

During Patrick's funeral, his 97 Smith housemates stayed in Puerto Rico for spring break. When they returned to the College of Charleston at the end of the week, one housemate walked into the neighbor's yard to see if the garbage truck had come yet. Under the beer cans in the trash, he found the two bags of GG249 pills he'd hidden while Patrick had died. He pulled the Xanax out and carried it to the house, and when another boy from the extended drug network texted him "Do you have any?" he responded, "Yeah, I have some." As he later admitted during the homicide trial, Patrick's housemate sold the two thousand GG249 bars to his and Patrick's mutual friend, a boy we'll call Turtle.

After Turtle bought the crime scene Xanax, he drove the bags to his new apartment. He'd just moved in with two strangers downtown, and when he got to his room he closed his door. Although he'd bought the pills to resell for a profit, he started to dip into the bag instead. Turtle was one of the dozen people who considered Patrick Moffly his best friend, and after Patrick died, his benzo use transitioned from "a queeb in the morning and a queeb when I'm drinking" to taking four or five bars a day. He didn't leave his room while he tried different combinations of Xanax, Adderall, and Lunesta. One afternoon he blacked in after driving his Honda Civic through a fence, and when he looked down his foot was still halfway on the gas.

By the end of the year he'd eaten the two thousand pills from the two bags, and he told me four years later that each GG249 bar had been a reminder of "how like sad and how fucked up this all is. I just lost my best buddy, and now I'm eating his pills nonstop." Turtle lasted through his benzodiazepine withdrawals, and he eventually found work in a restaurant downtown.

Turtle: Even now, I think about Patrick three, four times a day. If I smell hummus, or if someone orders something with no vegetables on it, or if someone starts ordering fucking rum and Coke. I think about him every time I do blow. Patrick was not asking to be saved, but he did tell me he was going to haunt me when he died. He said, "I swear to God, I will haunt you guys forever if I die, regardless of if you're to blame or not. I will be there haunting your shit, knocking your drink off at night, waking you up, fucking with you, making sure you have whiskey dick. I will be there. I will haunt you for an eternity." But he's not haunting me. That was just him being fucking funny.

After it started as a tropical wave off the coast of Western Africa, Hurricane Matthew gained speed through the fall of 2016. It followed the old Triangle Trade route across the Atlantic, drowning parts of Haiti and Cuba on the way to the southeastern United States. When the storm reached Florida in October, South Carolina governor Nikki Haley called for the evacuation of one million people along the coast. When the local TV started showing videos of horizontal palm trees, Mikey Schmidt was lounging at the Kiawah Island Golf Resort and suffering from a case of mononucleosis. He'd gotten sick after hooking up with a Charleston girl on the Fourth of July, and now he was losing energy and weight. Smoking Ultra Lights at the beach condo, he heard the governor's news and started to pack. The evacuation gave him a legal excuse to return home to the Atlanta suburbs, and with any luck his judge might let him stay there.

When Mikey came back to Dunwoody, his mom and step-dad asked him to see a psychiatrist. During sessions Mikey talked around his childhood and college years. At first he hated the conversations, but the doctor eventually gave him a Xanax prescription. Unlike the pressed GG249 bars, which put Mikey to sleep, the Pfizer-made Xanax made him feel like he was floating. In the morning he lifted weights, gaining back the muscle he'd lost when he was sick, and after breakfast he drove into Atlanta for his new job. Thanks to Biscuit's nightlife connections, Mikey had found work in the office of personal injury lawyers Harris "the Georgia Pitbull" Weinstein and Michael "Money Mike" Weinstein. Through Mikey's own startup, Peerless Promotionals, he designed and printed Weinstein Firm T-shirts, cozies, and golf balls. He also made Weinstein Firm cigarette lighters, explaining the blend of nicotine and promotional marketing as "When you do a giveaway item and mix in addiction, it installs [the brand] into your subconscious."

At home, Mikey worked to beef up his own legal defense. While Tim Kulp pressured the Charleston solicitor about Zackery Kligman, Mikey hired Steve Sadow to lead his case from Atlanta. Sadow had successfully defended a few of Mikey's heroes, men like T.I., Usher, and Rick Ross. Some Atlanta rappers called Sadow "the Fixer," and in Mikey's case he soon took a more aggressive tack than Kulp. Sadow wrote a long, fluent motion titled "Notice of Intent to Call Prosecutor Linder as Witness and Motion to Disqualify Her as Trial Prosecutor," announcing his plan to interrogate Stephanie Linder about her confidential informant network. Citing the relevant case law, he argued that a prosecutor cannot try a case in which she's also a witness (which she would be if Sadow successfully called her as one), and he asked the judge to recuse Linder from Mikey's trial. Sadow gave Mikey a reason to believe he might not go to jail, and so did the fate of the other boys in the narcotics network.

During the summer of 2017, the Charleston *Post and Courier* published its first article about the C of C Xanax network in nearly a year: "Charges Dropped against Suspect in Lucrative Drug Ring That Involved College of Charleston Students." It wasn't surprising to see the girlfriend of Citadel cadet Jake Poeschek freed from her charges; according to one source, the Charleston PD had mostly charged her as a way of pressuring Poeschek to cooperate. Still, Mikey had to feel some hope in September, when the *Courier* ran a mug shot of SAE Ben Nauss under the headline "First Suspect in Drug Ring Involving Charleston College Students Is Sentenced to Probation." Ben had hired David Aylor, a local defense attorney and former C of C KA known for handling high-profile cases and for his own branded wristbands and cozies, and even though Nauss had refused to cooperate with the Charleston PD, he had received a suspended sentence and five years' probation. After that, Mikey watched Poeschek and his own KA driver, Jonathan Reams, get off with probation too. In the two years following the bust, the only member of the narcotics network to receive any jail time was Kligman's associate Daniel Katko, a repeat offender who received a three-year sentence for six narcotics charges but went home after fifteen months.

The next summer, Zack Kligman got arrested again. This time, Myrtle Beach police raided his house and found 717 THC cartridges, 29.4 pounds of marijuana, and what an officer called a "multitude of edible THC food products." The arrest violated the terms of his cooperation agreement with Stephanie Linder, and it forced the state to charge him for his firearms, LSD, MDMA, and nearly 7,000 grams of Xanax pills. But South Carolina doesn't have a Xanax trafficking charge on its books—a storage locker of 3.5 million pills is worth the same "possession with intent to distribute" charge as a bag of five thousand—and most of his charges never went to a grand jury. I saw him working at Klig's Kites a year after his arrest, and during the 2020 lockdown I watched his Webex sentencing hearing. Sitting next to his lawyer, Zack pled guilty to possession with intent to distribute Xanax and cocaine, plus the unlawful carrying of a pistol. Facing the webcam, Zack's lawyer Kirk Truslow told the judge that his client was a local kid who'd gotten involved with drugs through friends. He added that Zack's cooperation "really made a difference with what he did in assisting state and federal authorities," and he said that he'd leased a space in his law office for Zack to run a new startup. (The business, Creative Labz, sells custom-printed marijuana packaging and carbon-lined, smell-proof duffel bags.) Presiding from his Webex square, the judge gave Zack two years of probation for the Xanax and cocaine, and he offered him time served for the pistol. Linder smiled at the camera, and Zack told the judge, "Thank you, sir." While Zack drove home to Myrtle Beach, his Xanax remained in a box at Charleston PD headquarters. After a few years, barring any appeals, officers would escort it to an off-site location and put it into a furnace.

In early 2019, a representative from Mulberry Hill traveled to Charleston and set up a booth on the C of C quad. Next to the other Greek life tables, he unfurled the Kappa Alpha flag. When boys walked up to him, he said his order offered a moral compass for the modern gentleman. After enough names filled his sign-up sheet, he organized a semester's worth of meetings for a Kappa Alpha provisional chapter. He taught the underclassmen to establish a philanthropic presence, develop relationships with sororities, and pay dues. According to the student president of the new order, the man from nationals only briefly mentioned what had happened to the C of C KAs in 2016. After a year of provisional status, the Kappa Alpha Order was allowed by the administration to return in November 2020. Also returning to campus were the Sigma Nus, who recolonized after violating the alcohol, drugs, and hazing rules, and the Pi Kappa Phis, who returned after former members had allegedly beat their brother unconscious. Setting up their own booths during C of C orientation, these chapters tried to catch up with the Pikes and the SAEs, who'd never left at all.

In 2017, the state dropped its felony charges against the AEPi brothers accused of assaulting a freshman girl at a day party. One boy's charge was dismissed after a detective didn't show up to his hearing, and the other walked in exchange for a misdemeanor plea. Later, the assault lawsuit against Pi Kappa Phi fizzled before it went to trial. The case had looked promising when the injured boy's attorney first had accessed the Pi Kapps' "Shotcallerz OG" Facebook group and found his attackers threatening to "bury" their brother and calling him "the biggest pussy to step foot on planet earth." The case fell apart, though, when the plaintiff's lawyer flew his client from the northeast for a deposition in Charleston. Seeing how the boy responded to a question about punching another Pi Kapp at a party, the attorney felt concerned. "He starts doing the whole, 'I mean, the bottom line, man, is that she wanted to be with me and he couldn't understand it, so yeah I bitch slapped him cuz he's a little bitch,'" the lawyer told me. The attorney had been a fraternity member himself, and when he got a sense of how his client would play in front of a jury, he settled for less than the mid-six-figure number he'd hoped for. "My kid was a freaking nightmare, dude. I mean, he was just a . . . spoiled, entitled, just, pussy, to be honest with you."

In May 2021, when I was almost done with the reporting for this book, I went to Mount Pleasant to retrace the path from Hardee's burgers to 97 Smith Street that Josh Bowman walked the afternoon Patrick Moffly died. Josh had since left Patrick's social world and changed his phone number, and the Hardee's where he'd waited for Patrick is now a Chase bank. Starting between its Greek columns, I headed through the smoke outside Melvin's BBQ and hiked up the Ravenel Bridge. When I got downtown the U-Haul center was overflowing with trailers, and King Street was full of bachelorette parties. A few blocks later I reached the Einstein Bros under McAlister Hall and passed through the gates of the College of Charleston.

During my recent visits to campus, the newer fraternity kids had seemed especially anxious about how I'd portray them. Many talked about not trusting journalists or not wanting to get canceled, and some presented their frattiness more quietly than the older guys before them had. This change seemed to be part of a bigger shift, which *Total Frat Move* described in a TikTok it shared comparing "frat guys in 2012" to "frat guys in 2020." In the first clip, a kid in a backward hat screams, "I'm FRATTING so GODDAMN hard in my VINEYARD VINES pink fucking BUTTON DOWN! Sperry's, NO fucking SOCKS." In the second, a kid in a forward-facing hat says, "Yo, if these parlays don't hit, I think I'm gonna take a queeb and just watch conspiracy videos in my room." When I'd asked a KA active if he felt like other students wanted the Kappa Alpha Order to return to C of C, he'd said, "Being in a fraternity, you don't brag about it."

But if they're not announcing themselves like they used to, the boys are still here. In 2021, there were an estimated 750,000 American college students in Greek life, which was only 50,000 members short of an all-time high. Every spring they bring ice luges to the Carolina Cup, and each fall they find new cabins for Mountain Weekend. Many alumni of the drug network—including Rob Liljeberg, the SAEs Ben Nauss and Russell Sliker, the Xanax dealer Johnny Drama, and the residents of 97 Smith Street—were allowed to graduate from C of C, and some of them still get bottle service on King Street. If the fallout from the drug bust has taught them something, it's that as long as you're one of the boys, you can usually go as hard as you want without having to learn anything. If someone tries to stop your fun, you'll find good lawyers and reasonable judges, and if the outside world sees you as a villain, you can always play the heel. As one fraternity lobbyist in a large state capital told me, although the young men he represents know they're seen as deplorables by some classmates, in private they assure him, "They'll all be working for us some day."

It's true that the first half of 2016 had seemed to lead to a kind of "bro reckoning," but then came the November election. Two years later, Mitch McConnell (Phi Kappa Tau), Mike Pence (Phi Gamma Delta), and Lindsey Graham (Pi Kappa Phi) helped successfully defend Brett Kavanaugh (Delta Kappa Epsilon) during his Supreme Court nomination hearings. Then, in 2020, a musician named Tophy released a viral song that mashed up snippets of Kavanaugh's testimony, the chorus of Avicii's "Levels," and the vocals from Waka Flocka Flame's "No Hands." In the song, the northern European synths start to build while Kavanaugh says, "I liked beer, I still like beer. Automatic, still is. But I did not drink beer to the point of blacking out. When I was in town, I spent my time working out, lifting weights, or hanging out and having some beers with friends. *Animal House*, *Caddyshack*, and *Fast Times at Ridgemont High*." Right before Avicii's EDM drop comes in, Kavanaugh's voice says, "Catholic all-girls' schools. Automatic, still is." While Avicii plays, Waka Flocka sings: "Girl, drop it to the floor. I love the way your booty go." A few guys told me they listen to it at pregames.

While other boys got off without jail time, Mikey Schmidt found Stephanie Linder unwilling to give him a suspended sentence. Linder showed little interest in Tim Kulp's homicide theories about Zack Kligman, and she defeated Steve Sadow's motion to have her removed from Mikey's trial. During pretrial hearings she branded Mikey as a narcissistic manipulator, the kind of boy who trafficked cocaine even though he came from money, and who refused to cooperate with the police while his lawyer played private eye. She also depicted Mikey as the central hub of the College of Charleston drug ring. During a private meeting she told Kulp and Sadow that the solicitor's office would give him fifteen years in exchange for a guilty plea. Kulp argued that Mikey was a young offender with no prior record, and after some back-and-forth Linder told him she couldn't go below ten years without parole.

In February 2019, after a motion hearing in downtown Charleston, Kulp and Sadow walked Mikey and his mother out of the courthouse. They went by a plaque marking the first meeting of the Pi Kappa Phi fraternity in 1904, and then they stopped under the oak leaves in Washington Square. They found two benches near the statue commemorating George Washington's 1791 trip to Charleston, where the first president had "enjoyed the hospitality of two fraternal groups." While Mikey sat next to Sadow, and Kulp sat next to Mikey's mother, the lawyers described Mikey's legal options. Mikey remembers Sadow leading the conversation, but Kulp claims he did the talking. Kulp told me he said, "Here we are. I have been hammering on these people for years, trying to find something that would blow the case up. It hasn't worked as well as I'd hoped. If they call this to trial, their offer of ten years is gone. And if Steve and I try the case and don't make magic, then the minimum mandatory is twenty-five years, and the judge may even apologize to you when he sentences you to the minimum that the legislature has enacted. So you've got a choice."

Sitting under the moss and shade, Mikey looked at the ground. At least as Kulp remembers it, Kulp kept talking: "To attempt to do better you have to risk doing far worse. If you're that kind of gambler, Mikey, let me know and we'll try it." Without showing what he was feeling, Mikey took his lawyers' advice. When they left Washington Square, Kulp and Sadow met Stephanie Linder's team and said their client would plead guilty if he could have sixty days to report to jail.

Mikey spent a good chunk of the next two months lifting weights. He kept working at the Weinstein office, and he continued to smoke weed and utilize his Xanax prescription. One of his Atlanta connections offered him a private flight to Mexico, and Michael Weinstein told me he encouraged Mikey to consider it. Mikey had seen his father leave his family, though, and he wasn't going to do the same thing to his mother. Instead he focused on getting his mind ready for prison and lifting even more weights. He prepared to say goodbye to his grandmother, who struggled to look him in the eyes, and to his two Havanese and his mutt named Bandit, whom he could reasonably expect to never see again. In his free time, he planned his last night out in Atlanta.

Mikey's going-away party started at Chops Lobster Bar in Buckhead. Chops was a private clubhouse with red velvet upholstery and red leather accents, and it'd become Mikey's favorite place to start the night with the Weinstein brothers. Lighting cigars around the table were Mikey, the Weinsteins, a few 808 Mafia members, and some KA brothers who'd driven in from Charleston. Mikey usually saw himself as a Macallan-18-with-an-ice-cube kind of guy, but at Chops he ordered white russians with shots of espresso. While the table ate steak and lobster, one of his 808 Mafia friends gave him advice for prison. First, the friend said, "You gotta let go of what goes on in the free world." Second, he said, "Don't let things that are out of your control upset you." Lastly, he told Mikey, don't get in debt. "You're small, bro. Don't let nobody put you in a situation where you have to defend yourself when it could have been avoided."

After more rounds of eating and drinking at Chops, Mikey's entourage went to Tattletale, the strip club off I-85. At some point they transitioned to the District warehouse nightclub, where the KAs got too drunk and tried to fight the guys at another table. While Mikey's fraternity brothers swung their bottles like weapons, Mikey told the Weinsteins that he wanted to leave. The three of them taxied to an after-hours venue, and after Harris Weinstein went home around two a.m. Mikey stayed at the bar with Michael Weinstein. When the two of them stepped outside at three a.m., Weinstein told Mikey that he and his brother would do anything they could for him. Mikey's face crumpled while tears formed in his eyes, and when he hugged the older man he said, "I'm so scared man. I'm fucking scared." Michael Weinstein hadn't seen Mikey cry before, and he started crying too. The older Michael told him their friendship wasn't going to change, and then Mikey's Uber pulled up. Looking in the mirror, the driver saw how inebriated his passenger was, and he asked, "What's the special occasion?" Mikey responded, "I'm going to prison tomorrow," and then he fell asleep. When they reached Mikey's cul-de-sac in Dunwoody, the Uber driver picked a sleeping Mikey up and carried him to the front door.

When Mikey and I started talking to each other in the fall of 2019, he was less than six months into his ten-year sentence. On May 1, his mom had driven him to the Kirkland Correctional Institution in Columbia and let him stop at a Waffle House and a Chick-fil-A. After a last chicken biscuit and cigarette, he'd taken three Percocets and two Xanax pills and entered for processing. His booking photo shows his hair cut to the length of the stubble on his chin, with no bangs to hide the acne on his forehead. After he'd been processed he'd used the prison pay phone, and when an inmate walked up to him holding what looked like a knife Mikey had turned and slammed the phone into the man's face. After the guards had broken up the fight Mikey had entered lockdown, and he'd curled up in a ball and sweat through his withdrawals. In July he'd been transferred to the Wateree River Correctional Institution in Sumter County, South Carolina, and in October I called his first black market cell phone.

For about a year, most of our calls revolved around Zack Kligman and Rob Liljeberg. Mikey predicted the results of Kligman's Webex hearing, and he wasn't surprised when, during the summer of 2021, Zack got arrested for domestic violence in Myrtle Beach and again walked away with time served. ("Let me just say, Zack Kligman is very special," Mikey said. "Whatever he is, he's learned the perfect formula for the system.") Mikey also foresaw the end of Rob's case, which resulted in what South Carolina calls a "Youthful Offender Act" sentence. Under the YOA, which is usually reserved for offenders aged seventeen to twenty-five, the twenty-six-year-old Rob lived in a special prison reserved for youthful inmates, and although his sentence was listed as six years he served for less than twenty-four months. During prison Rob worked as a commissary officer helper, and after his release he got a job as a sales representative at a diabetic medical supply company. On one of our early calls, Mikey asked me, "Have you ever thought about, like, do you think Rob feels bad? I don't know. I mean, it's probably more of a pride thing. Like when he wakes up, he looks in the mirror and thinks, 'I'm a fucking rat.'"

For the next two years, Mikey and I talked a few times a

month, except for the three times he got Covid and the nine times he changed phones. We texted during Georgia's college football playoff runs and Phil Mickelson's win at the PGA Championship, and we discussed Young Thug's arrest after a 2022 RICO "gang bust." I also happened to call him after the funeral of a friend's little brother who'd bought a pill that'd been cut with synthetic opioids. After that, Mikey told me about a C of C KA alumnus who'd died in 2018 of a heroin overdose and a younger KA brother who'd died from an overdose in 2020. We talked about these deaths exactly once, and it made me think of what an older Kappa Alpha had said after the first round of C of C KA funerals. "The friends would get together and stuff, and they'd have like a party to celebrate his life," this KA, who'd also bought pills from Patrick Moffly, had told me. "And like everyone would be crying and everything, but it's just like once that was over, it was right back to normal. It was almost as if everything was like a Xanax blackout. Just like, 'All right, next day, nothing happened, he wasn't ever even there.'"

For the most part, Mikey and I didn't talk about the hardest parts of life in Wateree. We spent more time discussing his business projects, which included mixtapes for the 808 Mafia and an iPhone app for campus deliveries and errands called Pledge. One time he said that a guard had sexually harassed him, and another time he told me that an inmate had been stabbed over a twenty-five-dollar debt, but he didn't go into details. Instead, we talked about University of North Carolina

Phi Gam, Kappa Sig, and Beta, three fraternities that'd been busted as part of a drug ring that shipped two hundred pounds of marijuana and two kilograms of cocaine across the country every week from 2017 until 2019. The fraternity dealers had coordinated via GroupMe and used the US Postal Service, and Mikey wondered if any of them would go to jail. We dug into their pending legal cases, but Mikey barely mentioned his own suffering in prison until January 2022, when he texted me from his fourth phone.

Mikey Schmidt: Shit gettin wild back here. Make sure you let the ppl know I kept it real if I die
Me: What's going on?
Mikey Schmidt: Shoot straight. You got me or not? Cause shit is getting wicked
Me: If something happens you know I'll do whatever it takes to get the story out there
Me: But what's going on? You got me worried
Mikey Schmidt: Make sure they know I never told on a soul that I was the only one that kept it all the way solid
Mikey Schmidt: It will be a miracle from god if I make it out of here

Later, Mikey told me that he'd watched a "bloodbath" with knives and axes while the Wateree guards had run away. He once again didn't say much about it, but he wrote that if he made it out of prison he'd need therapy. Without that option, though, he usually turns to his daily meditation instead. Around five a.m., before the other inmates in his converted horse stable get up to milk cows on the farm, Mikey lies on his back and concentrates on his breath. Without judgment or anger, he watches himself breathe in and out while his breathing gets deeper and slower. Feeling his spine on his cot, he hears the noise in his mind go quiet. Closing his eyes, he vows to give off such positive energy that evil can't get to him that day. Mikey learned this ritual from one of his first bunkmates, a Haitian immigrant who said that positive or negative thoughts will attract different energies in life. It's one of the lessons Mikey has learned in Wateree, like carpentry or how to drink moonshine. Now he knows how to lie there and slow his heart, focusing on the vibrations he gives and vowing to manifest something good. But when horseflies land on his skin and industrial fans blow in the Sumter County heat, Mikey sometimes opens his eyes and thinks, "I should've been an SAE."

ACKNOWLEDGMENTS

Thank you to my agent, Luke Janklow, for being a friend, guitar shop consigliere, and champion of this project since I was twenty-five years old. Thank you to my editor, Noah Eaker, for improving this book and my writing life one lunch at a time. Thank you as well to Jennifer Barth, who took the original chance on *Bros* and helped me see what it could become. I also want to thank Laurie Abraham and Denise Wills, at *The Atlantic*, for supporting the early days of reporting and writing. In addition, thank you to everyone at HarperCollins and Janklow & Nesbit who helped guide this story into the world: Andrew Jacobs, Claire Dippel, Michael Steger, Mark Poirier, Edie Astley, and many others.

Nearly every page of this book consists of stories that other people trusted me to tell. To each of you—from Captain Jenkins to Mikey Schmidt—thank you. I want to also specifically thank the Moffly family, who, like Joe Wilber and John Pitts, spoke with clarity and love about losing a son.

Thank you to the friends who read early drafts and made them way better: Jamie Fehrnstrom, Kal Victor, Charlie Marshall, Rachael Bennett, and Henry Green. Thank you as well to Tom Lake and the Chautauqua family for the group reads and late nights, and to Bronwen Dickey for suggesting this book's title before there was a story attached. Also, as always,

ACKNOWLEDGMENTS

I'm grateful to Steve and Janice Miller for their love and guidance, and to Skip Hollandsworth for the years of Preston Royal therapy sessions.

Now for a big list of names. Thank you to my teachers at St. Mark's: Ray Westbrook, David Brown, David Dini, Larry Cavitt, and Marsha McFarland. Editors at *Texas Monthly*, *GQ*, and *Sports Illustrated*: Jeff Salamon, John Spong, Anna Peele, and Adam Duerson. General encouragers: Wes Marshall, Jayne Litton, Jim Milan, Patti Beach, Adam Klein, Jacqueline Bennett, Amy Robinson, Ross Crawford, Holly Briscoe, Mark Rozzo, and Sidney Coren. Fraternity "brothers": Eli Geschwind, Tom Borgers, Gabe Merkin, Nick Perloff, and Robert Page. Topical guides: Annie Hecker, Helen Robertson, Justin Heckert, Niamh O'Reilly, and Tony Bartelme. I also want to thank Cyndi and Stephen Slade and Archie and Barbara Bennett for raising the woman whom this book is dedicated to.

Which brings me near the end. Thank you, Mom and Dad, for teaching me how to read, write, speak, and listen. Thank you, Charlie, for making me laugh harder and think more deeply every day since 1996. And thank you, Rachael, for sharing this house and life with me. Every sentence in here I owe in part to you.

NOTES ON SOURCES AND METHODS

This book draws from more than 180 interviews with 124 sources. Over four years of reporting, I spoke with C of C KAs, SAEs, Tri Delts, Sigma Nus, and Kappa Sigs, plus defense lawyers, prosecutors, investigators, benzodiazepine addiction specialists, NASCAR pit crew coaches, and many others connected to this story. Their quotes were edited for concision and readability. Because fraternity life is by its nature secretive, and because many boys told me about previously unpublicized wrongdoing, the majority of interviewees spoke on the condition of being identified as a source instead of by name. For the sake of clarity, I identified many of these Greek life sources by their chapter names.

It's important to note that the fraternity members I interviewed gave firsthand accounts of their own experiences. They spoke only for themselves, and their statements don't necessarily reflect their whole chapters or their national organizations. While these boys often discussed hazing each other and blacking out on all kinds of substances, it cannot be said that all members of their chapters engaged in those behaviors. (After all, national fraternal organizations forbid these activities.) In short, readers should not attribute the individual conduct I have reported in this book to groups as a whole.

The book also pulls from thousands of pages of police files, court transcripts, and DEA interviews. Some of these documents were provided by Freedom of Information Act requests, and others came from lawyers and investigators. In addition, I consulted text transcripts, police video recordings, third-party sources, and my own recollections. While the whole book draws from this mix of sources—interviews and documents, plus memories and third-party texts—a more detailed list can be found below.

CHAPTER 1: WOLVES OF KING STREET

Stories about Mikey's early years came from Mikey, in addition to interviews with high school and college friends. Press conference coverage came from the Charleston *Post and Courier*, the Charleston PD press release, and local TV outlets WCIV ABC News 4 and WCSC-TV Live 5. The *Aeneid* interpretation came from professor Tim Johnson on today.cofc.edu. As stated in the chapter, the oral history quotes came from eight recent C of C alumni and a criminal defense lawyer who represented one of the boys in the mug shots, and the storage locker police affidavit came from Tim Kulp. The affidavit listed the seizure as "6,947.62 grams of alprazolam" but did not specify how many individual pills they found. (At 2 mg of alprazolam per pill, 6,947.62 grams of alprazolam would equal 3,473,810 pills). On a phone call, Charleston Police Captain Andre Jenkins told me he couldn't remember the exact number of pills confiscated, but he confirmed the general magnitude of the seizure.

CHAPTER 2: MOUNTAIN WEEKEND

Mikey's scenes came from his recollections. The social reputations of different C of C fraternities came from alumni of C of C KA, SAE, Tri Delt, Sigma Nu, and Kappa Sig, as well as several non-fraternity members. (I also consulted fraternity members' public Instagram, Twitter, Facebook, and Venmo accounts.) The statistic from Cornell's Office of the Dean of Students website has since been removed, but it was cached via archive.org. I found the statistic about Greek life university donations via the Brechner Center for Freedom of Information and University of Oregon's Dean of Students website. The brief historical perspective came from Nicholas L. Syrett's *The Company He Keeps: A History of White College Fraternities*, and the observations on *Animal House* were influenced by Caitlin Flanagan's writing on fraternities in *The Atlantic*. As stated in the text, the account of Mountain Weekend came from two SAE alumni, a former Tugaloo employee, and two Tri Delt sorority alumni.

CHAPTER 3: RECRUITMENT

The opening scene came from Mikey's recollections but was aided by descriptions from other 7 Montagu housemates and my own observations of the house. The account of Rob's early years was based on interviews with his college friends, fraternity brothers, and a high school soccer coach, in addition to his own social media posts and résumé. I found his soccer statistics via elmhurstbluejays.com and the account of Rob's father's disciplinary issue from the North Carolina Medical Board's Quarterly Board Actions Report. The account of KA's social reputation was based on recollections from former members of C of C KA, SAE, Tri Delt, Sigma Nu, and Kappa Sig, as well as several non-fraternity members. Information about Rob's extended family came from *New Orleans* magazine and the *Times-Picayune*. The depiction of Mikey's rush was based on interviews with Mikey and other KAs, and my insights on rush at large come from personal recollections. The claim that "most eighteen-to-twenty-year-olds who join fraternities drink" is corroborated by the *Journal of American College Health* (which reported in 2009 that 97 percent of the 3,400 fraternity members they interviewed drank alcohol) and by the *Journal of Student Affairs Research and Practice* (which reported the same year that 86 percent of fraternity brothers binge drink each month.)

CHAPTER 4: PLEDGESHIP

My report on *The Varlet* came from the book's twelfth edition, which was published in 2010 and used while Rob and Mikey were in college. The other sections on C of C Kappa Alpha pledgeship came from the recollections of four C of C KA alumni: one boy who pledged in 2012; Mikey, who pledged in 2013; one boy who pledged in 2015; and another who pledged in 2016. My brief section on C of C SAE pledgeship came from three alumni: one who pledged in 2014 and two who pledged in 2011. The historical perspective came from *The Hazing Reader*, edited by Hank Nuwer, and John Hechinger's *True Gentlemen: The Broken Pledge of America's Fraternities*. The section on my high school friends' pledgeships was based on interviews with each friend.

CHAPTER 5: OLD SOUTH WEEKEND

The "Kidnap Night" story came from police files and interviews with a Kappa Alpha who took part that night. The section on weed dealing pulled from interviews with three Kappa Alphas, one SAE, one Kappa Sig, one Sigma Nu, one lacrosse team alumnus, and one GDI (non-fraternity affiliated student) who dealt marijuana to fraternity members. Stories from Mikey's first social semester as a KA active came from Mikey plus other KAs and fraternity and sorority members. My report on the KA and SAE social media presence came from LinkedIn and Instagram, and my section on rival dealers came from interviews, police files, and DEA documents. The section on the Carolina Cup came from Mikey and another KA, and the scenes from Old South came from two KAs.

CHAPTER 6: DOUSING THE TREE

As stated in the text, the section on Mikey's imprisonment drew from interviews with Mikey and his high school and college friends. The sections on Hawkins Wilber and Spencer Pitts came from Joe Wilber and John Pitts, respectively, plus obituaries and coverage in the *Post and Courier*. Ann Friedman's piece in *The Cut*, "How Do You Change a Bro-Dominated Culture?," ran on September 12, 2013, and the Kingsley Amis quote came from *Everyday Drinking: The Distilled Kingsley Amis*. To learn how Xanax worked, I interviewed Anna Lembke and Keith Humphreys at Stanford University and Donovan Maust at the University of Michigan, and consulted journal articles, including "Our Other Prescription Drug Problem" (*New England Journal of Medicine*, 2018) and "A Review of Alprazolam Use, Misuse, and Withdrawal" (*Journal of Addiction Medicine*, 2018). The first section on Xanax dealing came from dealer interviews and police files.

CHAPTER 7: QB SNEAK

As stated in the text, Mikey was the main source for the section on his home life. I also spoke with his ex-girlfriend, who asked to be identified as Alexis. The section on Rob came from interviews with his housemates and friends, plus his own résumé and *Odyssey Online* articles. For the bits on College of Charleston in the news, I pulled from the *Post and Courier*, Inside Higher Ed, *Charleston City Paper*, and NPR. The section on dark web dealing pulled from interviews with dealers and police documents. The sources on polypharmacy are named in the text, as are the sources on presidential elections. (I also pulled from my own memories from e-board voting.) The last section on Mikey drew from interviews with Mikey, Alexis, and Wilson Warren.

CHAPTER 8: BLACKOUT PUNCH

The first section was sourced mainly from interviews with Wilson Warren, Mikey Schmidt, Daniel Kuniansky, and Frat-Shows photographer Nick May, plus videos and photos from FratShows concerts. The account of Johnny Drama's robbery came from Johnny and a *Post and Courier* report, and the sections on Zackery Kligman and Robert Liljeberg pulled from police files, DEA files, court documents, and interviews. The section on blacking out drew from interviews with over a dozen sources, and the Title IX statistic came from the Department of Education's Office for Civil Rights.

CHAPTER 9: PURE WATER

The Number I's Leadership Institute scene was re-created via interviews with two former Kappa Alpha Number I's, in addition to documents and photos from the Kappa Alpha Order website and Facebook page. To understand the Fraternity Insurance Purchasing Group, Inc., I read through the FIPG's official literature and interviewed litigator Douglas Fierberg. (I also, once again, consulted Caitlin Flanagan's reporting in *The Atlantic*.) The section on Mikey in Atlanta pulled from firsthand accounts from Wilson Warren and other sources close to the situation, plus text screenshots from the police files.

The claim about the SAE leadership cruise was reported in University of Oklahoma President David Boren's March 27, 2015, press conference, and the writing on the Dallas Bubble came from personal recollection. I found Phi Delt's old "Aryan" blood requirement in *Commentary* magazine and SAE's in John Hechinger's *True Gentlemen*. The section on Kappa Alpha drew primarily from 1903, 1904, 1917, 1920, 1921, and 1922 issues of the *Kappa Alpha Journal*; the 1891 *History and Catalogue of the Kappa Alpha Fraternity*; the twelfth and thirteenth editions of *The Varlet*; the official 2019 Kappa Alpha *Convivium Guide*; and an interview with a C of C Kappa Alpha. The final section on pressed Xanax drew from police files and interviews with ten sources.

CHAPTER 10: UNCLE'S COKE

The section on cocaine dealing pulled from police files and interviews with twelve sources. The section on Eric Hughes's ring drew from DEA documents, police files, court transcripts, and interviews with dealers and local and federal investigators. Similarly, the final section came from interviews with seven sources, in addition to police files, social media screenshots, and text message transcripts.

CHAPTER 11: PATRICK

The sources in this oral history were either named or identified in the text. I interviewed twenty-six people about Patrick's life and death, and drew from police files, DEA interviews, and court documents.

CHAPTER 12: COUNT CRAZY

The opening section drew from Mikey's recollections, plus text message transcripts, Rob's résumé, and social media posts from the Greek life members on spring break. The paragraph on Rob's and Mikey's earnings pulled from police files, pretrial documents, and interviews with a Kappa Alpha dealer. The section on Xanax dependency drew from interviews with David and Elizabeth Moffly; Dr. Adam Downs from What Good Looks Like, LLC; Anna Lembke at Stanford; and interviews with Xanax dealers and users at C of C and in my own life. The statistic about benzodiazepine overdoses came from the CDC, which reported that "drug overdose deaths involving benzodiazepines steadily increased from 1,135 in 1999 to 11,537 in 2017." The sections on the April 2016 drug deal and bust came from police files, text transcripts, wire recordings, and interviews with two Kappa Alphas and two Charleston PD officers.

CHAPTER 13: I'M YOUR PLEDGE

Short of the Total Frat Move comment thread, the entire chapter pulled from text transcripts, police files, detective interviews, and conversations with fraternity dealers. The account of Mikey's graduation visit to Charleston up through his arrest also drew from interviews with Tim Kulp and Mikey.

CHAPTER 14: STORAGE LOCKER

The opening section came from Mikey's recollections and court documents. The section on the Moffly homicide pulled from police files, DEA files, court testimony, police body camera footage, and interviews with eyewitnesses and investigators. The "popular among his social circles" quote came from Charleston WCBD NBC 2, and the "well-known area surfer and skateboarder" quote came from FITSNews. The remaining sections on the drug arrests pulled from police files, DEA files, wire recordings, hidden camera footage, court documents, and interviews with investigators and dealers.

CHAPTER 15: SOME CONSEQUENCES

The opening paragraph came from interviews with Mikey, and the account of Mullen's press conference once again pulled from the Charleston *Post and Courier*, the Charleston PD press release, local TV outlets WCIV ABC News 4 and WCSC Live 5, in addition to court documents and police interviews. The paragraph on Brad Felder drew from DEA files, court transcripts, interviews with federal investigators and prosecutors, and coverage in the New York *Daily News*. The USC arrest paragraph that followed came from investigator and prosecutor interviews, DEA files, court transcripts, and coverage in the *Post and Courier* and the *Island Packet*.

The account of Kappa Alpha's 2016 closure came from an alumnus who took part in the membership review. The account of the other fraternity closures came from the *Post and Courier* and the complaint filed in the lawsuit against Pi Kappa Phi. The sources for the broader "bro" cultural reckoning were named in the text.

The account of Mikey's and Tim Kulp's pretrial preparations came from Mikey and Kulp, in addition to Kulp's documents. The section on the investigation of Zack Kligman also drew from these sources, in addition to police files, court documents, and interviews with the Mofflys and other sources named in the text. My sections on the Mungin trial and the Kligman meeting were firsthand accounts. The former also came from interviews with Jason Mikell, Evette Jamerson, and David and Elizabeth Moffly, and written correspondence with Stephanie Linder.

CHAPTER 16: PARTY NEVER ENDS

The account of Patrick's funeral came from four Moffly family members and seven of his friends. The section on Mikey's pre-prison time in Atlanta and Charleston came from Mikey, Tim Kulp, Steve Sadow, Michael Weinstein, and Demario Smith, in addition to post-conviction relief testimony from Mikey, Kulp, Sadow, and Mikey's mother. The account of fraternity reopenings came from the *Post and Courier*, Kappa Alpha social media, and interviews with a KA from that era. The 2021 Greek life statistic came from the *Hechinger Report*. The final section on Mikey's time in prison comes from texts and calls with Mikey, police files, and court documents.

ABOUT THE AUTHOR

MAX MARSHALL is a writer and investigative journalist. Raised in Texas, he attended Columbia University, where he graduated summa cum laude and Phi Beta Kappa in 2016. He served as a Princeton in Asia media fellow in Hanoi, Vietnam, and his work has appeared in *GQ*, *Texas Monthly*, *Sports Illustrated*, and the *New York Times*. He lives in Austin.